Symbols of Jesus is a systematic theology focusing on what makes Jesus important in Christianity. It studies six families of symbols about Jesus and shows how they are true for some people, not true for others, and not meaningful for a third group. Divine creation is analyzed in metaphysical as well as symbolic terms, and religious symbolism is shown to be wholly compatible with a late-modern scientific world-view.

Robert Cummings Neville, a leading philosophical theologian, here presents and illustrates an elaborate theory of religious symbols according to which God is directly engaged in symbolically shaped thinking and practice. Symbols are not distancing substitutes for God. Theology of symbolic engagement is defended as an alternative to doctrinal or descriptive theology.

This major work re-shapes the way we think about Jesus, and will be of value to students, academics, clergy with theological training, and others grappling with the meaning and importance of religious symbols in our age.

ROBERT CUMMINGS NEVILLE is Professor of Philosophy, Religion, and Theology at Boston University and Dean of the Boston University School of Theology. He is ordained in the ministry of the United Methodist Church. Neville has authored sixteen books, including *God the Creator: On the Transcendence and Presence of God* (1968; new edition 1992), *Creativity and God: A Challenge to Process Theology* (1980), *Behind the Masks of God* (1991), and *The Truth of Broken Symbols* (1996), and has edited a further seven.

SYMBOLS OF JESUS

SYMBOLS OF JESUS

A Christology of Symbolic Engagement

ROBERT CUMMINGS NEVILLE

WITH PLATES OF A PAINTING
FROM CAVES TO COSMOS
BY BETH NEVILLE

CAMBRIDGE
UNIVERSITY PRESS

BT
202
.N475
2001

PUBLISHED BY THE PRESS SYNDICATE OF THE UNIVERSITY OF CAMBRIDGE
The Pitt Building, Trumpington Street, Cambridge, United Kingdom

CAMBRIDGE UNIVERSITY PRESS
The Edinburgh Building, Cambridge CB2 2RU, UK
40 West 20th Street, New York, NY 10011–4211, USA
477 Williamstown Road, Port Melbourne, VIC 3207, Australia
Ruiz de Alarcón 13, 28014 Madrid, Spain
Dock House, The Waterfront, Cape Town 8001, South Africa

http://www.cambridge.org

First published 2001

Printed in the United Kingdom at the University Press, Cambridge

Typeface Baskerville MT 11/12.5 pt.   *System* QuarkXPress™   [SE]

A catalogue record for this book is available from the British Library

Library of Congress Cataloguing in Publication data
Neville, Robert C.
Symbols of Jesus: a Christology of symbolic engagement / by Robert Cummings
Neville; with plates of a painting From caves to cosmos by Beth Neville.
p.   cm.
Includes bibliographical references and index.
ISBN 0 521 80787 5 (hardback) – ISBN 0 521 00353 9 (paperback)
1. Jesus Christ – Person and offices.   I. Title.
BT202.N475   2001
232–dc21   2001035100

ISBN 0 521 80787 5 hardback
ISBN 0 521 00353 9 paperback

For Elizabeth Egan Neville

Partner in marriage, family, life, love,
and the engendering of our lives' works for
vision, wisdom, and culture:
companion for this brief run in eternity

Contents

Illustrations

xi

PLATES

From Caves to Cosmos, by Beth Neville, 1994, photos by Steve
Nelson/FAYPHOTO copyrighted by Beth Neville

between pages 158 and 159

Preface

The intellectual center of gravity in this Christology is the explication of
a number of religious symbols by which Christian traditions have
engaged God. Most of these are symbols of Jesus, although symbols of
God as Father and as Holy Spirit are also treated. Symbols are concepts
of a certain sort, as analyzed below, and they have many different media
of representation. Because this is a book, the main medium of representation here is verbal. But religious symbols such as these also have
been represented profoundly in visual arts, architecture, dance, music,
and crafts of many sorts. Visual representations can at least be reproduced and discussed in this book. The covers, Salvador Dali's *Christ of St.
John of the Cross* on the front and Matthias Grünewald's *Resurrection* on the
back, encase the entire Christological story in a symbolic sense. Because
of their integrated crucifixion/resurrection motif, they express the
central Christian point that makes all the other symbols of Jesus religiously interesting. Unlike most crucifixion representations such as
Delacroix's (figure 6, p. 83 below), in which the viewer looks up at the
hanging Christ, Dali's (following St. John of the Cross's drawing) looks
down from a God's-eye view, and the crucifix itself towers over the
reaped-clean landscape (see also figure 17, Wagner's painting of the Last
Judgment, p. 260 below) with its boat symbolizing Jesus' calling of disciples and the ark of salvation. Is the Crucified One ascending, descending, or hovering in majesty? His surreal cosmic position vibrates with the
realistic painting of Jesus modeled by the very human Hollywood actor
Russ Saunders, who could be the friend of any viewer and whose
humanity is symbolically continuous with the gospel accounts of Jesus.
Dali's atonement image compacts symbols as distant as the Cosmic
Christ, the descending Divinity, the historical Jesus, and the personal
Friend. The Grünewald Rising Christ, by contrast, transfigures all
those symbols, overcomes the limitations of stone grave and wicked
might, and blasts through to the aboriginal heat of creation. The Christ

breaking the gates of hell in the Chora fresco (figure 8, p. 100 below) has the same transfigured energy. All these symbols of Jesus make sense only in connection with the symbols of God the Father-Creator and the Holy Spirit. Esteban Murillo's *The Heavenly and Earthly Trinities* (figure 4, p. 28 below) makes this point on the vertical axis, while the horizontal axis (Mary–Jesus–Joseph presenting the Babe to the world) connects the human life of Jesus to the salvation of those who interpret God through him. The Christology here analyzes and amplifies the resonances of these and other symbols.

My positive thesis is that these symbols are true under certain circumstances. I spell out these circumstances, and urge their religious value in the circumstances of contemporary life where they are valid.

Surrounding the explication of the religious symbols are many philosophical considerations about the nature, use and validity of symbols. In other works, cited below where relevant, I have dealt with these issues in more detail. In this book I have tried to develop them enough for theologians who are more interested in the nature of this Christology than in its content to see what is new and might be interesting in this project. Part of the project is to show that the truth of religious symbols is related to context, and that it can be assessed by anyone sufficiently interested to analyze the context and the nature of the interpretations in which the symbols are involved.

Therefore two audiences are intended here. One is the Christian communities for whom I write as a Christian theologian urging the consideration of *our* symbols. The other is a wider audience of people who would never themselves employ these symbols for religious purposes but who can see how Christians might, and might do so truly. The line between these two groups is indistinct.

One theme of this book is the religious place of human beings and Christian interpretations of the human condition in the evolution of the cosmos. Christianity has no single symbol for this, and the theme is addressed in glancing discussions of other symbols, especially in chapter 3. But that theme is the exact center of the painting by Beth Neville, *From Caves to Cosmos*, which is reproduced in the plates here. The painting itself consists of seven canvases, each five feet high and seven feet long, which abut to constitute a large scroll-like work of art. The first panel, plate 1, represents the human view out from the birth-cave of prehistory and the last, plate 7, represents the entropic dissolution of the cosmos with things moving ever farther apart, losing relation, and reducing to irrelevant straight-line order. The legends under each of the plates give more details about representations and composition as I understand them. The artist herself has made several videos explaining her own intentions and understanding of the iconography, consistent with but not the same as mine; some of her early drawings for these paintings were published in my *Eternity and Time's Flow*. The artist is my wife, and our collaboration in nearly all things for many decades makes her painting an interpretation of my text and vice versa. For this, I thank her and dedicate this book to her.

The system of citation in this book employs titles in the text and footnotes of books and articles whose full bibliographical information is given in the bibliography on pp. 262–270 below.

Acknowledgments

All biblical quotations, unless noted otherwise, are from the New Revised Standard Version, copyrighted in 1989 by the Division of Christian Education of the National Council of the Churches of Christ in the United States of America.

I am grateful to Boston University for the sabbatical semester during which this book was begun at a retreat in Cambridge, England, and for my friends there at Trinity College and Wesley House. Topics in this book have been discussed with nearly all my colleagues at the Boston University School of Theology. Specific suggestions and reactions have been made to at least parts of the manuscript by my contemporary theology class, fall 2000, and by Loye Ashton, John Berthrong, Ray Bouchard (who has also helped in the preparation of the manuscript), James-Mark Lazenby, Byungmoo Lee, and Jay Schulkin (with whom I have discussed the topics here for twenty-five years). Wesley J. Wildman has been my closest interlocutor on the ideas defended here, challenging and refining their meanings, expressions, and existential significance. The anonymous readers for Cambridge University Press made many helpful corrections and I am particularly grateful to Kevin Taylor, my editor at the Press, for his encouragement from the beginning and his careful guidance throughout.

Prologue

The interesting Christian beliefs about Jesus Christ are mostly fantastic: that his blood saves, that he is the cosmic king, a divine being, the incarnation of God in history, each person's friend, and the final judge of human history, just to name a few. Most traditional Christologists have been uncomfortable with such fantasies, thinking fantasy to be untrue fiction, and have attempted to reconstruct those claims into something like literal descriptions. The result is doctrines that compromise the stark power of the fantastic symbols and still do not make much sense in terms of how we know the world works ("conceived by the Holy Spirit, born of the virgin Mary"?) or are foolishly false (washing clothes in blood turns them white?).

Whereas most Christologies are studies of doctrines about Jesus Christ, a more fruitful way forward in our time, I believe, is through studies of the major symbols of Jesus Christ and how they function to engage people truly or falsely with God.[1] Close behind this point is my conviction that even the classic doctrines have functioned in Christian life more often like symbols than like descriptions, explanations, or rules for belief. So this Christology approaches its subject through a theory of the ways symbols work or fail to work to facilitate truthful engagement. The theory of symbols in turn is justified in part by the felicity it exhibits in the analysis of that symbolic working.

Before discussing the profound and controversial symbols of Christology, however, it would be well for me to say as plainly as possible what I think Christianity is about and where Christology fits in with its symbols. The reason for this prologue is to forestall the criticism that the Christianity exhibited in these symbols is not what the reader recognizes, for the symbols are too intense, too extreme, and too much each

---

[1] See the magisterial analysis and summary of recent doctrines and symbols in *Jesus: Symbol of God*, by Roger Haight, SJ, which also advances a nuanced view of symbolic engagement. My only criticism of Haight's book is that it pre-empts the title that should name my book here.

a biased perspective on the whole, too fantastic, in other words. An abstract doctrinal system would not have such a problem. This overview is meant to be no more than superficial, because to get more profound would require the difficult symbols. Though superficial, it provides an important orientation.

Christianity first and foremost is about being kind. Love is the more customary word than kindness, but love is too complicated in its symbols, too loaded with history, to be a plain introduction to Christianity. In the end, of course, being kind opens into the profound ontological love that for Christians characterizes both God as love (1 John 4:8, 16) and the epitome of humanity and piety (Mark 12:29–31 and parallels). Nevertheless, being kind, though the bottom-line theme, is an ideal that often has been ignored within Christianity or seriously distorted, sometimes systematically as in the history of European Christianity with the Jews. The unkindness of Christians to Jews, and every other circumstance of unkindness, is a devastating reproach to Christian practice. But being kind is still the bottom-line theme.

Sometimes it is hard to tell in what kindness consists. Whether a social welfare system is ultimately kind if it creates a long-term dependent class of people is a debatable point at this stage, and how to amend it to make it more kind is also debatable. But some obvious and up-front meanings of kindness should be affirmed before stumbling on hard cases. These include being generous, sympathetic, willing to help those in immediate need, and ready to play roles for people on occasions of suffering, trouble, joy, and celebration that might more naturally be played by family or close friends who are absent (see for instance Paul's list in Rom. 12:9–21; or his song to love in 1 Cor. 13).

To be kind is also to be courteous, an extremely important and difficult virtue in a society as multifarious as ours. Courtesy means holding in balance two things. One is an articulate acknowledgment of who people are in all their differences, especially deferring to their differences from oneself. The other is an articulate and clearly communicated assumption that those others are equal to oneself in their importance for the community and in the cosmic assessment of things. Courtesy is especially difficult because its balance requires shared rituals of acknowledging and deferring to difference and also communicating acceptance and respect. Too often the necessary rituals themselves are lacking and to be kind to certain sorts of people is simply impossible. This is especially true in situations of sharp imbalances of power. The more powerful lack rituals for withdrawing their influence so as to open space in which, without their seeming to be abandoned, the less powerful can define and assert themselves. The less powerful lack rituals for asserting themselves in self-definition over against the more powerful without seeming to attack in order to take over. These failures in ritual are serious inhibitions to Christians attempting to be kind.

Kindness, especially as it depends on cultural rituals of courtesy, but also in many other contexts, is an ideal for a community. Communities should be kind to their members and their neighbors; they should enable their members to be kind to one another and to the communal institutions that make kindness possible and effective.

Christians believe that communities of kindness are the human ideal because of the nature of God. Being obliged to kindness in community and personal life is part of how Christians interpret being "created in the image of God." God is the ultimate foundation of kindness. Not that the created world is always a kind place to be, assuming for the moment the Christian claim that God creates the world. Rather, the "principles" expressed in creation are those that, in the human sphere, define kindness. Being kind, with all the personal and communal variations on that ideal, is being God-like (1 John 4:7–21).

Although Christianity has come to express this ideal as a kind of universal obligation, applicable to people across the board, it came to the ideal in very particular circumstances as a reforming insight within Second Temple Judaism. Jesus was a practicing Jew, observant of the Temple obligations, who assumed for himself a reforming and prophetic role within and for Judaism.[2] He taught kindness in his preaching, his healing, and in the formation of his community of followers, always stressing its continuity with historical Israel and contemporaneous Judaism, even when he loosened some of the commandments of Torah in the name of kindness. Continuity was important even when he criticized hypocrites for unkindness that they hid behind observance of the commandments (e.g. Mark 7:9–13). It's not that Jesus advocated kindness

---

[2] The theme of Jesus as a Jew, the ways by which he continued Jewish practices, or distanced himself and his movement from them, moved ancient principles to the center of his religious vision and displaced others to the margins, has been the subject of much recent scholarship. For a selection, see for instance Fredriksen, *From Jesus to Christ* and *Jesus of Nazareth, King of the Jews*; Meier, *A Marginal Jew*, volumes I and II; Sanders, *Jesus and Judaism* and *The Historical Figure of Jesus*; Theissen, *The Shadow of the Galilean* and *A Theory of Primitive Christian Religion*; and Vermes, *Jesus the Jew* and *The Changing Faces of Jesus*. Of these, perhaps Paula Fredriksen's *Jesus of Nazareth, King of the Jews* makes the strongest case for direct continuity of contemporaneous Judaism in Jesus' person and community, and Meier's *A Marginal Jew* stresses the opposite. Gerd Theissen's *A Theory of Primitive Christian Religion*, pp. 21–40, presents a clear, perhaps overly clear, catalogue of ways in which Jesus continued and modified a Jewish heritage.

whereas "the Jews" advocated legalism, as some Protestant commenta-
tors have liked to say.[3] Rather, whatever else he changed in emphasis and
direction, he carried over the focus on kindness and love in his summary
of the Law (e.g. Mark 12:28–34 and parallels) and in specific instructions
to his community about what is essential (John 14–17, especially
15:12–17).

To some degree Jesus may have seen his call to kindness as the initiation of a new world order. Surely his disciples saw it this way within a
very short time after his death. Jesus seems in all instances to have been
confident that his call to kindness, and his prophetic critique of unkindness, stemmed from God and was a continuation of the revelation of
God that had been laid down in the history of Israel. This conviction of
divine sanction and the power of his ministry made Jesus an extraordinary charismatic figure (Matt. 7:29).

The shock that his crucifixion caused among his followers led to an
extraordinary re-conception of the relation of their movement and
community to continuities with Israel. As expressed in the documents of
the New Testament, Jesus himself was a sort of divine figure and the
community he initiated, bound by the ideals of kindness, was a rewrit-
ing of the Old Covenant that foreshadows the coming of the completely
achieved kingdom of God. Although often justified by alleged pre-
figurements in the Old Testament and expressed in symbols mainly
deriving from there, the new Christian community looked not only to
the authority of the past but to the calling and fulfillment of the future.
How many of these new ideas were taught or at least hinted at by Jesus,
we cannot know for sure. Nearly all the New Testament writings reflect
directly or indirectly a tension between living out a given commandment
or program derived from the past – the religion of Israel and the teachings of Jesus – and the development of surprising new forms, often dis-
continuous with the old, that seem to be called for in order to be true to
the divinely sanctioned new community ideal of kindness, so charis-
matically taught by Jesus.[4] Clearly the most important new development
was the conviction that Jesus had been raised from the dead, had reconvened some disciples, commissioned them to spread the community in

---

[3] See Sanders' *The Historical Figure of Jesus*, chapter 14, for a careful discussion of Jesus and the law.
His general conclusion is that Jesus affirmed the law as a good Jew and that his disagreements
with Pharisees and others over its interpretation, applications, and allowable exceptions were
within the limits of acceptable first-century Jewish debate.

[4] The centrality of this point and its implications for current Christianity are brought out beautifully in Rowan Williams' *On Christian Theology*, especially in chapter 2 but discussed from various
angles throughout.

anticipation of his apocalyptic return, and would himself come again at any moment. The crucifixion therefore was not the defeat it looked like at first, dispersing the community who had failed to give Jesus even elementary support. Rather, for the early Christians it was the transition to the new order of divinely sanctioned community. Caravaggio (figure 11, p. 165 below) captures this sense by depicting even Jesus as a new man, ruddy, sleek, and youthful, not a man recently crucified, dead, and buried. Many images were used to express the relation between Jesus and the Church or new community, for instance that the Church was his body (Eph. 1:22–23) and he was its animating mind (1 Cor. 2:16), or that he was the bridegroom and she was his bride (Rev. 21:2; Gal. 4:26–29). But one of the crucial meanings of Jesus' resurrection is that he remains a somewhat external judge by which the Christian community and its members individually will be judged. Therefore the Church cannot look too authoritatively even to the past of Jesus but rather must look forward to its own time of judgment.

Meanwhile, given the understanding of Jesus as raised, ascended, and destined to come again as judge (see Memling's *Last Judgment*, figure 15, p. 226 below), the early Christians refocused the notion of the inspiring divine spirit as the Holy Spirit sent from God, especially in Jesus' absence, to help them understand Jesus and also to know what to do in their communities' new circumstances (1 Cor. 2:9–16, John 14:18–26). The Holy Spirit both interprets the witnesses to Jesus and guides the Church for the future. But the Holy Spirit is not organically bound within the Church and does not run things automatically. Rather it comes and goes ecstatically, and there is always a problem to discern the genuine leadings of the Spirit; the tests hover around the virtues of kindness (Gal. 5:16–26).

Thus within the New Testament documents lie the roots of what later would become the doctrine of the Trinity. The God of Israel, the Father, is the creator whose ideals for human life, by which the creation of the human sphere can be completed, is revealed by Jesus as a divine being, the Son of God (among other symbolic titles) who is the initiating and judging Lord of the Church. The Church is divinely attended during historical time by the Holy Spirit until the return of Jesus as judge (most of these notions are compacted together in Paul's salutation in Romans 1:1–6). These ideas and symbols competed with many others in the New Testament writings and they are not expressed there in coherent ways as would be sought in the later Councils attempting to define the doctrine of the Trinity. But they were sufficiently manifest that John's Gospel, the latest in composition, could represent Jesus as teaching mainly about himself and his authority as spokesman for the Father (for instance John 8:12–59), emphasizing the characters of love or kindness in the community of "friends" he had created (e.g. John 15:7–17), and promising both the guidance of the Holy Spirit and also the ultimate union of the community with him and the Father in the Holy Spirit (John 14–17, particularly 14:15–17, 26, and 15:26–27). John's Gospel ends (chapter 21) with Jesus cooking the disciples breakfast, charging the Church's leader, Peter, to remember and fulfill his love of Jesus by being kind to others (whom Jesus had claimed as his sheep), and to get on with it.

In getting on with it, the Church quickly discovered how uncomfortable it is to live in between a past that gives meaning and direction to its life and a near future that calls for the Church to be something new in order to be true to its risen (and therefore not fully past) Lord. That novelty might require rejecting some elements of the past, or at least displacing them from the center of attention. Instead of being able to think that Jesus had established the form of the Church and that all that then was required was faithfulness to his vision, the early Christian leaders had to invent new forms of life and community in order to be faithful to the revelation that was still coming out (through the Holy Spirit).

The first great issue came from the fact that Gentiles responded very positively to the ideal of the kind Church community with firm loyalty to Jesus as the Lord. Paul's first letter to the Thessalonians was addressed to a church community well established by the early fifties and the people addressed were Gentiles (1 Thess. 1:9). Whereas Jesus could orient his ministry to "the lost sheep of Israel" (Matt. 10:5–6, 23; 15:24), and expressed some astonishment that non-Jews had significant faith (Matt. 15:21–28), the Christians within a very few years included many Gentiles.[5] The first Gentile Christians might originally have been earlier converts to Judaism, but soon that was not the route to Gentile Christianity.

Jewish Christians could understand the Christian movement as a purification, rectification, but clear continuation of the revelation of God to Israel. For them the Old Covenant was clearly in hand when they adopted membership in the New Covenant and the earliest community continued to worship in the Temple (Acts 3, 4:1–31). But the non-Jewish Gentile Christians did not have the Jewish past to purify, rectify, or extend in continuity. Quite the contrary, they had their own various

---

[5] See Wayne A. Meeks' *The First Urban Christians*.

pagan and secular pasts to purify, rectify, and transform in becoming Christians. They could adopt a Jewish past in a kind of secondary sense, as the source of the symbols in terms of which they understood their faith, expressed in the Septuagint (the earlier Greek translation of the Hebrew Bible used by Hellenized Jews). They could use those symbols to understand Jesus as the Messiah, Son of Man, Son of God, and some of the sacrificial imagery for Jesus, and also the Holy Spirit. Nevertheless, their own past, with which they had to come to terms, was not Israel but something else entirely. Therefore very quickly they transformed their readings of those Jewish symbols from the strict history of Israel into new meanings that could apply to themselves. That Jesus could be represented as a divine being with cosmic dimensions for whom all people and nations are in the same family was congenial to Hellenistic paganism. But that representation must have been very hard for the anti-idolatry traditions of Israel that conceived God's revelations to be much intertwined with its national, tribal, identity. Jesus himself selected the Twelve as apostles so that they might judge the twelve tribes of Israel (Luke 22:29–30; Acts 1:21–26). Yet by Paul's time being an apostle had little to do with the twelve tribes; it was the office of carrying the community of Christ to new territory. The great Jerusalem Council (Acts 15:1–35; Gal. 2) decided that Gentile Christians did not have to become Jews or (in the case of the men) be circumcised. This meant that the Gentiles were recognized as full members of the community. It also meant that they could not worship in the Temple closer in than the "Gentile Court," a moot point after the destruction of the Temple in 70 CE. Peter made the point about the acceptance of Gentile Christians, not in terms of circumcision, but in terms of the dietary laws, proclaiming all things clean. He did so (Acts 10) with the authorizing citation of a new vision of Jesus as Lord and a confirming visitation of the Holy Spirit.

The second great issue for the young Church emerged more slowly than the almost sudden presence of many Gentiles. Apparently Jesus had been most particular about God's Kingdom coming very soon, in which he would be a kind of viceroy of God and the Twelve would rule the Tribes.[6] His arrest and crucifixion abruptly interrupted this expectation, but with the resurrection appearances and the Pentecost

---

[6] This eschatological emphasis was the general consensus of the first "quest for the historical Jesus," as summarized for instance in Schweitzer's *The Quest for the Historical Jesus*. See also Vermes' *The Changing Faces of Jesus*, chapter 6. For a careful recent summary of the evidence see Sanders' *The Historical Figure of Jesus*, chapters 11–12; he elaborates the symbol of Jesus as viceroy in the kingdom.

experience (Acts 2) his followers reconvened as the Church to perfect the community of love in preparation for his return on clouds of glory. They expected it within their own lifetime (1 Thess. 4:9–5:11) and, when some of the original members began to die, had to work out a new timeline (2 Pet. 3:3–13). Yet an indefinite eschatological postponement loses the immediacy of Jesus' conviction about the reign of God, and so a "realized eschatology" was developed, most notably in Ephesians, Colossians, and John's Gospel, according to which a present victory in Christ and unity with God in heaven was conceived to be concurrent with ongoing history. Realized eschatologies have become increasingly important as time has passed and the historical interpretation of Jesus' claim that the kingdom of God is "at hand" or "near" has proved empirically false. Even if Jesus understood it historically, later ages could not do so without giving up the immediacy of "soon." The Church gradually softened the notion that it was a temporary holding action until Jesus' second coming and understood itself to be an eschatologically judged way of life.

The condition of living in tension between an authorizing past and an open future calling for new forms of Christian life and truth is one of the clearest issues in the New Testament. We should read the New Testament not as a blueprint, for it has no consistent clear pattern of belief or practice, but rather for its tensions, for the very clash of symbol systems and the struggles to determine what new Way is faithful to the risen and future Lord, expressive of the guidance of the true Spirit.[7] The workings of the Spirit are better to be discerned in the dissonances of symbols rather than their consonances. We should see how that large text of texts embodies the extraordinary creation of the Christian Way.[8]

---

[7] See Williams' *On Christian Theology*, pp. 44–59, 93–147.

[8] Although many scholars attempt to reconcile the historical development of Christian ideas and symbols in the first generation, most recognize the importance of decisive break-points, for instance whether a text was written before or after the destruction of the Temple in 70 CE made Temple sacrifice impossible. One of the most consistent authors to read back from the end, for instance from the Gospel of John, toward the beginning to focus in on Jesus, sorting what must be later additions to earlier points, is Paula Fredriksen in *Jesus of Nazareth, King of the Jews*. It is to Fredriksen that I owe the chief hermeneutic principle of this study, namely, to assume that Jesus was solidly Jewish and to understand Christianity as a succession of additions and subtractions made to accommodate first the presence of Gentiles and delay in parousia, and then many other conditions to which Jesus' Jewishness did not speak. Scholars contest Fredriksen's point, noting that the tension between the present and the future permeates both Christian and Jewish writings of the period. The linear development from immediate expectation to realized eschatology might be overly simple. Nevertheless the earliest New Testament book, 1 Thessalonians, said "hold on and wait just a little longer," whereas the later ones such as Ephesians, Colossians, and John's gospel express realized eschatologies, and 2 Peter tried to explain the postponement. The result of this hermeneutic orientation is to see Christianity slowly coming into its own, and continuing to do so today. Chapter 5 explores this in detail in discussing the historical Jesus, still alive and not finished.

Our own situation is no different. Christians today are in tension about authentic Christianity between the authorizing past and a present and near future no longer served by the past's forms. To use the New Testament symbols, Christians urgently need the inspiration of the Holy Spirit to look realistically at our situation and search out appropriate forms, perhaps new, in terms of which to embody the divinely ordained community of kindness. We cannot name the crucified, risen, and future Lord merely by the biblical or magisterial record.[9] Christian fundamentalisms, institutional authorities, and theological orthodoxies are heavy millstones to drag along in a Church life responsive to the Spirit. Vapid liberalisms of quick adaptation of Christianity to late-modern society are equally destructive, especially in light of that society's very unkind culture. Yet the obligations of the Church today are addressed to the various existential situations of our time, and we struggle for revelation as to how to engage those situations.

The history of Christian life has seen the rise and fall of many symbols, and the movement of some to the center, displacing others, and then back to the margins. It has also seen the growing recognition of different kinds of signs and symbols, for instance the distinction between myth and history. Gerd Theissen says of myths that they usually "tell of actions of various gods in a primal time or an end time which is remote from the present world in which people live."[10] Myth is "a narrative the action of which is in a decisive time for the world, in which numinous subjects (gods, angels and demons) transform (or will transform) a fragile state of reality into a stable state."[11] In the religion of Israel, he notes, the mythical and the historical were blended, and in early Christianity this mixture was intensified with God, Satan, and Jesus all depicted as heavenly actors in a narrative that included historical time.[12] This mixture itself is a serious tension, which means that we should not take the mythic elements to refer and mean the way historical ones do (the temptation of fundamentalism), nor should we take the historical elements to refer and mean the way mythic ones do (the temptation of the liberal quest for the historical Jesus). An added complication is that the first-century cosmology, the rather widespread Hellenistic understanding of the structure of the cosmos, is greatly different from ours and looks more like the space (and time) of myth; yet the forms of its reference and meaning are not like those of myth, but rather like early

[9] Williams treats this important theme under the rubric of sacraments (among other ways); see his *On Christian Theology*, pp. 197–221.   [10] *A Theory of Primitive Christian Religion*, p. 3.
[11] Ibid., p. 325.   [12] Ibid., p. 3.

science. Although we can distinguish these various kinds of thinking, we cannot separate them in the thought of the early Christian community without doing violence to its actual life. Nor can we do that for the thought of any of the subsequent Christian communities, down to the present day.

Which symbols express the revelation for the Church best in our time and situation? We have our own conceptions of "truth" in history, myth, and science, and they bear upon the kinds of thinking that can embody revelation for us in our time. This book considers some of the most vivid of the historical symbols of Jesus and asks what they might mean today. Insofar as it is part of Christian theology (it is that and more), it is Pneumatology, inquiry into the Holy Spirit.

Introduction

A THEOLOGY OF SYMBOLIC ENGAGEMENT

A good way forward in Christology today, a way to engage God in Jesus Christ intellectually, know what we are doing, explain that to others, and make our claims vulnerable to correction and assessment of their truth, lies in the following four main ideas:

1. Certain important religious symbols are schematized images of an utterly transcendent and infinite ultimate reality in the terms of human experience. They present the ultimate, God, as relevant to fundamental human issues such as contingency, guilt, homelessness in the universe, and the meaning of life. Vast theological mistakes arise when the symbolic images themselves are confused with proper theological conceptions of the ultimate as such, as happens often in discussions of Christological doctrine. The idea of religious symbols as schematized images and the distinction of them from more metaphysical theological conceptions will be explained shortly and illustrated throughout.

2. A theory of religious symbols is available for understanding the ways in which religious symbols are schematized images of the ultimate. This theory shows two important things: how symbols engage people with their objects, including the ultimate, and how those engagements are sometimes true and sometimes false. A theology of symbolic engagement improves upon a doctrinal Christology.

3. Certain very important Christian symbols can be shown to be true under certain conditions, as explicated and assessed by the terms of the theory of religious symbols. Much of what follows is the development of a Christology, saying what is true about God in Christ as grasped through the Holy Spirit, under what conditions, and as involved in the symbols I shall analyze here. Much more might be said about Christology, of course, and other symbols might be analyzed.

4. Because the truth conditions of the Christological symbols will be

analyzed in the above ideas, the claims will be public to anyone who might be interested, not only to Christians. Although the topic here is Christology for Christian practice and belief, the argument is within the larger public of religious studies. In principle, symbols of other religions might be given a similar kind of analysis as schematized images, interpreted through the theory of religious symbols, and assessed as to their validity under the right conditions.

The distinction between responsible theological conceptions and the religious symbols of their objects is that the symbols are schematized images of the reality that the conceptions attempt to render in a more literal philosophical, even metaphysical fashion. People engage the ultimate directly through the symbols, not indirectly as if the theological conceptions were the real signs for engagement and the symbols represented the conceptions, not the object. Certain aspects of God and other ultimate matters can indeed be picked up through engagement with theological conceptions. But most of the existentially important things to grasp in God can only come through the schematized images of the religious symbols.

Theological conceptions in Christianity and most other religions take account of the fact that the ultimate, God for Christians, transcends ordinary determinations in important respects and is infinite, that is, non-finite, beyond determination. Thus theological conceptions work around a kind of in-built negation, "apophasis," to use the technical term. One instance of this in Christianity is the very ancient claim that God creates space and time as well as the things within space and time, and therefore God cannot be spatial or temporal. How can people relate to such an infinite God beyond space and time? Theologians might think through such relations, not a hard task for people who like intellectual play. But basic religious impulses such as worship, prayer, wonder, and longing for salvation, enlightenment, and harmony before God cannot be expressed through the metaphysical thoughts alone. For the practice of religion, including the reflective theological practice, religious symbols are necessary even in their negative character.

Religious symbols arise from complicated historical routes and rarely from their corresponding abstract theological conception. But they stand in the logical relation to theological conceptions of being the schematized images of their objects. The philosopher Immanuel Kant argued that conceptions of things that are not expressed in the spatio-temporal terms of experience need to be schematized into experiential terms.[1] A schema is a rule or formula for rendering a transcendent concept in experiential terms, for instance the formula for drawing a circle in a plane by making a continuous line all of whose points are the same distance from a point outside the line. Whereas a schema is a conceptualized rule, a schema-image is an imaginative representation that expresses the rule. Any circular thing such as a round dinner plate is a schematized image of the concept of a circle, as is a circle drawn with a compass on a sheet of paper.

Nearly all religions have schematized their conceptions of a non-spatio-temporal ultimate with the idea of Heaven as a space/time place where the ultimate is to be found and perhaps approached now or later. The schematized images of such heavenly places reflect many historical and cultural conditions.[2] Ancient Israel visualized Heaven with the imagery of a throne room (Isa. 6) and a heavenly court (Job 1) to which early Christianity added a dining room (Matt. 26:29, Luke 22:15–18), a dormitory (John 14:2–4), golden streets (Rev. 21:21), meeting with the risen dead (1Thess. 4:17), and harp music (Rev. 5:8). Muslims visualized Heaven more as an outdoor garden of delights, and Buddhists and Hindus show a preference for palaces set in large parks. Some Daoists imagine Heaven as immortal life in the sky at cloud level.

Historically the richly imaged religious symbols arise before sophisticated theological conceptions, and theology itself is stimulated by reflections on both what those symbols might mean and the conditions under which they apply. When the question of the truth of a symbol arises, as happens so often when conditions change or another symbol system is encountered, theological conceptions are developed to analyze the symbol as a schematized image of what the conception claims is true. So in one sense God really is in Heaven because God truly can be engaged by some people with the symbols of Heaven. But in another sense of course God cannot be in a place at a time and it was foolish of the cosmonaut to look for God above Earth orbit. The heavenly symbols are true as schematized images of a transcendent God to whom some people relate by means of them.

Most of the time people are not fooled by symbols, recognizing their

---

[1] Kant's discussion is in the chapter on "Schematism" in the *Critique of Pure Reason*, B 176–87. His discussion is particular to the technical details of his own transcendental argument. I have discussed it in the more generalized form used here in my *Reconstruction of Thinking*, pp. 139–42.

[2] See Colleen McDannell and Bernhard Lang's *Heaven: A History* for a treatment of Jewish and Christian conceptions.

symbolic roles and the contexts in which to use them. But theologians
are prone to confuse the symbols with the more abstract conceptions relative to which they are schematized images, developing bad hybrid theological conceptions. For instance, Christians have long symbolized God
the creator as a Father, following Jesus' injunction, and thinking about
their relation to the Father in terms of loving interaction, as in the
parable of the Prodigal Son (Luke 15:11–32). But they have also long realized that, as creator of the entire cosmos including the conditions for
interpersonal interaction, God cannot metaphysically be involved in
that kind of relation, and relative to the world God depends on nothing
at all to which a response might be possible. Confusing the symbol with
the theological metaphysics, they then have worried that a God who is
supposed to be loving and compassionate, ready to kill a fatted calf or
more for beloved wayward children, really is cosmically impassive,
allowing suffering. Or they have compromised the metaphysics of creation to make God a finite being capable of interpersonal interaction.
Much theology is stuck with confused conceptions that take a little from
the symbolic imagery and a little from the metaphysics of transcendence. These confusions lose both the power of the symbolic imagery
and the integrity of the theological conceptions.

Moreover the confusions compound their own difficulty by supporting an egregious opposition between so-called "biblical theology," which
adheres strictly to the language of symbolic imagery, and allegedly cor-
rupting "Greek metaphysics." Without some metaphysics adequate to
the day, the symbolic imagery cannot be related to the rest of what
shapes imagination; nor can there be much public measure of how the
symbols apply, with what range, and under what conditions. I will illustrate this in the next section. The confusions are resolved by understanding how the theological conceptions are grounded in metaphysics and
the religious symbols are schematized images of the religious object in
one way or another.

"Metaphysics" has meant many things and had different models in
Western thought. For most purposes of this book, a vague informal
notion is satisfactory to the effect that metaphysics is the study of, and
theories about, the common generic traits of all existence.[3] Because
many people believe that metaphysics is an illegitimate enterprise,
however, I should say that a thoroughly defensible form of it is the
development of hypotheses about the generic traits of existence,

[3] This is John Dewey's definition in *Experience and Nature*, p. 50.

hypotheses vulnerable to correction.[4] The metaphysics I present here is a hypothesis.

I argue that six important traditional families of symbols of Jesus Christ are true under certain conditions: these have to do with atonement, the Cosmic Christ, the deity of Christ, incarnation in the historical Jesus, Jesus as friend, and the eschatological savior. In addition to these Christological symbols, I will also analyze and defend the truth of symbols of God as creator and Holy Spirit, the latter only briefly.

The supposition about theological truth to be defended is that in Christology truth is less a matter of true description or explanation than of bringing people, under those conditions, into the truth about God as revealed in the Christological symbols. A good name for this general theological approach is a "theology of symbolic engagement," here specifically a "Christology of symbolic engagement." The symbols analyzed here, and perhaps others, can engage certain people with God in Christ, and under the right conditions can do so truly in ways that can be assessed. What it means to "be in the truth," to "actualize" or "realize" truth, will be explained and illustrated.

A theology of symbolic engagement needs a theory of religious symbolism that understands symbols to engage or connect their interpreters with their objects in the respects in which the symbols represent the objects so that interpretations can be true or false.[5] Interpretation is the engagement of the realities interpreted, as shaped by the symbols. The symbols are not distancing substitutes for their objects, as many theories of symbolism suppose, but are connectives that orient the interpreters for better or worse to those objects. Without symbols things cannot be engaged, only bumped into or missed entirely. Reality cannot be engaged in any ultimate dimension unless there are symbols for the ultimate such as "God," "Brahman," or "Dao" that articulate or at least vaguely identify this. Human life cannot be registered as having a predicament, or a salvation either, unless symbols exist enabling that interpretation. Human beings have evolved to possess the interpretive capacities to register not only social realities but the religious depths of existence.

[4] The conception of metaphysics as hypothetical draws its inspiration from Charles Peirce and his criticism of Kant. I have dealt with Peirce and defended this sense of metaphysics in detail in *The Highroad around Modernism*, especially chapters 1 and 6. I have defended the vulnerability of theory at length in *Normative Cultures*, chapters 1–4.

[5] This theory draws its main inspiration and many of its technical distinctions from the semiotic theory of Charles S. Peirce, the great American pragmatist. I have developed it at great length in my *The Truth of Broken Symbols*, which also contains the appropriate citations of Peirce.

A theology of symbolic engagement analyzes how particular symbols—Christological ones in this case—in fact connect interpreters of different sorts in different contexts with their objects, or fail to do so, and whether they do so truly. The two questions should not be confused: Do the symbols engage or not? If so, do they engage truly? Symbolic engagement is an enormously complex process whose complexity will be explained in more detail shortly.

SUPERNATURALISM AND METAPHYSICS

Religious symbols of the sort studied here presuppose some metaphysical construction of what is real and how the foundations and boundaries of the world are structured. The metaphysical construction supposed in the Bible and assumed by many Christians for whom the biblical world-view is important appears to us late moderns as supernaturalistic. God is supposed to be a supernatural being, for instance, Heaven is up, and entry can be gained to it after death, among other supernaturalistic suppositions.

Of course, what is "supernatural" depends on what is taken to be "natural." In the ancient world of St. Paul and Origen, the natural cosmology supposed a hierarchy of levels of reality with Earth near the bottom just over Hell, and a variety of heavenly levels above.[6] On each of the heavenly levels different rules of nature and causation obtained, for instance in different angelic types ("thrones," "dominions"; see Rom. 8:38–39, Eph. 6:12). Sometimes there occurred crossings of levels, as in angelic and satanic visitations to Earth or most important of all, in Christ's descent from and return to the Highest Heaven (Eph. 4:8–10, Phil. 2:6–11). With such crossings the deeds of the visitors from another level are "miraculous" in the sense of contravening the nature and causality of the Earthly visited plane. But in the large, the whole hierarchy of levels constitutes the totality of nature, and nothing was "supernatural," only un-Earthly. Heaven was indeed up, Hell down, God at the very top, and visitation by divine or heavenly beings a matter of descent and ascent. By the time of the European Christian medievals, the conception of the hierarchy of levels had softened, though the distinction between Heaven, Earth, (Purgatory), and Hell was observed (see, for instance, Memling's *The Last Judgment*, figure 15, p. 226 below). A crossing from Heaven to Earth was deemed supernatural, not merely atypical for

---

[6] For a systematic historical account of ancient worldviews, their imagery, cosmology, and metaphysics, see Richard Sorabji's *Time, Creation, and the Continuum*.

Earth, and a distinction was supposed between prevenient grace within nature and supernatural saving grace from God above. In the early-modern period nature was conceived in a radically continuous way, with one metric and sense of causation applying throughout the whole and a physicalistic definition of what can be measured. Late-modern physical cosmologies depart greatly from the commonsense early-modern conceptions of measure and physical things to be measured, but within the new conceptions of the physical cosmos, the radical closure of nature still obtains. Beth Neville's *From Caves to Cosmos* (between pp. 158 and 159 below) moves through the "levels" of below ground (plate 1), the Earth's surface (plate 2), atmospheric sky (plate 3), high orbit (plate 4), interstellar gases (plate 5), distant supernovae (plates 6–7), and infinite expansion to irrelevance (plate 7); though each "level" has a different scale of reality, with different typical causal patterns as in the ancient cosmology, the underlying metric physical cosmology is continuous and closed. Hers is a thoroughly scientific, late-modern vision. Much of what was religiously interesting in the Bible, for instance images of God as a super-being, miracles, and divine actions to save, including the advent of the Christ from Heaven, have to be regarded as supernatural from the perspective of late modernity.

In the present historical situation, there are three main options for response to the supernaturalistic metaphysics of biblical symbolism.

One is to adopt it with conviction and learn to see one's whole world through it. For people in late-modern cultures such as the North Atlantic countries, this means imposing the supernatural view on top of a scientific understanding of nature. For people with a fuzzy appropriation of the scientific world-view this is not hard, though better scientific education is always a threat to their religious imagination. For those who are equally committed to the scientific world-view it is harder, and this has given rise to one branch of the "science and religion" debate according to which the chief problem is to determine how a supernatural God, a being transcendent of nature, can act within nature without compromising accepted causal laws.[7] For people in Africa or parts of China, and in other places where the scientific world-view has not yet defined nature, Christian supernaturalism is imposed on top of whatever conception of nature they have. When that conception is already filled with spirits moving from one plane of reality to another, this imposition might not be difficult. For them the crucial agenda is not how to

---

[7] For an excellent collection in this genre, focusing on eschatological action, see Polkinghorne and Welker's *The End of the World and the Ends of God.*

reconcile supernaturalism and nature but how to discern the Christian
from demonic supernatural agents. Or rather, their situation is closer to
that of the early Christians, for whom the whole of nature includes
realms from which visitations might be made different from that of ordinary life, and the question is how to distinguish true from false spirits
and learn to live accordingly. The threat to this way of adopting
Christian supernaturalism is that modernization will lead to acceptance
of the scientific world-view and the situation will approach that of late-
modern Europe and America.

The second response to supernaturalism is simply to reject it and
those elements of Christianity that depend on it. The late-modern intellectual elite increasingly is making this response, in two main forms. One
adopts a very pale form of Christianity that usually focuses on ethics, liberation of the oppressed, domestic organization, and community building, and treats the Christian symbols as having the role and force of
Santa Claus, Jack Frost, the Tooth Fairy, and the Easter Bunny – something for children around which the family can gather. The second form
rejects Christianity outright because of its supernaturalism, often with
nostalgia and sadness.

The third response, which I shall defend in detail in this book, is to say
that some Christian symbols that are central to worship, community life,
cultivation of the spiritual life, and a Christian interpretation of affairs,
are compatible with a non-supernaturalistic metaphysics. Chapter 1 will
sketch some elements of this metaphysics, enough to show on the one
hand that it is compatible with the late-modern scientific world-view,
indeed with late-modern concerns for ecology, cultural pluralism, and
many other things that did not register in the world-view of antiquity.
On the other hand the sketch will provide the metaphysical background
for underpinning the valid use of the large symbols to engage God truly
in late-modern culture. These are not softened Christian symbols, but
the radical, often offensive, ones such as the atoning blood of Jesus, Jesus
as the Cosmic Christ, the Second Person of the Trinity, the historical
incarnation, a personal friend, the eschatological savior.

The metaphysics of antiquity is no longer viable. Nevertheless, metaphysical assumptions compatible with late-modern science can be articulated and used to provide the appropriate background for Christian life
with the affirmations contained within the symbols of its practice.[8] This
is the claim to be defended here.

[8] I have defended the viability of metaphysics in the pragmatic or process sense of systematic
hypotheses about reality, vulnerable to criticism and open to correction, in many places. Perhaps
the most succinct is throughout *The Highroad around Modernism.*

Now the ancient Biblical world-view that seems to us to be supernatural is only a schematized image in the sense defined above. It is a concretely imagined universe in which its symbols resonate throughout the structures and affairs of human life. In the ancient world, the accepted physical cosmology was more or less in accord with this schematized image. Therefore, little motive existed for articulating a separate metaphysics that could provide connections between the biblical schematized images of God, Christ, and salvation on the one hand and cosmological imagination on the other. The biblical and the physical cosmology could be taken together to be a more or less consistent icon for reality.[9] In our late-modern culture, the scientific view needs to be reconciled with the biblical schematized image across many cognitive dissonances. A viable contemporary metaphysics is necessary for this, interpreting both the scientific assumptions and the biblical schematized image (or rather many images).[10]

The contrast between a world-view, as a complex schematized image, and a metaphysics leads my Christology to a paradox. On the one hand the argument below takes itself to be a way forward in the late-modern world, overcoming the impasse created by the conflict between supernaturalism and science. On the other hand, the properly metaphysical claims to be defended seem to stand in stark contrast to, even rejection of, the biblical symbols interpreted metaphysically rather than as schematized images. For instance, I shall claim that God the Creator is not a being transcendent of the world, though properly imaged as such in some contexts. The metaphysical conception of God I defend denies any literal interior subjectivity, thoughts, or intentions to God and supposes no personal structure, let alone a personality, although in some contexts it is not only possible but requisite to personify God.[11] Jesus Christ should not be conceived to be a transcendent metaphysical entity breaking into the human realm, although in some contexts he should be symbolically imaged that way.

---

[9] Of course, most early Christian thought did not relate seriously to the abstract metaphysics in, say, Plato's *Parmenides*, which would have required dealing explicitly with the distinction between the schema and the schema-image See Robert S. Brumbaugh's *Plato on the One*.

[10] Alfred North Whitehead has shown how such metaphysics is possible. His major metaphysical works are *Science and the Modern World*, *Process and Reality*, and *Adventures of Ideas*. The latest and most magnificent development of his metaphysics, especially dealing with God and creation, is Lewis S. Ford's *Transforming Process Theism*. I believe that such process metaphysical theology is mistaken, and that my own improves upon it. My criticism is in *Creativity and God*. Whitehead is defended against my criticism by John H. Berthrong in *Concerning Creativity*. My own metaphysics is surely flawed as well and should be improved upon; suggestions to this effect are in Chapman and Frankenberry's *Interpreting Neville*.

[11] On personifying what is not intrinsically personal, see my *Religion in Late Modernity*, chapter 4.

To people who take the symbols to be directly metaphysical, the Christology presented here can be viewed as a rejection of Christianity. Those who insist metaphysically that God has to be conceived as a transcendent being, and Christ as supernatural, for instance, will think that this Christology abandons the very things that define Christianity. My philosophical answer, developed throughout, is that their response confuses the biblical schematized image with metaphysics, and that when properly distinguished, the perhaps supernatural biblical image is compatible with a naturalistic science-friendly late-modern metaphysics.

A more powerful argument for this Christology, however, is that its strategy justifies and guides the concrete practice of Christianity with its symbols, at least the symbols dealt with here, so that Christianity is true and its saving ways effective for those on its path. This is to say, Christianity is a vital, true, and saving religion (whether there are others is an open question, not discussed here) because its basic symbols engage Christians with God vitally, truly, and with efficacious salvation.[12] The proof of this claim, of course, is in testing the quality of Christianity in our place and time.

A THEORY OF RELIGIOUS SYMBOLS

The success of a theology of symbolic engagement depends on having a plausible theory of religious symbols that accounts for how engagement is possible through imagination, how the symbols might be used truly or falsely to interpret their objects, and how it is possible both in principle and in practice to assess truth and falsity. This section will summarize the theory.[13]

---

[12] For the record, I have defended a form of Confucianism as a viable set of symbols for certain conditions within the contemporary situation. See my *Boston Confucianism*.

[13] As mentioned in a previous note, the full theory is developed in my *The Truth of Broken Symbols*. There is a lengthier summary than here in *Religion in Late Modernity*, chapter 3, with an application to the issue of personifications of God in chapter 4. The theory of religious symbols itself rests with a more elaborate epistemological theory according to which all thinking is valuational in some sense, a theory laid out in the three-volume trilogy, *Axiology of Thinking*, which has five parts. Volume I, *Reconstruction of Thinking*, contains the first two parts. Part 1 argues the historical case against the fact-value distinction in the common European Enlightenment conception of thinking and details where, in interpretive judgment, valuation might lie. Part 2 presents an analysis of valuation in imagination and makes the case, supposed in the present book, that imagination enables engagement. Volume II, *Recovery of the Measure*, contains part 3, which is devoted to a theory of interpretation; whereas imagination presents engaging images, interpretation makes truth claims. Because truth is given a causal account as the carryover of what is important from the object to the interpreter in the respects in which the signs or symbols represent the object, subject to qualifications of biology, culture, semiotics, and purpose, the account of interpretation must be an integral part of a philosophy of nature. That volume

Truth or falsity occurs only within interpretations. A sign or symbol that is not taken to interpret something is neither true nor false. A proposition that is not asserted or assumed is neither true nor false. The overall vague form of interpretation, within which all kinds of interpretive judgments, assumptions, and so forth lie is the following: *An interpretation takes a sign to stand for an object in a certain respect.* Religious symbols, especially Christological ones, are the kinds of signs of chief interest in this book. An interpretation is an act of engagement. The interpretation can be formulated as a kind of complex proposition, as is necessary when we talk about interpretations in a book like this. But even here it is important to remember that the propositions are subjunctive acts; they *would* be true or false *if* used interpretively to engage the world.

The object of a sign in an interpretation is a logical object and need not be construed as an ordinary physical object among other objects. "Religious objects" are notoriously not like ordinary physical objects. When an interpretation picks out an object to represent in a certain respect by means of a sign, it selects and articulates the object as a focal element against a background of some sort. In order to pick out Jesus as a man with disciples working in Galilee, our interpretations can take fairly standard assumptions about distinguishing human beings in a physical and social landscape with other human beings. But to pick out God as the ultimate unconditioned condition for everything that has finite definiteness is a trickier matter: the background is a kind of dialectical movement through many kinds of conditioned things to focus upon an unconditioned conditioner, and in most theologies that reference includes an apophatic moment that says God is beyond even this argumentative focusing. It is far more complicated, then, to refer to Jesus' divinity, which must somehow focus on Jesus as a logical object against both of these kinds of backgrounds (as well as many others). The risen Christ in Caravaggio's *The Supper at Emmaus* (figure 11, p. 165 below) certainly did not look like the Jesus they had last seen the Friday before![14] Focusing on a logical object relative to a background is an element of the

details the philosophy of nature and its accompanying metaphysics. The present book supposes the philosophy of nature, but does not depend on it. Volume III, *Normative Cultures*, contains parts 4 and 5 of the *Axiology*, which are respectively a theory of theoretical reason and a theory of practical reason. Part 4 explains in detail the hypothetical character of all thinking and part 5 develops a Confucian theory of ritual to connect the theoretical and practical, personal and communal, and public and private. Between them the two parts make the case for the connection between symbolic interpretive reference within practice that is at the heart of the theology of symbolic engagement.

[14] On Caravaggio's dislocating of visual and bodily expectations, see Graham Hammill's *Sexuality and Form.*

act of interpretation, a function in part of its purposive context that will be discussed shortly. Ordinarily, our culture and its semiotic system automatically select the boundaries of objects against backgrounds. But in religious matters this is problematic.

Signs are the constructs of imagination as elements of ordered semiotic systems. Semiotic systems are codes that define the signs in terms of one another and provide syntactical and semantic structures for their possible connection. Within a culture's semiotic system, or perhaps layers of systems, scales exist from deeply presupposed elements, such as the structures for perceiving and thinking spatially and temporally, through archetypic structures, mythic elements, and matters of conscious attention and critical analysis.[15] The *extension* of a semiotic system is the set of possible grammatical connections of signs.

But only actual interpretations can be true or false, and this is the *intention* of interpretation, the intentional taking of some real object, identified as the logical object, to be as the sign says it is. In an actual intentional interpretation the sign is used to shape the engagement with reality, picking out things to notice and interpreting them in the respects involved in the interpretation. The sign is not alone; it carries with it its whole semiotic system, as it were, the system that gives it semantic and syntactic shape. So we say that our semiotic culture is the means by which we engage reality, transforming what would otherwise be bumps and shoves into discriminating responses that allow us to make our way purposively through life. *Civilized* semiotic systems allow for extremely sophisticated purposes, such as religious ones.

We should not think of human interpreters as fancy computers going through life making a zillion interpretations in rapid sequence. Rather people engage simultaneously in swarms of complex activities, each shaped by many levels of assumptions and purposes, guided somewhat by perceptions but even more by the cultivated structures of intentionality. Imagine driving a car in fast heavy traffic along a difficult road, but one you know. Your sensibility feels the state of your own car, its momentum and road placement. You watch the surrounding traffic in front and behind, interpreting other drivers' intentions, and you keep the car on the road, weaving throughout traffic to maintain your best possible speed, all the time thinking consciously about what you will do when you get to your destination. Countless interpretations are going

---

[15] See the discussion of levels of imagination in my *Reconstruction of Thinking*, chapters 5–8, and in *Boston Confucianism*, chapter 6.

on all at once, integrated by the complex intentionality focused on doing what you intend when you get where you are going. Each interpretation contributes to the shaping of your activity. Interpretation does not .mean only an explicit claim about something, but any kind of "taking" of reality to be the way signs represent their logical objects to . an interpreter.

Within religious practice, the special religious symbols play many such interpretive roles in the activities of life even when they are not noticed. Perhaps most often they are life-shaping assumptions about the way things are, not explicit claims. Of course the assumptions might be mistaken. So theology turns them into claims or hypotheses that can be examined. We can call these beliefs, but should not lose sight of the fact they are actual interpretations, and thus true or false, only when they are deeply embedded in behavior, not when they are listed in a creed as if they were mere extensional propositions.

The triadic character of interpretation—signs, their objects, and interpretations taking the signs to stand for objects in certain respects – gives rise to a threefold problematic for a theory of religious symbols: the definition of symbols, the nature of reference, and the significance of interpretive context.

First, religious symbols are defined within symbolic systems. For instance, the symbol of Jesus as Lamb of God is defined within the symbol of the atonement liturgy (Lev. 16) in which Jesus is like the scapegoat on whom all the sins of the priest and people are placed and who takes them away into the wilderness (see Jan van Eyck's *The Adoration of the Lamb*, figure 5, p. 66 below). This is a complex symbol system involving the Levitical sacrifice cult. But the symbol of Jesus as Lamb of God is also defined within the symbol system of the Passover (Ex. 12) in which the slaughtered lamb's blood was smeared on the doors of the Israelites in Egypt to ward off the angel of death who was sweeping through to kill all the firstborn of people and animals in the land. Then again, in the Book of Revelation the Lamb of God is not so much the one who takes away the sins of the world, or the one who wards off death, but is rather one of the several manifestations of Jesus – Lion of Judah, Root of David – who destroys the power of Satan and brings judgment on the world (Rev. 5:5–14). These three symbol systems are quite different, and will be analyzed in chapter 2. Yet they function together, resonating with each other, correcting, balancing, supplementing and complementing each other. Moreover, each of these systems involves symbols that take part in yet other symbol systems. The atonement ritual, for instance, is involved with symbols that distinguish intentional from unintentional sin and purity from impurity. The Passover was part of the much larger story of the Exodus and Yahweh's special relation to Israel. The victorious avenging Lamb is related to the several symbol systems defining Satan. No overall consistent theory or story puts together all these symbols, and systems of symbols, and systems of systems of symbols. Rather, they resonate together, or against one another, in the activities they shape interpretively. A mathematical symbol system, by contrast, aims to have every symbol consistently definable relative to the others. Much of what follows in chapters 1–7 is an analysis of the interactions of symbols and symbol systems.

Second, reference, as mentioned above, divides into primary and secondary reference, and of the first there are three kinds.[16] The most obvious kind of primary reference is through the conventions of a semiotic system. As a language determines what the references of a sign can be in this or that sort of interpretation, so the larger semiotics including gestures, sounds, visual signs, and so forth supplies the possibilities of extensional reference. Everything talked about in this book is at least conventional in its reference. The second kind of primary reference is iconic, that is, a reference that takes reality to be like the sign in some respect. Peirce's example was the cross on the church altar as an icon of the cross on which Jesus died, iconic by shape. Any description, however, is iconic in that it takes reality to be the way it describes. The positivists' dream of a formal scientific language with one-to-one mapping of reality is almost a caricature of iconicity. The third kind of reference is indexical, a "pointing" that establishes a causal relation between the object and the interpreter with the symbol such that what is important in the object comes across. This might be a mere turning of the head so that the interpreter sees what's coming. Or it could be the long process of the transformation of soul required to engage the object meaningfully with the symbol at hand. All of this will be discussed and illustrated in the chapters that follow.

Secondary reference is the readiness of qualification of the interpreter actually to engage the logical object with the sign or symbol at hand. Someone who has been abused by his or her father is likely to have great difficulty engaging God with the symbol Father. One also has to be at the right stage of spiritual maturity to use certain religious symbols

---

[16] This somewhat follows Peirce's classification. He wrote no sustained treatise on signs, but many of his writings are collected into what look like essays in the *Collected Papers*. See volume II, pp. 134–73. I have redeveloped these distinctions in *The Truth of Broken Symbols*.

actually to engage God, although one can understand their meanings readily enough without that maturity.

Third, interpretations are always made in actual contexts. The contexts have both purposive elements and given elements of time, place, and circumstance. The purposes are deeply shaped by cultural values and projects, by the needs of the circumstance, and also by personal considerations. The purposes lie within a complicated intentionality structure, analyzed in chapter 6, that gives direction to activity with interpretive components. In this book, especially in chapters 1–4, much is made of the difference between the context of the ancient world within which Christianity shaped its decisive symbols and the context of the late-modern period. There are also many differences in context between Christian groups at the present time, differences partly analyzed in chapter 5.

The hypothesis about truth here is that it is the carryover of what is important from the objects to the interpreters in the respects in which the symbols stand for the objects, as qualified by the interpreters' biology, culture, semiotic systems, and purposes.[17] The assessment of the truth of an interpretation thus is enormously subtle and complicated. It needs (1) to identify and sort the symbols involved in their systems, noting which possible systems are in play and which not, and how they interact, (2) to analyze the dimensions of reference involved, both primary and secondary, including how the interpretation identifies its logical object against a background, and (3) to detail the context of interpretation, the nature of the situation and how that affects the intentionality structure of the interpreter, thereby determining how the interpretation selects an object to be interpreted in a certain respect by certain symbols. The "arguments" in the chapters that follow work on bits and parts of this assessing analysis. In the long run, however, it is so complicated that only a community over time can make serious assessments. The purpose of this book is to invite that process to move ahead with the symbols analyzed here.

The question of truth is particularly complicated with regard to reference. A symbol such as "Heaven being up" might be iconically false and yet indexically true. Most religious symbols are iconically false if interpreted literally, because most are schematized images, not conceptual schemata or their underlying metaphysics. More subtle kinds of iconic descriptions that control for the distinction between schematized

---

[17] This is the thesis developed at length in my *Recovery of the Measure*, chapters 3–4.

images or world-views and their underlying metaphysics can be true, and might also have indexical reference as well. Whether an indexical reference is true cannot be decided by comparing the object with the interpretation of it, as was the hope with iconic reference. Rather, assessment needs to triangulate on both the logical object and the interpreter to see whether what is important is carried over in the proper respect. Religious "discernment of spirits" is extremely complicated. In point of fact, however, the Enlightenment supposition that truth is iconicity of mental form with the form of the external world, and could be judged by comparing them, has been revealed to be a fantasy, and the tests for iconicity are just as indirect as those for indexicality.[18]

In this book I aim to establish a normative and public defense of some central intellectual commitments of Christianity that have to do with Jesus Christ. Though there are many elements in Christianity beyond Christology, the most distinctive claims of Christianity have to do with Christ (and the Holy Spirit). In respect of interpreting ultimate reality, the human condition, and the kinds and critical characters of religious truth, the relation of Christianity to the other world religions is complex and interesting. But what is peculiar to Christianity is its Christology. What is true about Jesus Christ? Does the cult of Jesus Christ offer a way to salvation? These are normative questions of Christology.

The contemporary field of religious studies has established a proper public context for theology, namely, all the world's religions and their various secular counterparts in reference to which they need to make their cases. Public theology is an adventure in which identities rarely remain static. Hindu pundits, for instance, studying Christian symbolic meaning systems, might discover something that sharpens their imagination and corrects their culture, for instance, Jesus' inclusive table fellowship that implies an attack on the caste system. The Christian symbols then can be modified to apply to an Indian situation Jesus and his friends never imagined. Buddhist scholars, for instance, might discover that the kind of indexical reference involved in being "in Christ" is an improvement on the imitative indexicality of being a follower of Buddha embodying dharma. Confucian scholars might discover that the readiness of Christianity for contexts including bad families and broken homes, where love is learned outside the family, makes it an enticing supplement to the Confucian dependence on good families. In all these

---

[18] Richard Rorty's *Philosophy and the Mirror of Nature* is the most direct attack on the very symbols of Enlightenment commitment to iconicity as the only legitimate dimension of true reference.

ways, public theology about Christology might lead to greater empathy, perhaps syncretistic enlargements of other religious practices, perhaps even conversion. Of course it works the other way too: Christians engaged in public theology might be transformed to greater empathy, syncretistic appropriation of elements of other religions than Christianity, to multiple religious identity, or plain conversion. All of the world's great religions have transcended their own cultures to find their symbols' existential applicability and truth inculturated in new ways, and also to find new symbols for their own culture.

Secondary reference is particularly important for understanding the public character of theology because many people who can read and follow the arguments here cannot be appropriate secondary referents to Christological symbolic life for reasons of their own religious or anti-religious commitments. Scholars can come to appreciate how the Christology is true for the right kinds of people in the right contexts, but not true for themselves. For people, say from South or East Asia or from shamanistic traditions, whose cultures do not take the meaning-systems of Second Temple Judaism to be at the heart of their own cultural imagination, Christian symbols might be interesting but not engaging. For people whose cultural or psychic make-up disqualifies reference to ultimate things by means of the personifying symbols characteristic of Christianity, the Christian references might be interesting but not engaging. For people whose own existential contexts are simply not addressed by interpretations made possible by Christian symbols, Christian contexts might be appreciated as appropriate for others but not to the point of their own religious life. In these three senses, relating to meaning systems, reference, and existential context, people can say that the Christology is true for other people, namely, Christians with the right meaning systems in their imagination, the right readiness for reference, and the right contexts, but not true for themselves. The normative argument for a Christian theology in a global public thus requires making the case for the cultural, referential, and contextual conditions under which the Christology is true. This case can be made to anyone who can understand those conditions, even if they do not share those conditions.

If what I have argued so far is more or less on the mark, then there cannot be a neat and consistent genre for the analysis of the Christological symbols. In analyzing the meanings of symbols and the ways their systems interact, the genre of criticism as in literature and art is employed. Because of the difference in historical context between the symbols in their origin and that of their contemporary employment, historical analysis is involved. Sometimes the discussion calls for abstract metaphysics, although the heavy-duty arguments are finished by the end of chapter 1, only to be recurred to thereafter. Because part of the argument is to persuade readers to put themselves if only vicariously in the position of good secondary referents for the symbols, I need to make the symbols "meaningful" by preaching. Sometimes the argument is properly formal, with lots of passive voice. Other times the reader is addressed as "you." Sometimes the pronoun of address is neutralized but intensified as in "one cannot avoid ..." For the most personal parts I talk about myself in a confessional mode, assuming that the readers can substitute the analogies of their own heart. This multiplicity of required genres means there is no art to this writing, although it does imitate life.

THE CHRISTOLOGICAL SYMBOLS

This book will ask about how eight major Christian symbols can enable people to engage God truly and with salvific effects: God the Father, Jesus as the Atonement, the Cosmic Christ, Jesus Christ as the Second Person of the Trinity, the historical Jesus as the incarnate Word of God, Jesus as friend, the eschatological Jesus as Savior, and, briefly, the Holy Spirit. The first and last are not strictly Christological symbols but are presupposed by the others and will be treated in reference to Jesus: God the Creator as the Father to whom Jesus related himself and the Holy Spirit by which the Father and Son are made present (celebrated in the Trinitarianism in figure 4, p. 28 below). The second and third symbols are fundamental in the writings of St. Paul and have been thematized in many forms throughout Christian history (see the crucifixion images in the Dali cover and figure 6, p. 83 below and the Christ Pantokrators in figure 1 and figure 7, pp. 19 and 94 below). The fourth, Jesus Christ within the Trinity, was at the heart of the classical patristic creedal discussions and perhaps is the most difficult to justify in our anti-metaphysical and scientific age; the roots of deifying Jesus, however, are in the New Testament (see Sutherland's *Christ in Glory*, figure 9, p. 139 below). The historical Jesus, of course, has been the topic of much research and discussion for the last two hundred years, often as quite separated from the ancient claims about incarnation; I shall claim that the interesting thing about the historical Jesus is his ability to bear the symbol of incarnation (see Stella's *The Creche*, figure 12, p. 170 below Leonardo da Vinci's *The Last Supper*, figure 2, p. 20 below and Titian's *Noli me tangere*, figure 10,

Figure 1. *Christ Pantokrator*, detail, sixth-century encaustic icon, Holy Monastery of St. Catherine, at Sinai

p. 144 below). The sixth symbol, Jesus as friend, might seem to be of interest limited to popular Protestantism as nurtured by William Holman Hunt's *The Light of the World* (figure 13, p. 199 below) and Warner Sallman's *Head of Christ* (figure 14, p. 211 below), but in fact is at the heart of Jesus' self-identification in the Farewell Discourses of the Gospel of John: da Vinci's *Last Supper* is about evil discovered among friends. I will argue that friendship defines the heart of the religious quest: to befriend

Figure 2. Leonardo da Vinci, *The Last Supper*, c. 1495–98. Santa Maria delle Grazie, Milan

God. The ancient symbol of Jesus as shepherd (figure 16, p. 237 below) might have seemed in the nineteenth century to be a "friend" image; in antiquity it was an image of Christ as Savior.[19] The seventh symbol, Jesus the eschatological Savior, deals finally with the meaning of the cosmos and goal of human existence, the locus and point of Christian salvation; see Memling's *The Last Judgment* (figure 15, p. 226 below) for an indexical cosmic reference with Christian iconography, but also Roger Wagner's *The Harvest is the End of the World, and the Reapers are Angels* (figure 17, p. 260 below) for an alternative indexical cosmic reference with neutralized twentieth-century iconography.

Salvador Dali's painting of the crucifixion, chosen for the cover of this book, embraces all these symbols of Jesus in paradoxical ways. The crucifixion as such is an atonement topic. The perspective of the painting, however, is from above, looking down like God on Jesus towering over the world. More than most images of Jesus as the Cosmic Christ (for instance figures 1 and 7), Dali's asserts that the King of the Universe is the crucified one. At the foot of the cross is the boat of the fishermen, Jesus' first disciples, in whose train contemporary Christians find their historical identity.[20] By contrast, Grünewald's Resurrection from the Isenheim Altarpiece, on the back cover, simply blows apart any tidy set of symbols, an apophatic "More than This!"

From a systematic or scientific point of view, my selection of symbols is arbitrary. Many other symbols are also important and will be only glanced at here. I give no justifiable rule for selecting these rather than the others. To treat more symbols would make the book too long. The base-line arbitrariness is that these are the symbols that mean the most to me, of which I am most confident, and that have proved their truth in my own life and portion of the Christian community.

But the list is not entirely arbitrary. These are symbols that have been powerful in shaping Christian worship, spiritual practice, and community building. Other symbols that are more doctrinal have often been less important in Christian practice. The ecclesial orientation of this Christology dictates focusing first on the symbols of practice. Moreover, there is a rhetorical trajectory to these symbols, from Alpha to Omega, from Ground to Goal. Finally, these are among the most offensive Christian symbols. They offend the scientific-minded because they seem supernaturalistic, and they are often used by the supernaturalists

---

[19] For a fascinating study of conflicts in interpreting ancient Christian art, see Mathews' *The Clash of Gods*.

[20] For a historical account of this painting, see Gabriele Finaldi's *The Image of Christ*, p. 198.

to proclaim an offense to everyone else. If these symbols can be made vital, true, and saving in a liberal mediating theology such as this one, something serious and unexpected will have been accomplished.

Another dimension to the choice of symbols should be observed. Other symbols, such as the Word of God, and indeed most of the central doctrinal symbols in the creeds, are so multidimensional as to appear in different forms in many or all of the symbols thematized here. Such multidimensional symbols epitomize a large number of symbolic trajectories, overlying many different symbol systems. They are best elaborated in their different manifestations as interplaying with the symbols that are the primary focus. But in effect, many more symbols than the main eight, including major doctrinal ones, will be treated in this book. Each of the symbols of primary focus is analyzed in terms of several symbol systems, and subsystems of symbols.

Beginning with the chapter on God the Father, there is a constant interplay between the symbols functioning as schematized images for engaging God and the metaphysics that explains how they can have reference. Although chapter 3 will discuss the symbol of Christ as the visible image of the invisible divine creator, invisibility has not stopped artists such as Michelangelo in the creation scene from the Sistine Chapel (figure 3, p. 27 below) from representing the bearded Father. The discussion of God as Creator is explicitly metaphysical, and the consequences drawn out about the metaphysical nature of God there are employed to interpret the referential grounding of the other symbols in subsequent chapters. The development of a normative Christology requires this dialectical interaction of the symbols with the metaphysics, for reasons that have already been discussed. This means that the hermeneutical circle embracing the historical embodiments of the symbols and their current conditions of viability has a metaphysical dimension uncommon in hermeneutics.

The rubric for understanding all these Christological symbol systems is how they help flesh out the reality Jesus Christ has had as an operative transformative agent within Christian churches that engage God by means of Christ. That such symbols have been vitally engaging at various points within Christian history, if not continuously with equal emphasis, might be construed as a mere catalogue of once-vital symbols. But if the function of symbols is authentically to engage interpreters with their interpretive objects, then the question can be asked whether the symbols are true in their engagement. What is the truth about Jesus Christ? Perhaps the truth is limited to what gets conveyed to interpreters within their specific contexts, contexts we might no longer share. To assess that truth, theological scholars need to enter into those alien contexts. Without doing so they (we) cannot even understand the meanings of those contextualized interpretations of symbols. If the true engagement of symbols can be measured for alien contexts, then obviously it can be measured, at least to a degree, within our own context. The result is that the analysis of the reality of Jesus Christ as symbolically present throughout the Church can give rise to relatively testable contemporary normative Christology.

CHAPTER ONE

God the Father

THE GOD OF JESUS AND METAPHYSICAL ULTIMACY: HISTORICAL CONSIDERATIONS

The necessary starting point for a Christology is God, the God worshipped by Jesus through the schematized images of his religion and the God whom Christians further schematized by special relations with Jesus himself. As with all the Christological symbols to be studied here, the analysis will include both a metaphysical theological theory of the "object," God, and an interpretation of something in the human condition in terms of which God might be schematized, with a tracking of how the schematized images are legitimated by the theoretical conception relative to the human condition under certain specified conditions. Unlike the analysis of the other symbols, the preponderance of argument here will be on the metaphysical conception that in fact is at the heart of the theological ideas in the other symbols as well.

Paula Fredriksen, following E. P. Sanders and others, argues that we should assume that Jesus and his disciples were living as faithful Jews in most common respects except where there is specific reason to believe otherwise.[1] Jesus made many trips to the Temple according to the gospel stories, beginning with his circumcision (Luke 2:25–38) and annually during his youth (Luke 2:41). The synoptic gospels organize Jesus' ministry around a progressive journey to Jerusalem for the Passover confrontation at the Temple, whereas John suggests many visits for a variety of festivals.[2] Thus whatever criticisms Jesus might have made of Jewish practice and observation of the Temple sacrifices, they were the work of an insider, not an outsider.

---

[1] See Fredriksen's *From Jesus to Christ* and *Jesus of Nazareth, King of the Jews*, Sanders' *The Historical Figure of Jesus*, and Geza Vermes' *The Changing Faces of Jesus*, for a selection of scholars otherwise different who agree on this point.

[2] See Fredriksen's *Jesus of Nazareth, King of the Jews*, chapter 5.

The earliest Church constituted itself in Jerusalem and its suburbs. The Festival of Weeks or Pentecost (Lev. 23:15–21) brought many pilgrims to the city and it was they whom Peter addressed in his Pentecost sermon (Acts 2). The disciples regularly prayed in the Temple and got in trouble for teaching there so often (Acts 3–7). When Peter and the other apostles began coping with the Christian faith of Gentiles (Acts 10, 21, Gal. 2), it was in the context of the loss of the community's assumed practice of Jewish life, including Temple worship, because Gentiles could not advance into the Temple beyond the Gentile Court.[3] All of Paul's letters, and possibly (though not likely) the Gospel of Mark, were written before the destruction of the Temple in 70 CE when the possibility of Temple worship was ended.[4] The other gospels and later pastoral letters reflect a community in which the connection with Jewish Temple worship had been broken and Christians could see themselves as over against other sects of Judaism, though all those sects were having to cope with the loss of the sacrificial temple ceremonies enjoined in the Torah.

All this is to say that Jesus and the early generations of Christians presupposed the conception of God of their Jewish contemporaries and only slowly modified this in relation to the growing importance of Gentile Christians and their culture.[5] This Jewish conception was extraordinarily rich and shaped their imaginations through ritual life, especially use of the Psalms. Although scholars debate the specific content of this conception and its internal variations, at least five things stand out: (1) that God is creator of the universe; (2) that God is particular and definite as exhibited in the covenants, especially the Torah, not general and "all things to all people"; (3) that this particularity includes a specific history with Israel, as in the Exodus; (4) that the particularity also includes promises for the fulfillment of Israel; and (5) that God can be likened to a king under some circumstances and the nations to the kingdom of God, at least in their eschatological fulfillment. Each of these meant a great many things, not all compatible with one another. But the Christians took up all of them and developed them with their own many slants, also not always compatible.

---

[3] See ibid., pp. 42–73, especially p. 70.

[4] The most recent study of dating of Mark is in Joel Marcus's *Mark 1–8*, pp. 37–39. He dates it after the flight of the Christian community from Jerusalem following the occupation of the Temple by Zealots in 67–68 CE and possibly as late as 74–75CE.

[5] For a careful review of New Testament texts on Jesus' conception or image of God, see Roger Haight's *Jesus: Symbol of God*, chapter 4. See also Anthony J. Saldarini's "Ultimate Realities: Judaism."

If Jesus and his disciples had a special emphasis to lay on the conception of God, it was to stress the image of God as father, as in the Lord's Prayer, the Pater Noster (Matt. 6:9–13, Luke 11:2–4), Jesus' Farewell Discourses in John (14–17), and his claim, setting kinship family aside, that "whoever does the will of my Father in heaven is my brother and sister and mother" (Matt. 12: 50; see also Mark 3:31–35, Luke 8:19–21). Jesus was not the first in his tradition to call God "father" (see Isa. 63: 16 and 64:8, Wis. 2:16–18); that people, especially the people of Israel, are children of God was a common theme. But Jesus' teaching had the effect of placing God as father at the head of the kingdom of God ("Our Father. . .thy kingdom come") rather than God as warrior or king (e.g. 1 Sam. 8). Although he still employed the image of the king ruling the kingdom of God, in some parables (e.g., Matt. 22:1–14), the parable of the Prodigal Son (Luke 15:11–32) had overwhelming power to establish his rhetoric of God as father.

This conception of God the Creator as father of all people is different from conceptions of God as father of Jesus as Son of God exclusively. The Apostles' Creed (followed with variants by other creeds) expresses both senses of divine fatherhood. It begins, "I believe in God the Father Almighty, Maker of Heaven and Earth, and in Jesus Christ his only Son our Lord, Who was conceived by the Holy Ghost, Born of the Virgin Mary . . ." The first phrase identifies God's paternity with the creation of the entire cosmos. Michelangelo's famous image (figure 3) of the "Creation of Adam" on the ceiling of the Sistine Chapel symbolizes God's paternity of all people. In a different sense of paternity, God is father of only one Son, Jesus Christ. That idea of the generative relation between the Persons of the Trinity (see chapter 4) had a different ground from Jesus' Pater Noster image of God as father of all. In fact, the Apostles' Creed identifies Jesus' personal paternity with the Holy Spirit (and maternity with Mary). Murillo's painting of *The Heavenly and Earthly Trinities* (figure 4) illustrates four Trinities: the divine Trinity in the vertical line down from God the Father to the Holy Spirit (the dove) to Jesus, the human family trinity in the horizontal cross-piece from Mary to Jesus to Joseph, the "natal" trinity of Jesus in the center moving left to his mother's womb and up to the inseminating Holy Spirit, and the "epiphantic" trinity of Jesus in the center again moving up to the Holy Spirit and right to the viewer and all humanity through Joseph who presents him. The Trinitarian concerns arose some generations after Jesus and his disciples. For Jesus himself, the fatherhood of God related to God as Creator of the universe with whom people can be as children.

Figure 3. Michelangelo Buonarroti, *Creation of Adam*, 1508–12,
Sistine Chapel, Vatican, Rome

The theme of God as Creator is thus central to Jesus' own religious practice and assumptions, and to his explicit teachings that advocate relating to the Creator on the analogy of a father; this centrality was carried on and made more explicit in the early Church. The theme is so central, in fact, that any contemporary Christology that attempts to be faithful to Jesus and his early followers needs to come to terms with the symbol of God as Creator of the universe and to possess a metaphysical conception that explains what that symbol schematizes.

The symbol of God as Creator is correlative, of course, to the conception of the universe created. Psalm 95, for instance, celebrates God as creator of specific things, the Earth's corners, the mountains'

Figure 4. Esteban Murillo, *The Heavenly and Earthly Trinities*, 1681–82, National Gallery, London

strength, the sea, the dry land, and people who are the sheep of his pasture. Genesis 1 takes a more systematic approach, starting with the most elementary character of existence, the cosmic distinction between light and darkness, and moving step by step to the complex cosmos. Job (38–41) employs an architectural metaphor for creation, with the cosmos likened first to a great building. The conception of the cosmos reflected in the Noah story (Genesis 6–9) was of a domed continent surrounded by water with water under the continent as well as above the dome; the flood opened the gates of the dome and threatened to undo all the distinctions in Genesis 1 that had made human habitation possible. The Hellenistic world of which the early Christians were a part assumed a hierarchy of domes or levels of reality extending upward to a variety of Heavens and downward to Hell (Eph. 1:20–23, 2:6, 6:12, Rom. 8:38, Phil. 2:6–11, Col. 1–3). In a remarkable passage the author of Ephesians (Eph. 4:7–10) evokes the image of Christ knitting the entire broken cosmos together, ascending above the highest heavens and descending into the depths of universe. This cosmology of levels of reality was formalized in Christian thinkers such as Origen.[6]

A contemporary Christology needs a metaphysical conception of God as Creator that correlates with our contemporary physical cosmologies and that can be schematized into the biblical tradition's images of God as father and creator. Contemporary scientific cosmologies reject the ancient Earth-centered view, which has deep implications for notions of salvation history. And they describe a cosmos far older and larger than that imagined in antiquity, one that evolves according to forces that in principle can be described scientifically. Contemporary cosmologies are unanimous in rejecting the cosmology of antiquity. But they still are contentious among themselves on crucial points such as the origin and end of the cosmos, as well as the determinateness of communicability among parts of the universe. So, a contemporary metaphysical theory of God as Creator needs to be tolerant of a number of different cosmologies that might yet turn out to be true.

Beth Neville's *From Caves to Cosmos* (between pp. 158 and 159) is a late-modern play on the creation symbols. Most antiquely, it starts from the very Earth-centered view of a cave looking out (plate 1) and up (plate 3) to infinity (plate 7). But in plate 4 it reverses the direction of vision and

---

[6] See Origen's *On First Principles*; on ancient Mediterranean cosmologies, see Richard Sorabji's *Time, Creation, and the Continuum*; on the spiritual significance of ancient cosmology, relating as much to time and eternity as to spatial arrangement, see Peter Manchester's "The Religious Experience of Time and Eternity" and Jean Pepin's "Cosmic Piety."

looks down on the Earth, objectifying it as the origin but not destiny of humanity, a kind of space-port for a greater journey; subsequent plates do not have a located angle of vision. Plate 3 is the cosmic rainbow connecting the earthly playing field with the orbital perspective, a direct allusion to Noah's rainbow sign that says the original creation will not be undone by releasing the primeval chaos of waters. The plate is called "God's rainbow's really fire, not light and water" to mark the priority of the original creation, and the seriousness of the rainbow; it is painted in "fire" colors, contrasting red with green in combinations that blur boundaries like the Christmas advent of God. "Oh, what deaths are these, the supernovas," plate 6, uses the same colors to reverse the creative fire in tight circles that implode and disappear, not the rainbow parabola creating connection. The paintings are structured around the Alpha and Omega of creation. Yet Neville's vision is thoroughly modern in laying that structure on the evolution of the race from cave-dreamers to space-travelers tacking on time's river (plates 5–6).

The second element mentioned above in Jesus' and the early Church's conception of God is that God is particular and specific, as in covenanting with Israel. The metaphysics of this needs to account for the particularity of this created cosmos, why there is this world rather than some other. In human terms, relating to the image of the Creator as father, we need to recognize and account metaphysically for how God can give us our particular lives, with their specific joys and troubles. People do not all enjoy the same chances or take the same risks.

The way to frame this issue metaphysically is with the distinction between two ideas of what is ultimate in reality, the idea that it is symmetrical and the idea that it is asymmetrical.[7] The symmetrical idea supposes equilibrium at the base of things, a wholeness, or pure emptiness. Becoming attuned to the ultimate is losing one's particularity to be dissolved in the symmetry of the ultimate. The problem for symmetrical views of the ultimate is to account for the move from elemental symmetry to the determinate tilt of the particular cosmos.[8] In the history of

---

[7] I owe this distinction to conversations with Wesley J. Wildman, and believe it is he who first introduced it. Frank Close's *Lucifer's Legacy* is a witty romance on the hidden symmetries beneath the apparent asymmetries of nature, with Lucifer credited with the asymmetries that give us our determinate universe. The assumption here is that symmetry is ultimately what is most understandable, a mathematician's perspective. I shall argue, on the contrary, that asymmetry is the ground of rationality because it is the result of selective determinate creation, the making of something particular, and that such particular creation is what we most understand.

[8] Close's *Lucifer's Legacy* is precisely the attempt to give this account, reducing asymmetry to symmetry.

Western theology, the Aristotelian notion of the Perfect Substance, the Neo-Platonic conception of the One and of God beyond the One, the Thomistic conception of God as pure, simple, undifferentiated Act of *Esse*, and the Eckhartian distinction between God and the transcendent Godhead, all illustrate various ways of specifying symmetry. So do Buddhist notions of Nothingness.

The asymmetrical idea is that the aboriginal ultimate is the very particular act of creating as such, creating a particular cosmos and hence making itself a particular Creator. The cosmos as well as God has a determinate tilt from the very beginning. The divine act precedes and causes the divine nature, in some appropriate sense of "precedes." The Creator is not a being apart from creating, but becomes a singular God as Creator in the creating. On the asymmetrical view there is no difficulty in accounting for the particularity of the cosmos; the interesting question is how the cosmos is as regular as it seems to be. Attunement to ultimate reality is reconciliation to the particular ground of one's particular existence, not emptying oneself into the One or None.

The asymmetrical view has the distinct advantage over the symmetrical one in providing a metaphysics for a God of particularity in creation, and also in relating particularly to a people such as Israel or the Church, to creating a world with promise for fulfillment, and to justifying metaphors for God such as kingship. (These are the other elements of the conception of God assumed in late Second Temple Judaism and its early Christian forms.) The asymmetrical idea is classically illustrated in the conception of creation *ex nihilo* (so long as that conception is not interpreted to mean that God is a substance who creates the world out of nothing *except the divine substance*).

To put the point somewhat paradoxically: A metaphysics of asymmetry which denies that God is a being apart from creating the world is more friendly than the symmetrical idea to the particularistic schematized images of a personal God who creates just this world, relates differently to different people, and is wholly "unfair" where fairness means treating people with equality. A symmetrical metaphysics claiming that God is intrinsically a personal perfect substance has grave difficulty accounting for the particularity of creation expected of persons because particularity is a deviation from symmetrical perfection, wholeness, or pure nothingness. The serious question for Christology will come, however, when I ask whether the particularity of an asymmetrical Creator *ex nihilo* can indeed be used to ground the symbolic personifications of God involved in Christology. That question is in suspension for

the moment while I emphasize the difference between the biblical schematized image of God the Father as a person and the metaphysical idea
of God as Creator *ex nihilo* who has no reality apart from creating.

The philosophical or metaphysical ideas to be presented in the
remaining three sections of this chapter are to be regarded under two
rubrics. Under one, the metaphysics is only necessary to show it to be
possible to employ the religious symbols faithfully in the late-modern
age. As such, these ideas might be only one of several sets of adequate
metaphysical ideas that would perform that function. People deeply
committed to alternative metaphysical views can look upon these as only
a sample, perhaps a false sample, so long as their own metaphysical ideas
both are faithful to late-modern knowledge and richly ground the religious symbols.

Under the second rubric, the metaphysical ideas to be presented
should be looked at not just to see whether they allow the Christian
symbols to be applied today as their schematized images, but also to see
what is true of the world, understood in late-modern terms, that is religiously interesting. The scientific, philosophical, historical, and social-
scientific language of late modernity has flattened out what Tillich
called the depth dimension of reality.[9] Attention and recognition are
restricted to things that appear strictly in time. A good late-modern
metaphysics should be able to recover the depth dimension and thus
require something like biblical language to be its vitalizing expression.
The metaphysical ideas should identify and describe creation, and their
schematized images in biblical and other religious symbols should
convey their existential depth. Whereas the metaphysics of God as
Creator describes creation, the schematization of those ideas as the
religious symbols carries over what is important in the object of those
ideas for human religious life.

A CONTEMPORARY THEORY OF GOD AS CREATOR

At this point it is necessary to explain the idea of God as Creator *ex nihilo*.
The logical point here is not to "prove" this idea as a metaphysical
hypothesis, only to explain the idea in reference to others and show how
it is metaphysically plausible, tolerant of whatever science or any other

---

[9] See Tillich's essay "The Nature of Religious Language," which is chapter 5 of his *Theology of
Culture*; this essay discusses the depth dimension in direct relation to what is revealed through religious symbols. For more general discussions of "depth" see his *The Religious Situation* and *The Courage
to Be*.

mode of inquiry discovers, and what its structure is that might bear the reference of the imagery of God the Father.[10] The next section will continue the discussion into the topic of the temporality of the world relative to the eternity of God. The final section in the chapter will sketch a metaphysical ground for the symbols of the Logos and the Holy Spirit.

Suppose by hypothesis that God is the act creating everything determinate out of nothing (*ex nihilo*).[11] Without the act, there would be nothing. This would not be a metaphysically rich Nothingness, or a space-time empty of things. Just nothing. Of course, there is not just nothing, there is the world. And from the standpoint of the world looking back from its utter contingency to what would be if there were no creation, the nothing looks like the Abyss so intimate to the mystics.

The creative act itself is a sheer making, an asymmetrical creativity going from nothing to the determinate world. The act has a form, the particular form of the world created. Perhaps that form can be analyzed into interestingly different layers, with some elements of form being transcendental to all determinate things as claimed in the theory of the Logos put forward below. What is most interesting about the act, however, is its sheer creativity, the making of something.

The idea of creating something new is resisted by thinkers who believe that all ideas have to be about forms or patterns and that explanation means exhibiting first principles or forms.[12] They understand human creativity in terms of rearranging previously given elements, perhaps with a little randomness, so that creativity is only a changing of form. But any change within time involves at least a modicum of novelty. Consider all the elements that are real before the change. What is added to them to constitute the change? Whatever it is, it cannot be included in the prior elements or it would make no difference. If it is not included, it is novel, over and above the prior elements. The novelty might be a new form, or a partly new form (which is a new sub-form). It might be

---

[10] The conception of creation *ex nihilo* has been a preoccupation in my work since *God the Creator*, which developed the idea in detail with fairly comprehensive arguments relative to other options. Summaries and approaches from other angles are to be found in *Soldier, Sage, Saint*, chapter 5, *Creativity and God*, *The Tao and the Daimon*, chapters 3–4, *A Theology Primer*, *Behind the Masks of God*, and *Eternity and Time's Flow*. Because the exposition in the text here is so abbreviated, I shall give more specific references to places where I have discussed points in detail with more consideration of objections.

[11] This supposition is defended as a positive hypothesis in *God the Creator*. Chapters 1 and 2 reject alternative theories for accounting for being and solving the problem of the one and the many. Chapter 3 mounts a positive argument based on the categories developed earlier.

[12] See my *Creativity and God*, pp. 46–47, 62–63, for an exploration of this relative to process philosophers who reject the explanatory power of creativity as making.

little more than the repetition of the old elements in their old form, but the repetition itself is new. Even if the world were absolutely stable through time with no change of form whatsoever, there would be the novelty of each moment adding a new instance to its predecessors or there would be no time.[13] Contemporary physics has complicated this commonsense picture of endurance and change through time, though the point still holds: without novelty there is neither motion (and hence no passage of time) nor change.

Whereas in ordinary temporal processes change does involve antecedent elements that are rearranged with some novel additions, in the divine creative act there are no antecedent elements, according to the creation *ex nihilo* hypothesis. The act creates absolutely everything that is determinate. Whereas in our temporal lives we see bits and snatches of divine creativity (which is sometimes coincident with our creativity), in the divine creative act as such, the making of determinate novelty is total. The creative act does not make the world out of pre-existent matter. The Christian tradition has said that God has no co-equals.

Nor does the creative act make the world out of some divine stuff, although many theologians have said that. If the divine stuff is determinate, then we have to ask how God's nature got that way and the answer would have to be in terms of an antecedent divine will making it that way, which only repeats the problem back a step. If the divine stuff is simple and indeterminate, which is what most Neo-Platonic and Thomistic theologians have said, then whence arise the determinate things of the world? How do they get their boundaries and relations? To suppose that the divine stuff is pure fullness of being is to require that negations be introduced to delimit it into finite determinate parts. The negation of pure fullness, however, requires a positive act of limiting, the creation of positive determinations, in other words. Those positive determinations, or positive negations, are not contained within the pure divine fullness and so are novel and *ex nihilo*. Why then say that the creative act proceeds from pure fullness rather than nothing? The fullness has no character and is indistinguishable from nothing. Only an Aristotelian prejudice that you can't get something from nothing, "out of nothing, nothing comes," would incline a thinker to say that the divine creative act proceeds from fullness of being. Quite the contrary, what the divine creative act produces is precisely what cannot be found in the antecedent fullness, or nothingness, namely the determinateness

---

[13] See my technical argument of this point in *The Cosmology of Freedom*, pp. 151–54.

of things. So it is better to say that the divine creative act is simply the asymmetrical making of determinate things out of nothing determinate: nothing, nothing, nothing.[14]

The dialectical argument of the previous paragraph is likely interesting or convincing only to people who have attempted to conceive God prior to creation as the fullness of being in some sense, and its dialectical complexity is likely baffling to those who are not aficionados of abstract metaphysics. But there is an experiential appeal to be made to the creativity of the divine act. In everyday life we encounter countless instances of the existences of things. *What* is encountered might be expected forms, but *that* they are there and then, even if expected, is not reducible to what they are. Our pragmatic interests usually direct us to the what, where, and when of things, not to their that which we take for granted. But often enough, we respond to the thatness with wonder.[15] Poets make us attend to this regularly. Nature mysticism calls attention to the sheer existence of things systematically.[16] In the end, after we have absorbed all the principles of existence and change, final intelligibility involves locating and focusing on the making of the things exhibiting those principles.[17] Of course, the divine creative act does not have an internal nature that stretches through time so that we can understand steps in creation. It is simply the making of determinate things out of nothing.

The divine creative act results in the determinate things of the world. Those things constitute the terminus of the act, and hence its nature insofar as it has one. The determinate things do not exist in a medium apart from the creative act – that would have to be created too, and would be just another determinate thing. The world is the determinate achievement of the creative act, not something separate from the act but its completion. The world, of course, is temporal, a point that will be analyzed in more detail in the next section. "Completion," "achievement," and suchlike notions mean not temporal processes, but rather the act's result, which is temporal process itself (among other things). The integrity of the world consists in its being *what* it is. *That* it is means it is part of God.

---

[14] For this spelled out with many more combinations and alternatives, see my *God the Creator*, chapter 2.

[15] The distinction between the *what* and the *that* is elaborated in my *Soldier, Sage, Saint*, chapter 5, as the basis for the creation doctrine.

[16] On mysticism and nature romanticism, see *The Highroad around Modernism*, chapters 2 and 12, especially the latter, "Technology and the Richness of the World," my answer to Heidegger.

[17] On ontological and cosmological causation, regarding decision, see my *Religion in Late Modernity*, chapter 1.

What is the divine nature? God is the creative act that has nothing from which to begin and that makes the determinate world. The world is part of God because it is the act's own achieved nature and has no independent existence. At the "other end" of the creative act, as it were, is nothing. The nothing has no character. But because of the act's making of the determinate world out of nothing, the nothing is the source from which the world comes. Three interdefined notions are at work here: source, act, and product (or determinate world). The nothing would not be source without the act making it the source of the world. The act would not act unless from the source it makes the world as product. The product or world would have no determinateness unless it were made to be determinate from no determination. These three elements of God are symmetrically interdefined: each needs the others in order to be determinate. But what these elements together define is the asymmetrical act of creation of the determinate world from nothing.[18]

The three elements of God – source, act, and product – are the metaphysical rudiments of a Trinitarian theology.[19] The source is the metaphysical referent for God the Father, the act the referent for the Holy Spirit, and the transcendental elements of the determinate produced world the referent for the Son. Much needs to be done with these notions before there can be any serious religious equivalence. The last section of this chapter will discuss the relation of the Word of God or Logos to the rest of creation as well as how the comprehensive divine creative act can be identified with the specifics of the Holy Spirit.

God's nature, on this conception of creation *ex nihilo*, is one of the products of creation, a conclusion that will be surprising to many. This conception in a vague way follows the tradition of Duns Scotus that the divine will precedes the divine nature rather than the tradition of Thomas Aquinas that the divine nature determines the divine will. For thinkers like Thomas who are wedded to a substance theory of reality, God can only create as an expression of the divine nature. Action, on the substance theory, moves from a given actuality to a new derivative from that. It is on the basis of this action-derived-from-antecedent-nature principle that Thomas and others can argue from things in the world by analogy back to the nature of God.

---

[18] This point is explained in detail in my *God the Creator*, chapter 4.

[19] For a discussion of this distinction relative to the classical Christian doctrine of the Trinity, replete with an analysis of heresies, see *The Tao and the Daimon*, chapter 4, "Creation and the Trinity."

The belief that God's creativity must proceed from an antecedent nature funds the added metaphysical belief that God is a supernatural being apart from creation, which I am claiming instead is a schematized image. This implicit logic supports the common analogical inferences that God must create and act the way human beings create and act, but without limitation or imperfection. So, it is thought that, as we consciously entertain plans and choose, so God deliberates but with perfect wisdom. As we have an interior subjectivity that expresses itself in outer action, so God must have such an interior life. As we are addressed by others and respond out of our interior understanding and will, so does God who therefore can be addressed literally with petitionary prayer. The biblical images of God as a supernatural person, which evolved historically from naturalistic images of a storm-god, therefore can be projected onto a metaphysics of God as a substance who acts out of the divine nature. Although it is possible to see why supernaturalists gravitate to a model of God as substance, with divine will derived from divine nature and the products of will reflecting the divine nature, their analogies simply do not work.

To argue against this supernatural model of God it is helpful to consider the work of the contemporary theologian Keith Ward, who is only the latest in a great line of theologians from Thomas Aquinas to Austin Farrar defending the supernaturalist view. He holds that God is "a supernatural being of supreme power and value" who creates the world,[20] and he develops this idea through masterly discussions of central theological loci in *Religion and Creation*: divine creativity and power, wisdom, love, goodness, awareness, bliss, eternity, and the trinity. Ward's argument is the following:

God must have a given nature, which is not chosen, but which God possesses of necessity. It does not make sense to suppose that God chooses the divine nature completely, since there must already be a choosing nature in existence to make such a choice. For any choice to be made, there must already be knowledge of what could be chosen, power to choose, and some rational criteria of choice. There must therefore already exist a being with knowledge, power, and standards of choice. The divine nature cannot be caused by any other being, since then the Creator would not be the creator of everything other than itself. It cannot come into being out of nothing, since that would make it purely arbitrary and random. And it cannot cause itself, since a thing would have to exist in order to bring itself into existence, which is absurd.[21]

---

[20] Ward, *Religion and Creation*, p. 287.   [21] *Ibid.*, p. 171.

Ward's basic argument is that the creation of the divine nature by the divine will is an unintelligible idea, that *of course* you need an agent with a nature to perform a creative act. He appeals to an anthropomorphic model of choice to say there has to be a divine chooser with knowledge, standards, and so forth. But that appeal is mistaken if God creates the nature of being chooser by choosing, as the creation *ex nihilo* hypothesis proposes. He claims it is absurd to believe that a thing could bring itself into existence, although that is what is asserted by those who believe the divine nature is something determined by the divine creative act.[22]

Ward develops an extremely intelligent and up-to-date version of the Thomistic argument from analogy, according to which one begins with the claim that God is like a human person and then removes the limitations of finitude from human personhood, all in coordination with other analogies and considerations of divine transcendence. He needs the finite human side of the analogy of God as chooser in order to represent as absurd the view that God's choice or creative act creates the divine nature. He needs to say that God, like human beings, needs to have a choosing nature in order to choose, knowledge of possibilities in advance, and criteria of choice.

But there is something arbitrary about this. Why could we not just as well say that the difference between divine and human creative choice is that the former does not need possibilities, criteria or a creative nature in advance but simply and purely creates selectively, the creative choice being justified by what it brings about, including its own criteria? That is, why cannot the analogy with human creativity turn out to support the radical creativity of the creation *ex nihilo* idea? The reason is that Ward wants to keep a very close analogy between the human and the divine so that God can be rendered even at the fundamental metaphysical level as a person, thus maintaining a commonsense continuity with biblical talk of God as a person.

But the problem with arguments about God from analogy is that in order to know what to deny you need to know something positive and probably non-analogical, for instance Thomas' claim that God is simple and admits of no potentiality. What is the positive ground for saying that

---

[22] Professor Ward and I are in complete agreement on the importance of Christian theology being able to make sense of the anthropomorphic symbols of God as found in Christian scriptures, liturgies, and so forth, which is one of the motives of his position. We are also in agreement that such symbols are only symbolic in some sense and that God's nature transcends the finite application of those symbols to human choosers and makers. But we disagree on the weight to be given the anthropomorphic conceptions and their place in the development of conceptions of God.

God, like human beings, needs antecedent knowledge of possibilities, potential to choose creatively, and standards of choice, rather than that God creates all those things? The Thomistic tradition, of course, says that God contains all human powers and virtues eminently, without finite limitation.

Perhaps on the contrary the human need for antecedent knowledge, power, and criteria is not a virtue derivative from God but rather the fault of finitude and precisely what is without analogue in God. The point is, whenever analogy about God has an argumentative force so as to deny a contrary view, as is the case here, rather than a merely rhetorical or explicative force, it has an arbitrary moment in every instance when it decides what is analogous and what is dis-analogous. The technical way of saying this is that neither a three-termed analogy of proportion nor a four-termed analogy of proper proportionality can have non-arbitrary argumentative force because in neither is the determinate distance between God and the finite world knowable – in fact that distance is not finite.[23]

In conceptions of God drawn from analogy there is arbitrariness and special pleading for every analogy. Of course we do not want to say that God is the Big Guy in the Sky. But the analogical approach so often turns out to say God is just like the Big Guy in the Sky except somehow mysteriously transcendent in the places where that conception is embarrassing. The conception of God as personal on the analogy of human beings then is attended with a patchwork cover of qualifications, each designed to avoid the embarrassment of saying that God is just a Big Guy in the Sky but arbitrary from the standpoint of the analogy.

Only if we think God has to be a substance with properties, as Ward assumes, such that divine action is understandable in terms of those properties, would we think that God has a nature apart from and in any sense prior to creation. But we do not have to think that, because there is an alternative metaphysical hypothesis, that of creation *ex nihilo*. The following arguments go toward showing why the radical creation idea of God is preferable and serve to summarize and recapitulate what has been put forward so far concerning God the Father.

The *first* argument is to show its religious and Christian relevance. That God is creator of each and every determinate thing, with its determinate connections, means that each thing in its connections has an

---

[23] See my technical analysis of the analogy of proportion and that of proper proportionality in *God the Creator*, pp. 14–22. On the difference between argumentative analogy and rhetorical or explicative analogy, see pp. 138–40.

ontological contingency in addition to its cosmological contingency upon causal connections.[24] The sense of ontological contingency on God as creator pervades Christian teachings about the nature of the world and human beings. That God is the creative act upon which determinate things depend means that Christians can find God in and give thanks for everything when attention is called to that creativity. That God is the source of the created world underlies the dialectic of the mystics who contemplatively go beyond the world, beyond the dynamic act of its creation, to the fecund Abyss of non-being. The notion of the Abyss is paradoxical, as Tillich would say. First it says that God is nothing, nothing, nothing, not the Big Guy in the Sky. Then it says that the first point would be wholly unintelligible if there were no determinate creation out of the Abyss. The mystical paths all presuppose determinate characters of the world or some hierarchy of being in order to make the point of transcendence to the indeterminate. The three terms of the Creator-God – source, creative act, created world – thus coordinate many religious conceptual and experiential projects.[25]

A *second* argument for the hypothesis is that creative novelty is found in ordinary human experience and this gives rise to a different conception of God as personal from the supernaturalist one. To select only the fact that human experience always has antecedents and takes these into account in temporal process is arbitrary for understanding God. True, human beings always have antecedently formed character, act on prior knowledge of possibilities, and have canons of judgment in play as they act. Nevertheless, any creative human action always adds something to those antecedent resources, and that addition is novel, not to be found in the resources, and hence with respect to origin, *ex nihilo*. It is in respect of the novelty that finite persons are like God. In most human actions the novelty is wee. Where it is significant, the novelty might seem wild, out of character. Still, a person forms personal character and identity precisely by the novelty. People's responsible moral identity is formed by what they do creatively with the conditions of their lives, what they add to what they inherit, not merely by the given conditions of their existence.[26] God's creation of everything out of nothing is like what people do every day, with the exception that God has nothing given to deal with and creates only novelty.

---

[24] See chapter 1 of my *Religion in Late Modernity*, and on the experience of contingency see *God the Creator*, chapter 8.

[25] Many of these are detailed in illustrative fashion in *God the Creator*, part 2.

[26] See my arguments in *The Cosmology of Freedom*, part 2, and *Normative Cultures*, chapter 6.

A *third* argument for the hypothesis of creation *ex nihilo* is that its claim that creation is of everything that is determinate, including the determinations making up the divine nature, allows science and all other cognitive endeavors to find the world to be what it is, without any predisposition to infer from the nature of God that the world has to be anything in particular. This point is a tremendous relief in the religion and science discussions. Whatever any inquiry finds the world to be is compatible in principle with the concept of God as Creator *ex nihilo*. Empirical study of the world can reveal something about God in the sense that God is the creator of what is discovered. But nothing in the conception of a divine nature would require that the world be a certain way, for instance all good, devoted to the human, or completely orderly. The world has just the determinate character it has.

A *fourth* point is that the values of things can be conceived to be created, not derivative from divine goodness. There are different kinds and degrees of value, but it can be argued that nothing determinate is without some value.[27] If something is a disvalue from the standpoint of something else, as an exquisitely complex and self-defended virus is a pain to its host, still it has some intrinsic value. Therefore, the justification of the creative act is in the collective value of its product, not any antecedent motive. As Genesis 1 says, God looked at what he had created and saw that it was good. Similarly with human justification for choice: the act itself elevates some one among the several alternative possible motives to be the reason for the action. Moreover, nearly every human choice discovers that there are more value-laden elements in its outcome than anticipated in imaginative consideration of possible motives – we will more than we know in advance and create our characters in that existential leap.

Consider the traditional claim by Ward and others that God is a being of supreme value. On Ward's hypothesis, supreme goodness is part of God's given nature. But then there are the traditional difficulties in explaining how a good God can create a world with evil, suffering, and woes in it. The qualifications by finitist theologians that God might be limited in power, or purely temporal and thus at a loss to know and control the future, or that God creates free people with enough rope to hang themselves, are burdensome. To say that God is the source of all goodness in the world including standards for free beings, and that God

---

[27] This point was argued carefully in my *Cosmology of Freedom*, chapter 3, and in *Recovery of the Measure*, part 2.

is the collective goodness of the world in the sense that determinate things are the termini or results of the divine creative act, is far more convincing. Thus God can be acknowledged to be the source of the values in both the virus and its human host, one flourishing and the other threatened, intimate to both. There is no need to apply human moral criteria to a supposed antecedent divine plan, which trips on theodicy. Rather we acknowledge the multifarious values achieved in the particular, tilted, asymmetrical Creator God.

Consider the question of what makes something valuable. Ward argues that "value must consist in appreciation by some consciousness."[28] He grounds goods in their being appreciated by the divine consciousness. But when it is necessary to say *why* goods legitimately are appreciated, his argument becomes very complicated and in the divine case the final claim seems to be that they are appreciated because they are or might be created. Is it not simpler to say that there are some characteristics of things that make them valuable, for instance their harmonic determinate natures, and that God has created a world where everything determinate is of such a character?[29] From this hypothesis it is straightforward to understand how consciousnesses sometimes might be mistaken about and other times alert to what is valuable.

A *fifth* point in defense of the creation *ex nihilo* hypothesis is that it suggests a truly holy wildness in God. Holy wildness is obscured by conceptions of an antecedently good divine nature whose actions must be understood in the human analogates of what a good agent does. Human moral identity is defined in part by the fact that we have some control over the outcomes of our behavior that differ in value, and we are by definition better in moral identity when we behave better, and worse when we behave worse.[30] The criteria for human purposes are set by what is better and worse in our enormously complex fields of action. As the book of Job indicated, God the creator operates within no defining fields of action but creates completely. The divine purpose has no antecedent object but is the making of things with the values they in fact embody. The vast cosmos of expanding gases has values that are almost unrecognizable from the human sphere, and often

[28] Ward, *Religion and Creation*, p. 183.
[29] That value is to be understood in terms of harmony I have argued in *The Cosmology of Freedom*, chapter 3, and *Recovery of the Measure*, chapter 7. That human consciousness or judgment recognizes or discerns value in things, rather than projects value onto them (though it can do that too), is the argument of my *Axiology of Thinking*, the plan of which is explained in *Reconstruction of Thinking*, part 1.
[30] For arguments for this approach to moral identity, see my *Eternity and Time's Flow*, part 1.

inimical to human welfare. Part of the apprehension of the holiness of God is the recognition that divine purpose has very little that can be scaled to what is meaningful for human life, though within the human sphere the excellence of human life is its achievement of good moral identity.

In no metaphysical sense can the Creator be conceived to have an interior subjectivity, for instance to plot the success of the Israelites against the Egyptians, Canaanites, and Philistines, or to make the world safe for democracy. God's "purpose" is nothing more than creating the world created, with whatever values it has, and this is an unusual sense of purpose in light of the denial of antecedent reflection. But by the same token, what is interesting about human purpose is not so much the inherited motives clamoring for attention but the creative initiation of actions that nearly always bear more value or disvalue than anticipated – we too are wilder than would be expected by our commonsense Aristotelian myth of deliberating about the means but not the ends.

The result of this discussion is a conception of God as creative act that produces a particular world. The divine nature itself is singular and particular, resulting from the work of creation. To call this God wild is to acknowledge the freedom and particularity of creation, a condition called for in the previous section. That the wild, particular, God creates a particular universe means that science and other forms of inquiry are needed to find out what the universe is, without prior commitment from a conception of the divine nature. The lopsidedness of our world, its unfairness from the standpoint of human moral judgment, its chanciness to put us on our small planet with our strange evolution, is what one would expect from a willful God.

A bonus of the discussion is that it has yielded suggestions for an unusual conception of human choice and creativity, one that emphasizes freedom and human wildness, though limited by the given materials of environment and antecedents. This too will be important in subsequent chapters when we inquire how we might relate to Jesus.

The conception of God as Creator *ex nihilo* has been defended piecemeal against the more traditional metaphysical alternative of a supernatural being. The strength of that alternative, however, is that it seems to accord easily with the images of God in biblical religion, images to which Jesus and his followers appealed. I still need to show how those images are better justified in reference to the conception of God as Creator *ex nihilo*, the point of the following section. The biblical symbols are best understood as images schematizing the radical Creator *ex nihilo*, and the conception of a perfect, supernatural, personal being is a confusion of the two.

In accord with the earlier observation that the conception of God as Creator is correlative with the conception of what is created, it is appropriate now to look more closely at the fundamental structures of the world that reveal important elements of God. This section focuses on the temporal structure of the world, the singular eternal character of the divine creative act, the sense in which people have eternal lives, and what this means for petitionary prayer in light of the fact that God is not in time to interact with the petitioner. The next section will elaborate these considerations into a rudimentary doctrine of the Logos to be incarnated in Jesus, and the Holy Spirit.

The most elementary thing to say about time is that it has three modes, the past, present, and future.[31] These modes are radically different from each other in their essential features. The past is essentially fixed achievement. Nothing in the past changes except perhaps significance brought about by later developments. The past is the locus of realized actuality, including realized values; it embodies the choices that had been made to exclude other possibilities from being realized. The present, by contrast, is essentially creative actualization, the transformation of a field of possibilities to a singular, definite, actual, state of affairs. Though limited in one sense by the past providing its material and in another sense by the future providing its possibilities, the present is spontaneous and creative, the temporal mode of making novelty; for the present makes determinations for a partially open future and adds actuality to that which is contained in the past. The future is essentially form and value, structuring what is possible for the present to make out of the past. The formal structure of future possibilities constantly shifts as the actual state of affairs for which it is the possible future changes, with different values to be realized in each of its possibility sets. The essential characters of past, present, and future are very different from one another: achieved fixed actuality, spontaneous creativity and choice, and formal possibilities for value.

---

[31] This analysis of time is carefully constructed to draw from but go beyond that in Whitehead's process philosophy. See his *Process and Reality*, and my *Recovery of the Measure*, parts 2 and 3, and *Eternity and Time's Flow*, part 2.

The modes of time are obviously interconnected, however, conditioning one another in their own natures. Most of these important conditions have already been mentioned. The past, for instance, is conditioned by the future because it embodies those formal possibilities that have been chosen for realization, and it has the value achieved by realizing those possibilities rather than others. The past is conditioned by the present because the present chooses the possibilities to realize and does so in ways that add to the past moment by moment. The past continually grows as the consequences of present realization fall out. The present, in its turn, is conditioned by the past because the past provides it the resources or potentials with which to be creative; the present must actualize possibilities that cohere with what previously had been realized. The present is conditioned by the future that gives it the formal possibilities for doing something with the potentials given by the past. The future is conditioned by the past because its formal possibilities are always relative to the actualized things for which they are possible transformations. The future is conditioned by the present because the present continually makes new actualities, thus shifting the structure of possibilities.

Time's flow, the perdurance of a temporal thing through a stretch of time, is a function of all three modes of time together. It is not sheer accretion of actuality, or sheer spontaneous creativity, or sheer unfolding possibilities for realization. Rather it is the integration of the three senses of dynamism in the modes of time: the past growing, the present spontaneously bringing possibilities to actuality, and the future unfolding a kaleidoscope of possibilities. A temporal thing is "in" all three modes of time, changing with the three different dynamics. At a moment of present actualization, it still is essentially defined by its past to which the present is adding something and by the future that provides its possibilities of identity.

For most things in the world, the conjunction of past potentials and future possibilities may not allow much leeway for creative novelty. A rock repeats its rockiness moment by moment, usually changing slowly in relation to variations in temperature, pressure, and wear around it. Some things change blindly, randomly, in response to adventitious occurrences that suddenly shift their combination of past potentials and future possibilities. Whatever spontaneity most things have, so far as we know, is either extremely constricted in scope or random without meaning. Human beings, however, sometimes have significant choices because they can relate intelligently to real possibilities outlined by their symbolic meaning systems. Human beings engage their world by means of signs, which means they can pick up on both past actualities and future possibilities that are inaccessible to rocks and stupid things. Whereas the spontaneous creativity of most things is limited to inertial trajectories and sudden bumps, or other patterns of causal determinism, human beings can pose different possibilities for themselves, possibilities that would actualize different values. Those different possibilities can function as alternative motives for choice, and choosing is the adoption of a course of possibilities and its value as the motive for action. Free choice, to use the moral language appropriate to human beings in these circumstances, is the adoption of a value-laden course of action which in turn defines one's chosen moral identity: to choose is to make oneself the one who has the motives chosen. Motives are not impelling forces from the past – that would reduce human moral choice to a deterministic inertial vector of forces. Rather, because of the spontaneity of the present, shaped by the extraordinarily complex biological and social structure of human life, people can in part choose what they will do and be.[32] Of course, from a physical point of view, 90 percent of a person's life is determined like a biological organism. But there are little decisions that begin to be made in childhood that add up in the long run to big decisions about character and career. Mature people decide about the conditions of their biological lives, and people are interesting because of the accumulated moral characters they achieve as they face the options in life that only humans, so far as we know, can conceive. Within the limits of their pasts, their environments, and what the future allows, people make themselves and their world, and this is the basis for responsibility.[33] As pointed out in the previous section, God is like this except for having no limits or potentials from past identity, an environment, or future structure.

Broaden attention from the human zone and think of the cosmos as vast streams of temporal processes that interact with the expansion of the universe. Suppose the Big Bang theory is correct and the universe will expand to a final dissipation when nothing is close enough to relate to anything else (or alternatively that it will reach a farthest point and then contract). From an initial cosmic soup to the formation of galaxies, suns, and planets, most things are still little more than expanding clouds of gases with adventitious clumpings (see plates 4–7, between pp. 158

---

[32] See my *The Cosmology of Freedom*, chapters 6–7, for an analysis of causation, spontaneity, choice, and the elevation of motives to determining reasons.

[33] Chapter 6, on Jesus as friend, will develop this very general idea of human responsibility into a theory of intentionality structures evolving from infancy.

and 159). The astrophysical forms of causation involved are not those of common sense taken from the observed mechanics of the human scale of things. But the vague categories of temporality sketched above apply to all those forms of causation. Within the cosmos lie vast expanses of minimal order in which only the bare principles of physics are exhibited. But pockets of tight order also exist such as the environment of Earth in which biological evolution is possible and human societies give rise to meaningful history and personal life. The cosmic streams of temporal processes exhibit many degrees and kinds of order, all to be understood in terms of the temporality of the integrated growing past, spontaneous creative present, and shifting structure of future possibilities.[34]

How are the modes of time together? In a sense, they are together in each of the modes, thus in three ways. So, the present and future are in the past as conditions for its growth. The past and future are in the present as the limits and forms of its creative making. The past and present are in the future as the grounds for its determinateness and continuously shifting structures. In this sense, however, the modes are in one another only as conditions. How are they together so that they can condition one another in the first place? They are not *temporally* together, before or after one another. Only temporal things are temporally related to one another. A temporal thing has dates that flow from future (through many transformations) to present actualization to past achievement: the modes of time do not do that.

The answer is that the modes of time are together *eternally*. Eternity should be conceived as the ontological reality or context in which the modes of time are together and that allows for the time's flow in temporal things. This recommendation about how to think of eternity runs against the grain of the modern world. Modern philosophers from Kant to Whitehead have thought of eternity as a matter of pure static form, as if it were a slice of future possibilities, or as the sum total of possibilities (as in Whitehead's notion of eternal objects). Other thinkers, such as Augustine, have thought of eternity as a very broad vision of the present, so broad as to get the past and future in view as a *totum simul*. Many modern scientists have thought of eternity, though they might not use the word, as the deterministic stretch of time unrolled like an actual past, with the principle of the conservation of energy interpreted to mean that time could move either forward or backward, or not at all. None of these views of eternity does justice either to the ancient sense

---

[34] On different forms of causal patterns, see my *Recovery of the Measure*, chapter 12.

of dynamism in eternity or to the need to understand how the modes of time are together.[35]

To conceive eternity as the togetherness of the modes of time is to give it an extraordinarily dynamic interpretation. Eternity contains within itself the dynamics of actual growth, of spontaneous creativity, and of the shifting kaleidoscope of possibilities, all ordered by the progressive shifting dates of the present in cosmic processes. But the ordering of the progressive dates of the present, which defines a temporal thing's time structure, does not reduce eternity to a singular complex story. On the contrary, in eternity a given date for a thing, say Nelson Mandela's election to the presidency of South Africa in 1994, has all its modes of time. It has its mode as present, the day it happened. It also has all its forms as past time, the day after it happened, the year after, and its significance centuries hence. And that date in eternity has all its forms of future time, when it was not a very structured possibility at all, say before Mandela's birth, when it was a possibility for leadership but before the office of President was defined, when the election was in doubt, and so forth. In eternity, every date of every determinate thing is together with all its different forms in different modes with every other date of every other thing with respect to which it is determinate. In eternity, the openness of one's youth is together with the fixity of one's old age, although at any present moment one is in the past and the other future. In eternity, every thing in all its modal temporal forms is together with everything else. Otherwise, the finite temporal flow of time would be impossible.

Eternity, so understood, is the divine life. God's creative act produces all the determinate things of the world in all their temporal conditioning relations to one another. God does not create a static world with everything completely determinate at once; that obviously is not the world we have. Nor does God create a world with nothing but little bursts of creativity; we do not have that world either. God does not create a world of pure possibilities, for the possibilities are structured in our world by what is actual and by what happens. Rather, God creates the world with the integrated temporal structure something like that described here. The reality of God is in what God creates, and that is the cosmos with its eternal temporal structure.

Because of the super-dynamism of eternity as the togetherness of the temporal modes, this can legitimately be called the Divine Life, schema-

---

[35] This argument about eternity is the main thesis of *Eternity and Time's Flow*.

tizing to what we know of life. God is a living God precisely because of that dynamism. God is not living in the sense of being a temporal thing within time, changing in reaction to the world, or even in response to prayers. Occasions might arise when it is appropriate to think of God that way, and I will discuss shortly how this is so. But from a metaphysical point of view, the Living God has the dynamism of eternity, not of a temporal thing. God has neither a present, nor a past, nor a future, but a Life embracing all determinate things in all their shifting temporal modes. The creative act is singular, giving rise to the singular cosmos of dynamic eternity within which time flows for temporal creatures.

The full togetherness of the temporal modes with the temporal things in those modes constitutes the Divine Life, eternal and more dynamic than any temporal thing at a given time. But there is a sense in which temporal things have eternal identity within the Divine Life. This is of crucial importance for understanding the relation of human beings to God and Jesus' role in that relation. The moral identity of a human being is the most obvious case to make for the eternity of temporal things.

When a person is a baby very few dates lie in the person's past, and the person's character so far is determined far more by genes and external nurture than by any personal choices. For a small child, the future dates are wide open, determined by little more than those genes, familial and social environment, and whatever historical destiny obtains; even how many future dates that person will have is an open issue. In middle age, that proportion of fixed past and open future has shifted; many things in the child's future are now fixed a definite actual way, and even those that still lie in the future are far more determinate. At the end of life the proportion shifts again, with most significant things, including choices, lying fixed in the past and little future except what final circumstances dictate.

Who is the person? Temporalists are likely to say that the person's identity is always fixed by a present date; so the person as a baby has little moral identity, as middle-aged has some fixed past with moral consequences and also a somewhat open future with some moral commitments and surprises, and as elderly has a fixed character for better and worse with little possibility of change. Religious temporalists are likely to say that the person's only full identity is at the end of life when the entire character has been achieved. But that cannot be the whole story. Even at the end of life, those things for which a person can be held morally responsible are the ones where earlier in life the person faced an open option and made a choice. That is, as a youth, the person chose a career or made a commitment the consequences of which are parts of that person's moral identity. If the choice were not open in youth, the person is not responsible for the choice and its consequences. So in a sense, at the absolute heart of moral identity the late moment of fixed accomplishment has to be together with the earlier moments of open choice. Late in life, the person no longer is the one who has the choice.

Looked at backward, the person's life is all fixed, all determined, including the moments spontaneously determined by the person; there is no single moment in the past that is not wholly determinate; as past there are no open choices. But the very meaning of moral identity requires a togetherness of earlier moments of choice with later moments of achievement for better or worse. The future as well needs to be together with moments of present choice in order to make sense of the moral bindingness of commitments to do things in the future. The togetherness of early choices, subsequent actualized character, and future commitments is not a temporal togetherness. The past has no present spontaneity or open possibilities, the present has lost the past and not gained the future, and the future is uncertain even about length of life. Rather the togetherness of all the moments of a person's life is eternal. The real moral identity of the person is the eternal togetherness of all the dates of the person's life in their future forms, all the dates as they are lived in the present, and all the dates as they are actual past. This can be restated to reflect the three kinds of dynamism of the temporal modes. The real identity of the person is the eternal togetherness of every date as it is shifting its possibility structure relative to what is happening, of every date as a present creative moment adding to the past and resolving future possibilities, and of every date as a growing addition to the achievement of actual historical value for better or worse.

At no finite time does a person have a full moral identity, only in eternity. Every finite present within the person's life is an abstraction from the full eternal connection of personal identity. To be sure, at any finite time the person's future is somewhat open, very much so in youth, much less in old age. There never is a time, a date, at which the future is fully fixed. God does not exist with a date at which the future is more closed for God than it is in fact at that date. God cannot "predestine" things because God is not temporal and thus not "pre" anything. By the same token, no individual is fully alive at a finite time, however vital that might feel. Full life, full identity, life abundant, is eternal.

I have spoken here as if persons were isolated with dates and careers all their own. In point of fact, people share their dates with all the rest of the cosmos in various ways and are fully conditioned by the world's past, by their environments, and by futures that they share with other things. Nearly all significant human actions are conjoint actions with other people, taken in community and shaped by semiotic systems that spread beyond their communities. So the eternal identity of an individual is part of a larger eternal identity of the cosmos, with the connections among all the parts like the many streams of processes proceeding from the Big Bang, some with very thin connections and some with tightly integrated pockets of order. The human moral sphere is a tight pocket of order where the causal elements are determinative enough for people to have some control over their actions and thus be able to make morally significant choices. This human sphere, and all the people in it, are part of the eternal identity of the Living God.

We now have conceived of God metaphysically as eternal creator of a temporal world whose singular creative act contains as its end-product the eternal togetherness of the unfolding world. And we have conceived human life, individually and communally, in its moral spheres and beyond, to be temporal in the sense that it is lived out in present moments that succeed themselves one after another and eternal in the more important sense that all their dates are together in all their temporal modes.

How shall we understand the application of religious imagery to all this? Should we imagine people to meet God as they are at the moment of death, wholly defined by their past? Or will everyone in Heaven be imagined to be thirty-three (Jesus' traditional age) at the prime of physical and spiritual vitality? We could just as well adopt the Daoist image of Heavenly life as the playroom of infants, a swarm of putti. All three are images schematizing eternal identity into some mode of temporal identity. In a brilliant essay, Kenneth R. Dutton has analyzed the Christian vacillation between ascetic and heroically perfectionist attitudes toward the human body, contrasting with non-West Asian religions that usually lacked the latter. With the European renaissance the perfectionist attitudes won out in art as well as in most other cultural modes of Christianity (note the natal build on Adam in figure 3).[36] This accords well with the view that a proper image for schematizing eternal life is one that seeks to combine the beauty of youth, the strength of maturity, and the wisdom of age, all involved in the heroic model.

[36] See Dutton's *The Perfectible Body*, chapter 2, "The Body Re-born."

Leave the eschatological images for a moment and consider the relation of persons to God within temporal life. How is a person in an existential situation, fully present, to relate to the eternal God? If the existential situation is calm, reflective, and meditative enough as Christians hope to attain, and if the person is a practiced metaphysician, it might be possible to rehearse something like the philosophical reflections in this chapter. The person can meditate on the place of the present time in the person's more concrete eternal identity that is partially hidden in God, and on the eternity of the Divine Life itself, especially as focused at the person's part of the world. The language of Christian antiquity is replete with imagery of eternity, both for God's divine life and for human fulfillment in that. Although late-modern language has debased those symbols of eternity, the meditative metaphysical person can recover the vitality of the symbols of eternal creation and eternal life, acknowledging a metaphysics interpretive of the scientific world but correcting pallid late-modern imagery with the ancient religious symbols. The metaphysics itself, integrated with the schematizing ancient symbols, can be a complex symbol guiding and enabling meditative engagement with God the Creator and one's own eternal destiny, if one is a metaphysician with meditative practice.

Most people, however, and metaphysicians most of the time, engage God, if at all, from the temporal perspective of some present. Whatever their eternal identity, they are ultimately concerned about what their present situation holds for that identity. The extreme case is where life itself is in jeopardy. A person is in imminent danger, as from a skidding car or a threatening disease. Or something else that really signifies life to the person is at stake, say the life of a threatened child, a love-affair, a meaningful career. Christians are taught to pray to God in these circumstances for whatever signifies life, the heart of petitionary prayer.[37] Popular Buddhism also has petitionary devotions, although theologically most forms of Buddhism deny any God to pray to; nearly all religions have a place for petitionary prayer. Even the most die-hard modern secularists sometimes cry to God in emergency, though it might be hard to tell a prayer from a curse. How can petitionary prayer be understood, knowing that it is the heart's cry for life?

To address such a cry to God as if God were a temporal companion is quite proper because part of the meaning of the prayer is the desire for something to happen in time. It is a cry for how the petitioner wants

---

[37] This is the heart of James P. Carse's *The Silence of God*.

the future to be resolved. From the temporal standpoint of the praying present, the future is still open, at least to unexpected miraculous possibilities that might be imagined. If God is imagined to be in the present, then the future is just as open to God and the petition is for God to act favorably. Of course God is eternal and not located in that present. This means that God has not, in the present, foreordained the future; in the present it is really open, or at least the petitioner hopes it is; whether the future is open is an empirical issue. A true prayer of petition is a cry from the bottom of the heart for the Creator of the Universe to do something!

Not only is it proper to cry to God as if God were in time and responsive to prayers like a person, it would be improper not to do so, at least in the Christian perspective. Not to do so would be to suppress the deepest passion of the heart. It would be to pass that present situation failing to express what is most significant, most engaging. Not to cry for what one most wants, or to express one's heartfelt rage at misfortune, or joy at the abundance of life, would be to withdraw from fully engaging life and its circumstances. The courage to engage life as it comes requires the capacity for the deepest prayers. One cannot occupy the present in a fully human way without a prayerful cry for life. Similarly one cannot fully occupy one's past without present prayers of thanksgiving and for forgiveness, and one cannot fully engage the future without present prayers of hope and promise. To occupy time *in extremis* is to require a schematization of the eternal creator into one who can be addressed now.

Thus temporally full life demands a resonance of tuning that time's attention on temporalizing eternity with understanding the divine life and creation as eternal. To commit oneself to the time requires unconditioned thanks and repentance for the past, insistence on life in the present with appropriate responses to its joys and woes, and a launching of oneself and one's community forward in hope. So people rightly imagine God as receiving thanks, forgiving sins, responding to petitions, and carrying out promises hoped for. But we know also that God creates the whole of time and that the temporalizing imagery for God is a function of our own present relations to past, present, and future. Christians do not seriously believe that their prayers manipulate God into doing something that God would not do otherwise. And they often conclude their prayers with some formal recognition of this as "not my will, but thine, be done," Jesus' prayer in Gethsemane (Luke 22:42, KJV) when he sweated blood crying for life.

A critic might say that prayers addressed to God personified as within time are simply false in their assumptions, reminding us that there is no supernatural God companioning us through time who might listen and be moved by what we pray. The critic is right if the references to the temporal personal God are metaphysically descriptive or iconic; God is not temporal but the Creator of time, not personal with a deliberating responsive emotional intellect but the singular creator whose life is the eternal dynamism of the temporal world. But the critic is wrong because the reference in those prayers is indexical as a schematized image. That is, the reference orients the petitioner very truly to the eternal God. By imagining God as a temporal supernatural companion in the context of prayer the petitioner is able to accept and engage the ultimacy of personal life and the depths of divine eternity. How is it that persons should live before the eternal Creator? By engaging with ultimate seriousness the lives given them, including joys but also the suffering and inevitable death that comes with temporal life, an engagement made possible by the personifying image of God, the object of prayer. Knowing full well the late-modern metaphysics of eternity and time's flow as understood by science, the symbols for prayer that truly schematize the eternal Creator into the present context of our temporal situation are something like, "Our Father, who art in heaven . . . ."

Simple people who do not relate to late-modern culture can use those personifying symbols naively, as do many people practicing the Christian life of prayer and worship. The only caveat for them is that they not make inferences that would seem so easily to follow of the sort that supposes that God is a moral agent intending things to happen his (or her) way. That would pose impossible problems for theodicy, requiring people to ask why God sent Grandma the fatal cancer, or caused the earthquake that killed thousands. Cancer, we know, is caused by a combination of genes, stimulating substances, and the immune system; shifting tectonic plates cause earthquakes. Sometimes good spiritual direction can prevent inferences such as these, although oftentimes that has not happened. To blame God for suffering increases the suffering. To think that God wants your country to conquer its neighbors, or your ethnic group to exterminate some other, is much worse. Personified notions of God coupled with people's sense of self and sense for the righteousness of their desires have done much evil. Against this, late-modern culture is an important and vital corrective.

The metaphysics developed so far gives a straightforward interpretation of divine presence in this sense. All finite things, all collections of finite things, are parts of the overall cosmic terminus of the divine creative act. They cannot be separate from that act. Taken together in all their temporal as well as spatial and other relations, the things of the world are God's fulfilled creative act. They are parts of the Divine Life.

Divine participation in things of the finite world is manifested in many ways. Apposite the previous discussion, any prayer that comes from the heart, spontaneously and creatively, is God praying in us (Rom. 8:26–27). This illustrates the metaphysical point that the creativity in the present is a portion of the divine creativity. Anything from the past that functions as a potential for present self-constitution also was the locus of a spark of divine creativity when it was present. So we encounter nothing that has not had God the Creator in it. God creates a world in which the law of contradiction obtains and also the other laws of mathematical order. So any orientation to the formal future encounters God resident. These points ring the changes on the metaphysics of temporality, showing how God is resident in past, present, and future relative to a moment of present experience. God is of course resident eternally in things considered in their full eternal identity in which all their dates are present, all future, and all past, all together.

THE LOGOS AND THE HOLY SPIRIT

The idea of the Word of God has complex histories that do not need to be rehearsed here. Vac (Voice) is one of the creator-gods of the Vedas. The Buddhist Dharma is the enlightening speech of Gautama Buddha, spoken also by all the Buddhas. The talismans and sacred characters of the religious Daoists are written words of Power. Probably one of the roots of the metaphor is the power of the King to get things done by speaking out orders: "Let there be . . ."

In Christian imagery creation (Gen. 1:1–3) takes place when the divine Word is added to the deep stuff roiled into formless chaos by the divine breath or Spirit. The same imagery is used in the synoptic gospels' accounts of Jesus' baptism (Mark 1:9–11, Matt. 3:16–17, Luke 3:21–22): he went down into the water and when he came up the Spirit came (in the form of a dove) and the Voice spoke saying "You are my Son, the Beloved; with you I am well pleased." With the beginning of Jesus' ministry, a new creation begins. That baptism was construed by the early Church to be more ontologically significant than mere washing, is indicated by the claims in Colossians 2 and 3 that, in their baptism, Christians have already died with Christ, as if returning to primeval chaos deeper than the elemental spirits of the universe; and in being absolved of their sins the Christians have already risen with Christ in glory. The Gospel of John begins with the famous prologue (John 1:1–3a):

In the beginning was the Word, and the Word was with God, and the Word was God. He was in the beginning with God. All things came into being through him, and without him not one thing came into being.

Jesus is called many things in the New Testament. But his identification with the Word or Logos has been powerful even to this day, especially in Reformation thought. At some remove, in the form of witness, the Christian scriptures are the Word of God. The purpose of preaching the Word is to create something of a new heart in the congregation. Peter and Stephen's early sermons are creative of the nascent Christian community (Acts 2, 7). The idea of the Word of God, usually called Logos, will weave in and out of most of the chapters of this Christology.

The question for this section is whether the metaphysics of creation developed above has an ontological referent that can sustain the symbols of the divine Word or Logos, of which Jesus is called the incarnation. In the sense noticed at the end of the previous section, God is intimately present as Creator in every determinate thing created, in all the temporal shifts of the dynamic universe. But this does not select out any element or set of elements as either especially definitive of God's nature or as that in and by which the creation is accomplished. Much less does it select out anything that can be especially intensified or exemplified or brought to actuality in Jesus.

We can ask, however, whether any universal or transcendental traits characterize all determinate things such that without them the things could not exist and such that their existence is accomplished by making them determinate in relation to these traits. The search for such transcendentals has been common in Christian (and other) philosophy. What follows is a hypothesis proposed as appropriate to late-modern culture. Other hypotheses might improve upon this one, but this at least exhibits the possibility of a contemporary interpretation of the Logos.

Every determinate thing is a harmony of its features, some of which are essential to the ownbeing of the thing and others of which constitute its conditioning of and being conditioned by other things with respect to which it is determinate.[38] These things as harmonies are located in the

---

[38] The distinction between conditional and essential features, employed above in the interpretation of time, is a central metaphysical theme. See *God the Creator*, chapter 2, and *Recovery of the Measure*, chapter 5.

space-time flow of the cosmos, and they each have the value, for what it is worth, of harmonizing just these components in this place. From these observations it follows that there are four transcendental traits:

the order or pattern with which the component features are harmonized,

the component features themselves,

the existential location of the things (bearing in mind dynamic shifts and interactions that continually change conditional features), and

the value achieved in the great scheme of things.

The transcendentals are: (1) form, (2) components to be formed, (3) existential location, and (4) value. Nothing exists without these four traits, and things exist only by having them. At this very abstract level God's character as Creator is to be a maker of things with form, components, existential location, and value. While these seem so abstract as to be almost trivially true, we can imagine a universe with a physics and chemistry only slightly different from ours in which nothing would bond with anything and so nothing could have ordered components, things could not be related as regards space-time dynamics, and nothing would be achieved.

From the religious point of view, this metaphysical Logos is uninteresting unless related to the human condition. The situation for humans is that they have some control over what they do, make, and become. This control requires some degree of right understanding of conditions and the capacity to imagine alternative outcomes, and it requires capacity to affect causal processes in line with intended outcomes. Human beings therefore need to relate to the transcendental traits of the Logos insofar as they can influence what happens.

With respect to form, people need to ask whether they are fostering the better or worse form, the right or wrong one.

With respect to components, people need to ask whether their actions show proper respect for the values and careers of the components or reduce them to only their roles in the larger pattern.

With respect to existential location, people need to ask whether they are rightly related to their existential context, taking account of what is real and relevant, or are in some kind of denial, escapism, or bad faith.

With respect to value, people need to achieve a value in the great scheme of things, to the extent they can influence that which is their eternal identity within the Divine Life; or to put the point the other way, how people understand themselves before God or in the Divine Life bears upon what values they set their lives to achieving.

Where people have options, they live under obligation to do the best. It is always better to do better, and the people who do better are better people. Therefore regarding the Logos,

>   With respect to right form, people lie under obligations we describe as justice, righteousness, fairness, and so forth.
>
>   With respect to components people lie under obligations we describe as natural piety or deference that acknowledge things for what they are.
>
>   With respect to existential location people lie under obligations we describe as faithful engagement, courage to embrace the situation, or authenticity.
>
>   With respect to value people lie under the obligations of hope for a right relation to the Creator, or the religious quest.

The Logos thus becomes not only ontologically descriptive but problematic for human life, and normative.

The cardinal ontological virtues, then, are justice, piety, faith, and hope, to use shorthand expressions for very complex normative characters. I follow a long Christian tradition to call the integrated combination of these virtues, love. Love not only creates things (through form, components, existential location, and value), it makes normatively good things. Projected back on God as creator of things with form, components, existential location and value, we can say that the integration of these transcendental traits of creation is ontological divine love. Much more than this abstract schematic is involved in the notion of love, to be sure.

The schematic of the Logos, however, is sufficient to lay out the bare bones of the religious situation. The human condition is that justice, piety, faith, and hope (as defined) are often hard issues. The human predicament, according to Christianity, is that perfect virtue is impossible, in part because of contradictions within human nature and also of what people have made of themselves. Thus people ordinarily live in sin: injustice, impiety, faithlessness, and ontological despair, in sum, in unlove; and the sin prevents its own rectification. Salvation means what can correct this predicament of bondage to sin, to use Paul's words, so that people can be virtuous, including being holy before God. Jesus' role as savior, as incarnation of the Logos, has to do with his setting people right before God so that they can attend to the cardinal virtues. This bare-bones schematic will be fleshed out in following chapters, picking up next in the last half of chapter 3.[39]

---

[39] It is in fact the organizing structure of my *A Theology Primer*.

The connection was made earlier between the act of creation itself and the Holy Spirit. The only thing metaphysically unsatisfactory with this connection is the seeming arbitrariness of using a symbol thick with Christian meaning to refer to the fact that everything determinate, and all of its determinate connections, exists by the act of creation. In the metaphysical sense the effect of the creative act is in everything's reality. If creative presence is so universal, is it not a trivial truth?

The religious meaning of the Holy Spirit is not only the presence of God in all creation as Creator but the special ways by which that creation manifests itself so as to fulfill the normative side of the cosmos. Several levels or instances of this can be pointed out as an orientation to what is to come.

Close to the universal sense of the Spirit as creator is the particularity of creation itself, its tilt off any symmetrical center. The Spirit blows where it will. The particularity of the universe has a wildness to it, a freedom and unexpectedness. Whereas Islam has emphasized the order of the cosmos as expressing the unity and absolute sovereignty of God, Christianity has been more open to the chanciness of process, to the accidents of meeting, to spontaneity and serendipity. The cosmos exhibits principles of both order and chaos. As the cosmos as a whole is wild in its eternal singular reality as the product of a divine act that gives itself its own nature, so the processes within the cosmos are wild. The Holy Spirit is not a force for stability.

The images of the Holy Spirit in the Hebrew Bible include the wild nabis, the prophets who would be seized by divine frenzy, as well as the still small voice announcing the presence of God. Jesus promised (John 15) to send the disciples an Advocate, a Comforter, after his ascension. The Holy Spirit is to guide the disciples through times of persecution and into a new kind of community of friendship. That is, the Holy Spirit will bring to fruition a new reality in the community of disciples, not a nation or clan or people but a community of those called to relate to Jesus' love and in so doing to learn how to love one another.

The principal appeal to the Holy Spirit in the Christian tradition is to God's special creative power that allows people to be related to Jesus, to understand his religious significance, and to join with him and others in the new reality of the Church. However we articulate the sense in which Jesus is the incarnation of the Logos, Jesus cannot be that in saving ways unless people are transformed to accept him as such, and that transformation is the most special work of the Spirit. All subsequent chapters will explicate this thesis.

CHAPTER TWO

Jesus the Lamb of God: blood sacrifice and atonement

What are the symbols of Jesus that most engage contemporary Christians with God? That is still an open question at the present stage of this inquiry. Nevertheless, for the earliest Christians, Jesus was seen centrally, if not always most importantly, as the sacrifice that allows Christians, Gentiles as well as Jews, to approach God, or to turn back to God, or to be "at one" with God, the original meaning of the English word "atonement." Because this might be a surprising claim, some introductory historical considerations are in order.

The surprise would come from the fact that we customarily take the gospel accounts of Jesus' life to reflect the earliest stage of the church, followed by the accounts in Acts and in Paul's letters of the fledgling Christian community in the first generation without Jesus' personal presence. The gospels contain very little discussion of Jesus as a sacrifice, even the Gospel of John which has such a sophisticated theology of Jesus' identity and goes so far as to quote (1:29) John the Baptist saying "Here is the Lamb of God who takes away the sins of the world" (figure 5, p. 66 below). In point of fact, the gospels, with the possible exception of Mark, were written after the destruction of the Second Temple in 70 CE. Accordingly, the Christian communities for which they wrote did not enjoy the continuity of life within the Temple centered on sacrifice. They did, however, acknowledge that Jesus, his family, and disciples participated in the sacrificial life of observant Jews of the time.

The letters of Paul, by contrast, were written earlier while the Temple was still functioning and Paul was preoccupied with the involvement of observant Judaism in the Christian communities. And Paul was deeply committed to interpreting Jesus as a sacrifice. Paula Fredriksen notes that Paul's sacrificial imagery was not consistent, but that he and his readers were immersed in a world where sacrifice made sense.[1]

---

[1] See her "Ultimate Reality in Ancient Christianity."

Among the earliest practices we know about in the nascent Christian communities was the Eucharist, which is a celebration of Jesus as a sacrifice in some sense or other. Of course the Eucharist is about much more than sacrifice.[2] It is the paradigmatic communal meal, as depicted in Leonardo's *Last Supper* (figure 2, p. 20 above), which only looks ahead to the betrayal and sacrifice of Jesus. The story in Luke 24:13–35 of the post-resurrection encounter with Jesus on the road to Emmaus centers on a meal with the breaking of bread in which the identity of Jesus is suddenly made known (see Caravaggio's painting of this, figure 11, p. 165 below), an early Christian reference to the central meal as an epiphany or celebration of the presence of Christ. The Eucharist remained at the heart of Christian worship long after Christian participation in Jewish sacrificial life had become impossible and, for increasing numbers, undesirable. The Eucharist and its attendant symbols is a way forward in asking why Jesus was so special in those early generations, especially to those who had not been his personal friends. A focused exploration of the Eucharist as sacrifice will allow us to ask what issue in the human condition it addresses.

THE EUCHARISTIC SACRIFICE

The central liturgy of Christianity is the Eucharist or Lord's Supper and in form it is a symbolic cannibal rite. The bloody power of this symbolic act, endlessly rehearsed in all sorts and conditions of Christian existence, has rarely been acknowledged for what it is. This is obviously true of recent liberal Christologies that limit their focus to the Jesus of social justice and moral rigor. It is also true of the Christologies that emphasize Jesus the teacher. Jesus can be construed in more classical ways as priest, king, and prophet; yet this still gives no clue as to why Christians should eat his flesh and drink his blood. Atonement Christologies can be bloody, so bloody that today they seem gross, childish, and wicked: they say Jesus substituted for humanity in the bloody divine execution of the wicked, or that Jesus ransomed humanity from Satan, or that Jesus was the sacrificial lamb causing the Angel of Death to pass over sinners, or that as a sacrifice he purified humanity on the temple altar, or that as a scapegoat he carried away the sins of the world. Cosmically bloody as these atonement Christologies are, they do not explain, justify, or even put into place the Christian rite of symbolic cannibalism.

---

[2] In *The Truth of Broken Symbols* I discuss nine layers of meaning in the Eucharist, only one of which is cannibalistic sacrifice.

Christology should do better; so we can start with the cannibalism of the Eucharist and ask what problem requires such a serious ritual response. Lest it be thought that I exaggerate the cannibalism, however, we should review some of the basic texts, not esoteric rites hidden from the world and revealed only to initiates, but widely and early published material closely involved with defining the Christian faith. Of course the Eucharist has many levels of meaning over and above the cannibal one, and it has meant different things in different historical and cultural contexts. In all its forms of celebration, however, the cannibalistic aspect is explicit in word and gesture.

Probably the earliest written instructions for the rite come from St. Paul in 1 Corinthians 11:23–26:

For I received from the Lord what I also handed on to you, that the Lord Jesus on the night when he was betrayed took a loaf of bread, and when he had given thanks, he broke it and said, "This is my body that is for you. Do this in remembrance of me." In the same way he took the cup also, after supper, saying, "This cup is the new covenant in my blood. Do this, as often as you drink it, in remembrance of me." For as often as you eat this bread and drink the cup, you proclaim the Lord's death until he comes.

Note that Paul ascribes the words identifying the bread with Jesus' body and the wine with his blood to Jesus himself delivered directly to Paul, a powerful ascription indeed because Paul was supposed not to have known Jesus in the flesh. As noted, Paul was instructing liturgical practice in a Christian community before the destruction of the Temple in 70 CE, a time when sacrifice in the Temple was still an option for Christians and when questions were raised about other pagan sacrifices (see his extensive discussions in 1 Cor. 10 and 11).

The next biblical examination of the Eucharist was likely to be the account of the last supper in Mark's gospel (Mark 14:22–25), written shortly after the destruction of the Temple or perhaps a little before:

While they were eating, he took a loaf of bread, and after blessing it he broke it, gave it to them, and said, "Take; this is my body." Then he took a cup, and after giving thanks he gave it to them, and all of them drank from it. He said to them, "This is my blood of the covenant, which is poured out for many. Truly I tell you, I will never again drink of the fruit of the vine until that day when I drink it new in the kingdom of God."

Matthew's (26:26–29) small differences from Mark include a special reference to the disciples, both at the meal and at the anticipated heavenly meal, and an explanation of the blood of the covenant as poured out for many for the forgiveness of sins. A more important difference is Jesus' explicit instruction not just to take the bread but to eat it, and an imperative to drink the wine which is his blood. Luke's account of the last supper (22:15–20) is similar to Mark's and Matthew's except that the order of things is a little different, they drink both before and after the bread, and Luke's Jesus is more loquacious.

The Gospel of John has no account of words such as these at the last supper although Jesus is recorded as making a major speech on that occasion about who he is and how the disciples ought to behave after his death, the so-called Farewell Discourses (John 13–17). But in the sixth chapter of John (6:53a–58), in the midst of explaining the sense in which he is the "bread of life," Jesus says to his Jewish opponents (not the disciples as in the other gospels, though they were there and later discussed it with him):

Very truly, I tell you, unless you eat the flesh of the Son of Man and drink his blood, you have no life in you. Those who eat my flesh and drink my blood have eternal life, and I will raise them up on the last day; for my flesh is true food and my blood is true drink. Those who eat my flesh and drink my blood abide in me, and I in them. Just as the living Father sent me, and I live because of the Father, so whoever eats me will live because of me. This is the bread that came down from heaven, not like that which your ancestors ate, and they died. But the one who eats this bread will live forever.

Scholars now suppose that the differences among these texts reflect different liturgical practices in the communities primarily addressed by their authors. Because the gospels were written after the temple was destroyed, the sacrificial imagery was a symbolic degree removed from the possibility of actual Levitical animal sacrifice. One thing is clear in each to one degree or another and reinforced in the collected texts: the community is to eat the bread as a symbolic substitute for Jesus' body and drink the wine as a symbol of his blood. Christians in the twenty-first century, who are almost entirely removed from ancient Mediterranean and Second Temple Jewish sacrifice sensibility, still celebrate the Eucharist.[3]

True, the ritual is only a *symbolic* cannibal act. But what is symbolized

[3] See Gerd Theissen's *A Theory of Primitive Christian Religion*, chapters 7–8, for an outstanding account of the nature of sacrifice rituals, particularly the Eucharist. He points out that the escalating violence in baptism, from washing to dying with Christ, and the escalating violence in the Eucharist, from sharing a meal to eating symbols of Jesus' flesh and blood, corresponds to a diminishment in violence in external Christian practice, from constant ritual washing to one baptism, and from many animal sacrifices to the one completed sacrifice of Christ, resulting in a community (ideally) where many ritual taboos, such as mixing men and women, social classes, ethnic groups (Gal. 3:28) are overcome.

is *cannibalism*, eating human flesh and drinking human blood, indeed not that of just any human, but of Jesus, the founder of the Christian faith. Animal sacrifice was common in the ancient world and was prominent in Jewish worship in the Temple. Sometimes animal sacrifice involved eating the sacrificed animal. Animal sacrifice is not *human* sacrifice, however, a practice widely abhorred, especially in Judaism, which prohibited even the drinking of animal blood.

If the early Christians needed a ritual to mark their special communities, they could have used the foot-washing ritual established by Jesus against the background of common customs of hospitality, for instance. This was John's version of the rite Jesus performed at the last supper (John 13). But they did not. They chose the cannibal rite of the Eucharist, despite the facts that they could not talk directly about its cannibal symbolism and that they were sometimes accused by hostile neighbors of practicing cannibalism.[4] Though variously enacted, this is the rite central to Christianity in all its forms from earliest times until now.

Although the symbolic cannibalism in the Eucharist is suppressed in most theological accounts, the sacrifice imagery is not. In the background of all that imagery was the participation of observant Jews in the sacrificial rituals of the Temple, all of which were intended to render people pure enough to participate in the Holy Temple rites. Leviticus 1–6 details how the various sacrifices were to be carried out, including burnt offerings of animals and grain offerings, sacrificial offerings of well-being to join with God in gratitude, sacrificial sin offerings to atone for unintentional disruption of one's own or the community's purity and hence accessibility to God, and guilt offerings in which damage has been done to others for which restitution must be made as well as the offering of an animal for sacrifice. To participate in Temple ritual on special festival days, Jews had to be purified, and the business at the Temple of purificatory rituals must have been brisk. Fredriksen describes the hundreds of priests in dozens of altars performing sacrifices to prepare pilgrims to be pure and ready for a feast such as Passover.[5] The blood and fat of animals were especially dear to God, and the priests dashed the blood of dying animals around the altar and burned the fat away. In some deep sense, the blood of the sacrificed animal substituted for the blood that might be demanded of the person making the offering (Leviticus 1:3–9). According to Genesis 9:4–6, in the Noah story, people

[4] See ibid., p. 345.
[5] See Fredriksen's *Jesus of Nazareth, King of the Jews*, chapter 2, for a physical description of the huge temple, and its purifying and sacrificing rituals.

are allowed to eat the flesh of animals, but not the life of that flesh, namely its blood: blood is a deep symbol for life itself, and that passage can be read as citing blood as the image of God in humankind; it also says that the lifeblood shall be required of any person who sheds the blood of another person. In this vague, though deep, sense, Jesus substitutes for us so that our "sins are covered," the meaning of atonement in Levitical religion. It should be remembered that sins in the Levitical context are not primarily what we would call immoral, but rather are failures to observe the commandments with the result that the person is rendered unclean and unable to approach God; unclean persons can render those they touch unclean. Moral commandments are included among those the breaking of which alienates the person or the whole community from God; a person alienated from the community is not only unclean but unholy and hence alienated from the community's worship.

Beyond its contents including instructions for sacrificial offerings, the Mosaic covenant itself, the giving of the Law, is sealed with a bloody sacrifice (Ex. 24:3–8). In the event, Moses had twelve oxen sacrificed, one for each of the tribes of Israel. He caught half of the blood in basins. He dashed the other half of the blood against the altar, which was usual in other animal sacrifices. Then he took the blood in the basins and dashed it over the congregated people to whom he had just read the covenant, saying, "See the blood of the covenant that the Lord has made with you in accordance with all these words" (Ex. 24:8b). When Paul in the Corinthians passage quoted above cites Jesus saying "This cup is the new covenant in my blood" (1 Cor. 11:25b), the resonating reference is back to the blood of the "old" covenant. When the author of the letter to the Hebrews laid out his extensive interpretation of the new covenant, he paraphrased the old covenant sacrificial ceremony in detail (Heb. 9:18–22).

In one sense, first-century Jewish Christians were extremely decorous compared to the temple sacrifice culture because they symbolized the blood with a cup of wine rather than having real blood, hot from a living creature, dashed over them in buckets. In another sense, the blood of Jesus dripping from the crown of thorns, from the nail holes, from his pierced side – all recalled in the cup – is far more gory than the ox blood commonplace in temple worship (Delacroix's crucifixion, figure 6, p. 83 below is a very sanitized representation compared with the more familiar crucifixion by Grünewald). That the Christians drank it rather than were splashed by it internalizes the covenant in an extreme way. As Jeremiah (31:33) said in reference to the new covenant that the LORD

Figure 5. Jan van Eyck, *The Adoration of the Lamb*, after 1426, lower half of the central panel, Ghent Altarpiece, St. Baafskathedraal Gent

promised, "But this is the covenant that I will make with the house of Israel after those days, says the LORD: I will put my law within them, and I will write it on their hearts; and I will be their God, and they shall be my people." Written on their hearts rather than on the frontlets before their eyes like splashed clothing. Nevertheless, there is an even more powerful separation of the blood of the old covenant from that of the new. Blood itself should not be consumed, one of the "kosher" laws: Leviticus 17:14 (and see Gen. 9:4–6) says "For the life of every creature – its blood is its life; therefore I have said to the people of Israel: You shall not eat the blood of any creature, for the life of every creature is its blood; whoever eats it shall be cut off." By drinking blood, even symbolically, early Jewish Christians were willfully risking being cut off from the old covenantal community.

The letter to the Hebrews details differences between the old and new covenants, quoting the Jeremiah passage cited above. One of the chief of these (Heb. 9) is that the Aaronic priest can go into the Holy of Holies, an area of the tent in the Exodus account (which Hebrews follows), and a room in the Temple much later. But Jesus as the High Priest can go straight to Heaven. Another and even more interesting difference is that Jesus is not only the priest; he is the sacrificial victim (Heb. 9:11–15; see also Van Eyck's *The Adoration of the Lamb*, figure 5). Jesus' blood, not that of sheep or goats, constitutes the sacrifice. For the author of Hebrews

(10:10 and elsewhere), as for the Torah, the function of sacrifice is to purify those making the offering and to sanctify them so that they might approach God.

Two special senses of sacrifice associated with the liturgical calendar should be mentioned, the festival of the Passover and that of Atonement itself. Passover literally means the Angel of Death passing over the houses of the Israelites in Egypt when on its way to kill the firstborn in every other house, barn, and flock (Ex. 11–13). The reason the Angel passed over was that at God's command the Israelites had slaughtered a lamb (or goat) and smeared its blood on their doorposts and lintels. The images of Jesus as the Paschal Lamb associate him with the slaughtered lambs that prevented the Angel from taking the firstborn of the Israelites. Yet ever after God claimed that the firstborn children and animals belong to Him, and further animal sacrifice is required to substitute for firstborn children.

The atonement ritual is described in Leviticus 16, beginning with Aaron's need to atone for the sins of his two elder sons who had approached God without being commanded to do so and had been struck down for it, thus defiling Aaron's whole house. The ritual is described as an annual event in which with proper sacrifices the sins of all Israel are placed on a goat. Then the goat is sent out of the people into the wilderness, bearing their sins away (Lev. 16:21–22):

Then Aaron shall lay both his hands on the head of the live goat, and confess over it all the iniquities of the people of Israel, and all their transgressions, all their sins, putting them on the head of the goat, and sending it away into the wilderness by means of someone designated for the task. The goat shall bear on itself all their iniquities to a barren region; and the goat shall be set free in the wilderness.

This is the origin of the term "scapegoat." But because goats and sheep were often inter-changeable, as in the Passover sacrifice, Jesus was identified as the lamb of God who takes away (into the wilderness) the sins of the world, as in John 1:35b.

We have found here three sacrificial symbol systems for Jesus. The first is Jesus the sacrificial victim who establishes the new covenant with spilt blood. The second is Jesus the Passover sacrifice who keeps God's Angel of Death from taking the firstborn of Israel, and by extension protecting Christians. The third is the atonement rite itself whereby human sins are transposed onto Jesus, atoning or covering the sins of the people, and then sent with Jesus into the wilderness, sometimes interpreted as the hell of death, from which he rose back into the Holy of Holies.

But we have not found why Christians so emphasize the conjunction of eating the sacrifice and the human character of the sacrifice eaten. For this we must change directions and ask what these symbols suppose about the human condition that needs atonement. From there we can ask how the atonement symbols schematize God to that condition.

THE NEED FOR THE BLOOD OF THE LAMB

René Girard has developed an entire theory of religion based on his analysis of sacrifice.[6] His main idea is that society is founded upon elementary violence that, even in the most just society, forcibly imposes social order on natural disorder. Perception of this violence lurks in each person below the thresholds of consciousness producing a tension, a blind pressure. Societies as groups of pre-consciously communicating people feel this pressure as unfocused guilt. Every social order, including the goods that society enjoys (if not justice itself), is built upon violence, and the guilt is deeply distributed among individuals. So the social response is to find a scapegoat, something like the scapegoat in the Levitical atonement ritual. But for the pressure to be released, the scapegoat is more often a person to whom violence is done for the sake of the group. Often this person is innocent of any explicit crime, in fact, the more innocent the better. In some ancient societies, the cycle of revenge was broken by the sacrifice of someone related to the feuding parties but not involved in the feuding revenge cycle. After the violent sacrifice of the scapegoat, the pressure of guilt-violence is lowered and society can resume with less tension. Girard makes his case mainly through literary analyses of the myths and practices of Greek and Semitic religions.

Surely this thesis has much to it. But something even deeper is involved in sacrifice, something in the evolution of human physiology. The "old brain," the "reptilian brain," at the core of the humanly evolved brain programs violent bursts of action, the selfish lunge and grab for food, the rage to fight, the instinct to flight, the overwhelming urge to copulate in season. Sensory signals are quickly interpreted with such violent bursts of action. Human life, of course, requires much more cooperation than is possible with such reptilian responses. So the human (and higher mammalian) brain evolved with mechanisms to check the immediate violent responses and actions, to slow them down with cues that they might not be necessary. Whereas reptilian brains interpret only

---

[6] See his *Violence and the Sacred*. Theissen makes many of the same points in his *Theory of Primitive Christian Religion*, chapter 7.

the surface of objects facing the animal, mammalian brains can rotate the object in imagination and thus think of objects as inhabiting a larger world than what immediately faces the animal: maybe the Other is engaged in a harmless activity and need not be eaten, fought, fled, or forced. The amygdala in particular has the function of registering instinctual violent responses and turning them off when other evidence justifies cooling it. Just as Purkinje brain cells smooth out jerky reptilian motion, so the higher brain organs in mammals, particularly the temporal lobes and frontal cortex, provide a sensible display of the environment as a field of many actors and conditions within which measured responses are advisable. With this possibility, the advantages of cooperation at elementary and more advanced levels are also possible.[7]

As primitive human groupings arose, with elementary semiotic systems of language and gesture, human perception and responses came to be organized by meaning structures as well as the connections of the nervous system. The nervous system to some degree took on the behavioral structures of human semiotic codes, expressing human purpose and reading the natural environment in terms of such purpose.[8] Thus families could be formed, cooperative hunting and gathering established, and rudimentary political life organized. With the development of semiotic systems a vast new avenue of sophisticated civilization was opened. The late-modern culture that seems so scientific and religiously problematic works with the same brain structure that served for Neolithic hunter-gatherers. The difference lies in the content of the semiotic structures.

We can imagine human behavior as a hierarchy of levels of neural and social development. Higher neural organs, which mediate its violent responses and make possible the imagination of a field of interrelating actors, overlie the primitive reptilian brain. Elementary signs are already involved in this as cultures differ in how they envision space-time fields and dynamics, and how they identify objects against backgrounds. As semiotic systems become more elaborate and culturally specific, human society forms with shared and taught sign systems. Social behaviors arise and reward the use of higher level brain functions, setting strong controls on the cruder and more violent lower functions. Social controls not only employ higher-level brain functions but take shape in terms of the

---

[7] See any recent introductory neurology textbook to spell this out. For advanced discussion of biological determinants of behavior by means of hormones, see Jay Schulkin's *The Neuroendocrine Regulation of Behavior*. See also Terrence Deacon's *The Symbolic Species*.

[8] For a speculative scientific account of this, see Deacon's *The Symbolic Species*.

semiotic systems, with conceptions of control stemming from purposes for community. Political organization imposes political controls on group behavior, limiting the reactions of individuals and clans. Essential to the *polis* are the police.

Confucians would point out that these levels of behavior, each imposing its order top down on the lower levels, are functions of ritual, at least where semiotic codes are involved.[9] The human organism is highly underdetermined in its movements. Whereas pigeons get food only by genetically stylized pecking motions, humans can get food to their mouths in a seemingly indefinite number of ways. A parental culture has to teach some one definite way. Eye contact can be made any number of ways; a culture has to teach some definite set of ways. Gestures not only make possible finite action, they take on other meanings as well, so that styles of eye contact indicate respect or brashness. The origin of syntactically structured speech is a higher level of ritual. Political organization involves a ritual that determines kinds of speeches, and so on up to explicit ceremony that articulates fundamental human roles and the relation of human communities to the natural and spiritual environment. Thus human life is made possible by the development and exercise of rituals that, level by level, coordinate physiological processes into civilized human behavior.

But at the core of the brain is the snake.

The higher supervening ritualized levels of human behavior impose order on the lower levels but they do not exhaust their energy or eliminate their native behaviors, only coordinate them. The energies and native behaviors of the lower levels threaten to break out. The police-enforced rituals of civil justice pressure the inertias of clan revenge to submit to arbitration before the law, but sometimes fail in that. The rituals of clan organization subordinate the interests of particular families for dominance and power, but sometimes fail in that. The rituals of family life coordinate the behavior of individuals who otherwise seek personal gain, but sometimes fail in that. The rituals of personal style and sense of self coordinate personal impulses, but sometimes fail in that. Sometimes the snake's limited repertoire of violent responses breaks through cultured impulses, personal self-control, obligatory family roles, the organized destiny of a clan, and the rules of civilized behavior. The white-knuckled driver pulsing road rage is not just exhib-

---

[9] For an elaborate argument to this effect, see my *Normative Cultures*, chapter 7, and *Boston Confucianism*, chapters 1–2, 5, and 10.

iting a resurgence of clan revenge, or a bid for family power in the clan, or the assertion of personal interest in the family, or even an untamed impulse. That driver is a velociraptor in a Mercedes.[10]

We can speculate, therefore, that ritual has another dimension. Ritual is not only a set of horizontal dances, as it were, integrating lower-level behaviors into a higher coordinated pattern, though it is that. It is also vertical dancing that seeks to harmonize the force of the higher levels with the destructive energies of the lower. When the rituals involve sacrifice, this is especially so. The religious and political organization of Israel could have been celebrated with rituals of lecture and refreshments, not with slaughtering an ox for each tribe and the throwing of blood on everyone. It was not, however, and the reason likely was the recognition and legitimated expression of the violence involved in that political organization. The rituals celebrating the changes of season could be celebrated with a ceremonial change of clothing or diet; but across the ancient world they were celebrated instead with animal sacrifices, acknowledging the destruction in human consumption, breaking the land, burying seed, cutting off its growth, and consuming it; nurturing the life-cycle of herds and flocks, and then slaughtering the animals. The Exodus could have been commemorated with a great freedom party; but instead it is commemorated today in the Seder with a ritual remembering the sacrifices of lambs and goats, and the deeper sacrifices of the Egyptian first-born. Sacrifice is a symbolic way of letting the energies of the lower-level behaviors of life find expression outside the higher controls and yet in coordination with them.

Consider the point more generally. The entropy of the universe is such that the maintenance of order requires an input of energy. An increase in order, as in the development of personal integrity, a nurturing family, a social community, or a civilization, requires an even greater price in energy. One need not know Newton's physics to have a sense for the prices paid at many levels of personal and social organization. Human metabolism consumes life. Personal identity consumes energy to contain impulses. Family energy is required to coordinate individuals, communal energy is spent organizing families, and civil society is hugely expensive in holding to even a modicum of justice. No social economy whatsoever would exist without some social organization, some differentiation of roles, class, power, duties, and prestige. Each of these requires

---

[10] The biblical tradition records the situation of the first people who had ancestry of guilt. See Regina M. Schwartz' *The Curse of Cain*.

something of a violent price. Even the worst off, the oppressed in society, are better off with some social order rather than none, and so are hardly less guilty for the price paid than those on top. The greatest achievements of human civilization, the art, the science, the perfection of local domestic communities, the expressions of genius – all exist because heavy prices have been paid. The greater the excellence of order, the greater the entropic price. In this respect, Michelangelo's representation of the creation of Adam (figure 3, p. 27 above) is deeply misleading because it suggests that the vivifying transfer of energy comes without price from an infinite divine reservoir; the real costs are to finite things.

How does all this feel to an individual human being, or to a community? It feels like blood-guilt, I wager. Not in the first instance is it the guilt of immorality, which is a disruption of civil and social order, although blood guilt can grow into that. Nor is it in the first instance the guilt of personal responsibility. The Levitical sacrifices of guilt and sin offerings (Lev. 1–7) are for *unintentional* sin. Rather this guilt is for the prices paid for the way things are, especially the good things, and it is stimulated and given energy by dim awareness of paying those prices again in personal and communal life. Who has not resented the inhibition of revenge, the limiting placement of one's family in a communal hierarchy, the demands of the family on one's wants, the discipline of personal control over impulses? Who has not felt blind rage and the counter-violence of blocking it? Most conscious guilt needs specific objects, and surely we are aware of the consequences in morally reprehensible but personally responsible behavior that arise out of our resentment and rage. But I mean here to call attention and assign the name "blood-guilt" to the felt prices paid from which our conscious resentment and rage arises.

To the modern sensibility such blood-guilt seems childish in comparison with guilt for things for which we are morally responsible. Who should feel guilty for the structure of human physiology, or for family life as such, or even for social and political structures beyond one's capacity to influence? Late-modern culture has rejected what it interprets as the superimposition of categories of moral responsibility on matters for which there is no individual responsibility whatsoever. But in point of actual fact, the late-modern attitude is mistaken. The prices of civilization have been paid, we are the beneficiaries, and we bear that cumulative blood-guilt. Late-modern culture in the nineteenth and twentieth centuries has warred with greater violence than any predecessor, perfecting mass murder and the mindless destruction of culture and wealth.

Enlightenment rationalism seeking only personal responsibility boggles before such behavior. Economic competition, which is supposed to increase wealth, is utterly contradicted by the martial and other kinds of violence that it has made acceptable. Dismissing sacrificial rituals as superstition, and thus lacking acceptable sacrifices as ways of coming to terms with the blood-guilt of high civilization, late modernity unwittingly legitimates more blind and unmeasured violence.

Consider the role of blood-guilt in personal spiritual life. I might begin by acknowledging with Paul (Rom. 7:15) that the good I would, I do not, and that which I would not, that I do. These are not necessarily moral mistakes. They are not rational valuational miscalculations. They are the destructive eruption of the lower demanding behaviors of life into the higher. Those behaviors the tradition analyzes as sins – for instance sex, pursuit of wealth, love of food, protection of one's own – are all good and necessary when coordinated by the civilizing law of God written in our hearts. They are sins when they break out of that coordination and become lust, greed, gluttony, and selfishness, and take on lives of their own that cannot be coordinated.

Contemplating my blood-guilt, however symbolized, and my inability to handle that guilt within civilized life, I note that this is not a matter of mere personal mismanagement. Rather, it is a breaking of the founding orders of my life and civilization. However symbolized, the founding orders that give life meaning are among the most important ways that the ultimate impinges upon me. God the Father creates me in my civilized context by means of those levels of ritualized foundation. They are thus sacred. The sacred becomes vivid in contrast to its profanation in the breakthrough of violence, level bursting level. The Levitical code recognized this in saying that sin was not just moral evil but the breaking of the law of God as such. Sin is first of all impurity and stain, as Ricoeur argued, an offense against the sacred for which rituals might be restorative.[11]

Christianity radicalized the Levitical sense of sin and sacrifice. Sins are deeper in the human soul, are universal to all people and societies, and cannot be atoned for by any finite sacrifices of oxen, sheep, or pigeons. Even if the ancient Israelites were right that God's great mercy on Sinai gave laws for sacrifice that restore sinful people fully to the purity required for approaching the sacred, those laws do not help the Gentiles. And they do not in fact help the Jews, Paul thought (Rom.

[11] See Ricoeur's *The Symbolism of Evil*, part i.

9–11), because they still were caught in bondage to their alienation from God as he saw it. So Paul found in Jesus a sacrifice fully efficacious, not for Jews only but for Gentiles too. How can this be understood today?[12]

If the above analysis of levels of personal and social constitution is at least partly on the mark, then in every one of us lies something like what is symbolized as blood-guilt in the biblical tradition. That symbolism is peculiar to this tradition, of course, and does not make immediate sense to cultures that have long since abandoned blood sacrifice and suppressed its memory. Chinese culture, for instance, makes little of guilt and rather interprets misbehavior as something that shames a family and that ought to be corrected with education. Nevertheless, the shame that can cause the ostracism of an entire family, or its physical punishment, is not unrelated to blood-guilt. The ancient Chinese emperors did conduct blood sacrifices. And the terrific conflict between pro-ritual Confucians and anti-ritual classical Daoists, a conflict likely internal to nearly everyone in Chinese culture, bespeaks the oppressive and sometimes bloody price paid for ritual harmonization. The Judeo-Christian tradition keeps that symbolism alive despite Enlightenment rationalism.

How does the symbolism work? Blood-guilt can only be understood and appreciated personally. So I shall answer in the first person, supposing that readers can tell their own story and ask whether the analysis applies to them.

Reflecting on myself in view of the Ultimate, standing before God, *coram deo*, what am I? A husband, father, householder, professor, academic administrator, churchman, writer, theologian, philosopher, now with a long career of mixed achievements and failures; I am not a lawbreaker, violent, systematically deceitful, or intentionally wicked (at least in big things); the personal sins I enumerate and confess that harm family, friends, and institutions come from ordinary selfishness, self-deception, weakness, cowardice, and perversity. All in all, not too good but also not too bad, because I was born into a loving and competent family, was well-educated, lucked into a miraculous marriage, have found a few deep friends, have held good jobs, have been either too young or to old to go to the wars of my time, and have lived in a rela-

---

12   See Paula Fredriksen's "Ultimate Reality in Ancient Christianity," for a defense of the thesis that Paul's main contribution was to claim that through Jesus Christ God extended to the Gentiles the possibility of participation in the promises of God to Israel. Whereas in older Judaism, the Jews were holy (in varying degrees) and the Gentiles common or profane, in Christianity Christ's sacrifice makes the Gentiles holy as well and thus able to approach God.

tively stable and wealthy society with high culture to whose wealth and culture my family has had access. Precisely because of this modest but genuine goodness I stand before God blood-guilty.

The extraordinary high civilization of late-modern Western culture giving my life context was built upon its imperial domination of virtually the entire world and is sustained by an oppressive global economic market that is ruining the environment. (Perhaps Paul had analogous feelings about his civilized world that gave him Roman citizenship, a passport, a classy education, meaningful work, a circle of colleagues famous even today, and access to a generally fair judicial system of which he took full advantage, all supported by the efficiency of imperial legions.) I feel the price paid for my civilized context. If I were a victim of my civilization, I might feel the guilt of resentment and a desire for revenge. Favored as I am, I feel the reverse guilt ("liberal, white, male" is my kind) of self-contempt projected from the imagined eyes of the victims (and sometimes from their actual words and deeds). The civilized context for my life's modest achievements, failures, and satisfactions makes me guilty for the devastating wars protecting national interest, the unjust global market economy, and the ruined rain forests. Not personally guilty, to be sure – I vote against all those things and recycle as well. But blood-guilty – I am made of those things, they are my life-blood.

I have also been favored by a well-ordered society, which is to say, my community has been structured so that the crucial roles are played and things work. For instance, I was able to get into an elite system of higher education from a lower middle-class background, marry someone similar, and move into jobs and a social class that give satisfying access to culture and power. My children are well educated and I have a growing retirement fund. The community works, more or less. Even the least favored in my community are better off with it than with social chaos. As to price, members of families have been forced to play social roles, such as single mothers being forced to work, and the good of the families has been subordinated to those social roles, sometimes with devastating consequences, especially for minorities. For the prices paid for social roles, I am blood-guilty.

My families, too, my family of origin and my own family, fine as they are and so full of satisfaction, have come with a price. My parents sacrificed much of their own happiness to provide a responsible and economically stable home. My wife and I have struggled to compromise two careers into the management of our household. The prices paid in petty resentments, frustrations of opportunities, losses of friendship, and conflicts about taking out the garbage color moods too much of the time. Here too I am blood-guilty as well as personally responsible.

What price have I paid for my own discipline and organized self-identity? I work hard and play hard (because I schedule the play along with work) and am very self-reflective. Like a Confucian, I spend much energy cultivating myself and, as Plato pointed out, the personal force that integrates the self is spiritedness or anger directed against the self's waywardness. Such personal stability and effectiveness as I have comes from deflecting, redirecting, drawing out, displacing, suppressing, repressing, and bottling up the impulses of a healthy human animal. For that I am blood-guilty.

From the white knuckles on my steering wheel, I see that I'm still the snake.

So when I stand before God the very best that I am is intrinsically impure and unholy because of the blood-guilt expressed in reptilian rage, frustrated impulses, suppressed individuality, resented social conformity, and feelings of revenge for the price of civilized life. Rarely if ever do I reflect on this analytically when standing *coram deo*. But the feelings are there. And the more honest I am, the deeper and more painful that layered blood-guilt is.

How can I engage God, so guilty as this, so impure and unholy? Of course I cannot by any ordinary means. Can I then avoid God? Can I stay permanently distracted from ultimate things? Can I flee into proximate worries and troubles so as to avoid who I really am from an ultimate point of view? Should I take drugs, stay drunk all the time? Run to the power games? Devote myself to money? Give myself over to unbridled lust? All the avenues for flight from God lead to binding sin and add personal responsibility to my blood-guilt. And those flights never work. The avenues never lead out of creation. Nothing we can do can separate us from the Creator. Before the Creator we stand in ultimate perspective: we are who we are, and who we are is blood-guilty. I am blood-guilty.

So ask again, how can I engage God, blood-guilty as I am? This is to ask, with what symbol can I as such a sinner engage God, with real and true engagement taking place? The obvious symbol is that I should be punished so as to suffer the price in blood for the blood-guilt that I bear. That's what a criminal really is in ultimate perspective: a person whose dignity lies in being worthy of punishment. For most peoples (and not only in Christianity), this punishment has been further symbolized as Hell, and cultures' imaginations are rarely more inventive than in appointing the accommodations and implements of Hell. Such bloody punishment unto death, which I deserve, is the only successful way of engaging God, namely, the only successful complete flight from God. To stand before God blood-guilty is to accept the merit of punishment unto death, and will it. That is the way to engage the ultimate truth about oneself in ultimate perspective. But that clutch at the dignity of truth by means of willing one's own punishment unto death is not a profitable way to carry on as a child of God.

What if I engage God with the symbol of someone who undergoes penal suffering unto death *for* me? The witnesses of the Church give me Jesus.

Jesus would have to pay the blood price for civilization: he was executed by Rome as an accident, not deserving punishment but the adventitious victim of the political need to contain the Passover crowds excited about a Messiah.

Jesus would have to pay the blood price for social order: his disciples, his new community, abandoned him.

Jesus would have to pay the blood price for family: while hanging on the cross (John 19:25–27) he deconstructed his kinship family, and that of the disciple John, to create the artificial family in which Mary became John's mother and John Mary's filial son.

Jesus would have to pay the blood price for personal integrity: he sweated blood praying that crucifixion's cup, the blood-filled cup of the new covenant, would pass from him.

Jesus would have to pay the blood price of reptilian rage: when no angels came, when he was too tired to heave more against the nails, when he saw the guards dividing a dead man's clothes, he knew he was gone and cried, "My God! My God! Why have you forsaken me?" Rage. Despair. Terminal loneliness.

If Jesus had deserved punishment as a matter of personal responsibility at any of these levels, from being a real threat to the political order to being unfaithful to God at his heart's core, he would not be a symbol I could use to engage God, because it would have been his personal sin, not our common sin, that was punished. The blood-guilt I bear for my portion of the sins of the world, the guilt for the price paid to have the world in all its levels of evolved achievement, that is the guilt for which Jesus died.

But how does his tortured death become mine? How can his substitute for mine? Why was not his death just the price he had to pay, as I too have to pay mine? The meaning of these questions is whether Jesus' death can be a symbol that allows me to engage God, standing before the Creator blood-guilty, without dying myself and willing that death.

The answer in the atonement symbolism is that I eat Jesus and drink his blood, becoming that death. Or rather, because his flesh and blood have become mine, I have been punished unto death in his death. So I can stand before God having taken my punishment. The act of cannibalism is not merely a symbolic way of getting Jesus inside me, metabolizing his flesh and blood into mine, although of course it is that. More important, the act of cannibalism is a kind of taboo murder that violates every level of human existence. It is a reptilian strike at a brother, an unleashed forbidden impulse, a sick abuse of a dead man for one's own salvation, a defiant rejection of social order, the mocking transformation of civilized sensibilities into a terrible joke. In order for Jesus' punishment and death to become mine, I must will it as I will my own, and in the worst way. Cannibalism is the worst way. If it were not a curse, it could not be a blessing.

Christianity says that human guilt goes far beyond matters of personal responsibility and that because of it we are dead before God. We can be saved from that death, however, and returned to God, made pure again and worthy to approach the Holy of Holies, if we engage God with the symbol of Jesus whose death becomes ours. This is the meaning of substitutionary atonement. "And can it be that I should gain an interest in my Savior's blood?"[13]

Atonement is only one aspect of salvation in the Christian tradition, although I have somewhat artificially abstracted it from the rest at this early stage in the argument. Notice that the reality of this aspect of salvation is a matter of engaging God by means of a symbol that allows that contact to be maintained by a blood-guilty sinner. It has little to do with whether Jesus in fact died in the way that the gospels say, or was the person they describe. It has little to do with whether Jesus had the metaphysical status of being Son of God or the incarnation of a Person of the Trinity. It has nothing to do with whether God is in reality a supernatural person with an ill will toward sinners, demanding their death like a judging king administering justice. It has little to do with whether there is a real Hell or a real Heaven, or whether people go to one or the other in an afterlife. It has only to do with whether we have a symbol that allows us to present ourselves to God, to stand in ultimate perspective, given our blood-guilty identity as sinners. This is the Christian develop-

---

[13] Charles Wesley's hymn, number 363 in *The United Methodist Hymnal.*

ment of the Levitical theme of divine holiness and human impurity. The crucified Christ is such a symbol, and those other symbols are significant for atonement only insofar as they extend this and are also meaningful. Their greater significance lies elsewhere.

The truth of the symbol of Jesus' crucifixion lies not in its iconic descriptive reference. Jesus the Galilean had no idea who I would be and did not die for my sins in any literal sense. Rather, the truth of the symbol lies in its indexical reference: by meditating on God through the symbol of Jesus' crucifixion I am changed so as to be able to engage God and live, being blood-guilty. The symbol of the crucified Christ schematizes the divine Creator who creates me blood-guilty.

RESURRECTION

What is the result of engaging God with the symbolic act of consuming the crucified Jesus Christ? Without that act, or something else that performs the same function, we are like dead people in the ultimate meaning of our lives. With it, we have new life as resurrected sinners. We can live before God with our blood-guilt, but with it atoned, having received and survived the merited punishment. We have died with Christ, and have been raised with him (Eph. 2, Col. 2–3).

Resurrection is a symbol that itself has many systems of meaning. Among them are the resuscitation of a dead body to life and also new life in a heavenly place after ordinary death. Neither of these is the meaning of resurrection here except insofar as they supplement the symbolic meaning of atonement-resurrection. Atonement-resurrection is the new life Christians have after they have come to engage God, blood-guilty as they are, with the symbol of the crucified Christ, an engagement that means living "in Christ."

Resurrection in this sense is interpreted by what is called a "realized eschatology," that is, an eschatological state of affairs realized in ordinary life, not in an afterlife. Perhaps the most direct statement of this sense of resurrection is in Colossians. Following a statement of a very high Christology according to which the world is created in, through, and for Christ (Col. 1:15–16, topics to be discussed in chapters 3 and 4), the author asserts the following (selected from Col. 2:8–3:11):

For in him [Jesus Christ] the whole fullness of deity dwells bodily, and you have come to fullness in him, who is the head of every ruler and authority. In him also you were circumcised with a spiritual circumcision, by putting off the body of the flesh in the circumcision of Christ; when you were buried with him in baptism, you were also raised with him through faith in the power of God, who raised him from the dead. And when you were dead in trespasses and the uncircumcision of your flesh, God made you alive together with him when he forgave us all our trespasses, erasing the record that stood against us with its legal demands. He set this aside, nailing it to the cross . . . If with Christ you died to the elemental spirits of the universe, why do you live as if you still belonged to the world? So if you have been raised with Christ, seek the things that are above, where Christ is, seated at the right hand of God. Set your minds on things that are above, not on things that are on earth, for you have died, and your life is hidden with Christ in God . . . Put to death, therefore, whatever in you is earthly: fornication, impurity, passion, evil desire, and greed (which is idolatry) . . . These are the ways you also once followed, when you were living that life. But now you must get rid of all such things – anger, wrath, malice, slander, and abusive language from your mouth. Do no lie to one another, seeing that you have stripped off the old self with its practices and have clothed yourselves with the new self, which is being renewed in knowledge according to the image of its creator. In that renewal there is no longer Greek and Jew, circumcised and uncircumcised, barbarian, Scythian, slave and free; but Christ is all and in all.

This passage has many themes in addition to the atonement symbols mentioned so far, some of which will be discussed in later chapters. Instead of the blood of the Mosaic old covenant, this author cites the circumcision of the earlier Abrahamic covenant, and says that in Christ Christians of whatever kind and heritage have a new spiritual circumcision. This author treats baptism as a death for Christ and for us with Christ; rising out of the baptismal water is a resurrection from the dead. Although the author assumes an afterlife in which the full glory of God, Christ, and resurrected Christians will be revealed, the point is that the resurrection has already taken place. "You have died, and your life is hidden with Christ in God." "When you were buried with him in baptism, you were also raised with him through faith in the power of God, who raised him from the dead." Christians are raised with Christ while still in this life. They have a new life in Christ, or Christ in them. And therefore they should get their act together and behave as Christians should. They should put to death the old ways of sin and attend to improving such habits as rage control, disposition of will, and ways of speaking with others. The author goes on after the passage quoted to advocate the positive cultivation of compassion, kindness, humility, meekness, patience, love, and gratitude, and finally gives advice about family life (including, alas, the view that it is fitting in Christ for wives to be subject to their husbands). A similar view of death and resurrection is expressed in Ephesians 2.

The other sustained locus of realized eschatology in the New Testament is the Farewell Discourses in John, chapters 13–17. Without denying immortality and life after death, Jesus talks rather of eternal life that involves a right relation to God in which the alienating powers of the world are overcome. Jesus says, in prospect of his imminent arrest and crucifixion, that he has already overcome the world. He will leave the company of the disciples to be with God in Heaven and will send the Holy Spirit to guide them through the course of life, not later after death but within this life of the disciples. The eschatological transformation is not something that comes later in subsequent history, or at the cataclysmic ending of historical time. Rather it is like an overlay on top of ongoing historical existence. More is going on in history than we are wont to notice when we attend only to temporal affairs. History has an eternal dimension too. Jesus in these discourses explicates this in terms of love between God and himself, himself and the disciples, and the disciples with one another; the theme of love is the topic of chapters 4–7 below.

St. Paul was fully committed to the view that Christians are a new creation that consists in being in Christ and Christ being in the Christians. Like the author of Colossians he said (Rom. 6:1–4) that we die to our old selves in baptism, being baptized into Christ's death. But he tended (see Rom. 6:5–11, 1 Cor. 15, for two instances) to reserve the resurrection symbol for the afterlife, believing in a cataclysmic ending of history with the second coming of Christ. Paul's own expectation was that Jesus would come again in the near future, at least within his lifetime. So his metaphors for living now "in newness of life" were about "walking between the times," with postponement of serious changes of life.[14] He advocated moral and holy living as the proper way to respond to God until the end comes, not as the way of living out the resurrected life. Colossians and Ephesians likely were written later than Paul's other letters, either by himself toward the end of his life when he might have given up hope for a fulfillment of history or by one or more disciples even later who had abandoned Paul's tension between unfulfilled and fulfilled history.[15]

The point of the realized eschatology is that the central saving sense

---

[14] See J. Paul Sampley's *Walking between the Times*, a study of Paul's interim ethics.
[15] I am quite willing myself to attribute Colossians and Ephesians to Paul on the grounds that smart people like him can modify their theories in the face of contrary evidence. Neither of those letters denies a future Second Coming; they realize, however, that the intensity of eschatological expectation cannot be pinned on indefinitely future hope, only on eternal consummation.

of resurrection takes place within this life and that the subsequent business of life is the cultivation of holiness in the Christian community. This sense of resurrection is compatible with another sense in which there is an afterlife, and the authors of Colossians, Ephesians, and John assumed that latter sense too. But it is also compatible with the contrary view, more common today, that there is no afterlife: the saving resurrection is a state possible in the midst of life in consequence of which Christians should cultivate sanctification.

The Eucharistic symbol of the atonement is a genuine possibility for engaging God in the late-modern world. Such engagement does not require belief in an afterlife, or in a God with inner subjectivity and a personal will. It does require an ability imaginatively to configure the senses of sin, analyzed here as blood-guilt and the more nearly personal guilt that comes from the consequences of resentment and rage, that obtain from just being alive in human civil society. This is not difficult for the late-modern imagination. Eucharistic engagement also requires an ability imaginatively to identify with the sufferings of the crucified Jesus in the sense of taking his suffering and death to be what we deserve. So in prayer and meditation late-modern Christians can picture themselves and the cross in vivid detail. Visualizations of the gruesome crucifixion have often been extreme, especially in Western European medieval and early-modern Christianity.[16] Delacroix's "Christ on the Cross" (figure 6) is violent but not gruesome. The wind whips clouds and garments, the soldiers and their mounts are pistons of energy, the women are at extremes of grief and adoration, and a disciple in the lower right corner buries his head in guilt. But Jesus is an immensely strong man who could be holding up the cross instead of hanging on it, looking to heaven with his face in shadow, a man of transcendent importance on whom to depend.

Atonement in this radical sense is not compatible with the common late-modern belief that we bear guilt only for those wrongs for which we are personally responsible. In fact, atonement in this sense, at least as analyzed so far, does not touch personal responsibility and its guilts, only the blood-guilt that comes with the human condition itself, although blood-guilt often leads to responsible guilt. As to personal guilts, Jesus

---

[16] Mitchell B. Merback's *The Thief, the Cross and the Wheel* details the extremes to which Christianity can go in presenting models in art and in the practices of public execution for identification with penal suffering and death. The extremes are violent enough to our own sensibility to justify rejection of the entire thematic of blood-guilt and the atonement. But something else must be found to deal with blood-guilt, however redescribed.

Figure 6. Ferdinand-Victor-Eugène Delacroix, *Christ on the Cross*, National Gallery, London

would not be a good substitute because he is represented as himself not guilty in that sense. The blood-guilt of the human condition itself has been interpreted in the Christian tradition as original sin. Augustine thought it was inherited through the act of sexual intercourse by which people are conceived. We do not need to buy into that quasi-genetics, especially its interpretation of sex. But real genetics is part of the source of guilt for the human condition, along with the institutions of family, society, and civilization. The doctrine of original sin was more right than wrong about the human condition.

The radical symbol of Eucharistic atonement is also incompatible with the common view that sin is not so bad, that it is at worst a problem of immaturity or bad education and at best a spur to improvement. This doctrine of the atonement is incompatible with the view that there is no real sin at all, only victimization. Although the blood-guilt atoned for is not generally a matter of personal responsibility, the very meaning of blood-guilt is that people take responsibility for it. If people do not accept themselves as constituted by the processes that have exacted enormous prices of the sort discussed above, they cannot conceive themselves as in need of punishment. Of course we are indeed constituted by those processes. That is the human condition. And the recognition of this is an essential part of what it means to be human, for which we take responsibility.

The strong symbol of the atonement is also incompatible with a common view of God as a Really Good Guy who would never hold sin against us. Many Christians in our day extrapolate from the symbols of God as a loving Father to an "I'm OK, you're OK" image of God. The centrality of divine mercy to Jesus' teaching is misconstrued as God not taking sin seriously. The opposite is the case in the real logic of the symbol of mercy. Mercy is significant only if judgment is prior, exact, and radical. The tendency to personify God as a benevolent parent works contrary to the saving significance of the atonement symbols. Life's common injustices and vicissitudes give the lie to that easy image of the benevolent parent. Atonement is far more resonant with a non-personifying image of God as simply the Ultimate before whom we are exactly what we are, blood-guilty.

The Christian message of resurrected new life in the blood of Jesus Christ can be put to the most secular sensibilities of the late-modern world this way: If you can identify with bloody suffering and death so that it imaginatively becomes your own punishment for the price your life has cost, you can accept this as your ultimate identity – blood-guilty, but paid up and redeemed. Then all the powers of creation that have constituted your natural environment, your biology, personal integrity, family, community, and civilization become your powers. The powers of creation in nature and the human sphere flow through you like a river. The orders of your life are for you to enjoy, enhance, and improve when you flourish as a warrior against entropy. Your life's many parts are each to be delighted in and deferred to, each the result of great prices paid: you are part of many flows pulsing larger and more ancient than yourself. You can seize your rhythmic place among your people, in history, and in the cosmos as the miraculously evolved arena to be yourself. And you can find satisfaction, exultant joy and the peace that passes understanding in the unique achievement in value that is your song, with your orders harmonizing your parts in your place and time. The structures and orders of your life might not be very good in comparison to others or to what you might like, but they come to you through the trajectories of the whole creation. You might have preferred a life of different parts, more wealth perhaps, more intelligence, talents, luck; but your parts make you part of a mesh of cosmic processes that connects you with whatever might be enjoyed. You might have just complaints about the place and time into which you have been thrown to live your life, but it is your situation and your identity is how you engage it. The whole might not add up to much compared with history's heroes, but it adds up to you, a unique value achieved by creation's pricey evolution poured into the nexus of your place and time, the specific components of your life, and the patterns by which you hold all together against entropic dissipation and the dark. Thoughtlessly you might enjoy the thrill of existence on a sunlit day after a long string of good luck. You cannot seriously begin to appreciate what is wrought in you and yours, however, until you feel the prices that have been paid – ruined stars, bound snakes, suppressed impulses, subordinated interests, social duties, history's losers. The weight of that load of prices cannot be borne when you accept it as constituting yourself. Only if you can see that the burden is assumed by the heart of the creative process itself, and can make that part of you, can you face your identity within creation. That Jesus is the heart of the creative process is the central supposition of the atonement symbols, and this thesis will be explored through all the remaining chapters.

No secular language carries the force of this. Better to say that the price paid for you and yours is blood-guilt, that identification with the paying of it is ingestion of the crucified Christ, and that the freedom you then have as heir to creation's processes is resurrected new life. If the symbols of the atoning Christ can set you free, invest in the Christian life. If other symbols can do that as well, or instead, marvelous. If no symbols allow you to engage life fully, embracing the prices paid, then you are damned to resent, diminish, flee, and rage against the very powers that would give you being.

THE CHURCH AS RITUAL SUSTENANCE

The extreme symbols of the atonement, the acceptance of blood-guilt, the cannibalistic participation in the suffering and death of Christ on the cross, and the resurrection to new life, are anti-Enlightenment. They are exorbitant and fantastical. Meditating on the wounds of Christ is a little sick. Imagining myself washing in the blood pouring from Immanuel's veins is a condition for which one should call a psychoanalyst or at least an S&M master. Cannibalism is a great crime, and symbolic cannibalism is symbolic crime.

But the cannibalistic atonement symbols are not alone in the Christian life. They are nested with other symbols that limit them and give them new meaning. God cannot be engaged through those symbols without also setting those other symbols into resonance. Many layers of symbolic meaning are compacted in the Eucharistic celebration itself. The cannibal act might lie at its core, but it does not lie there alone. Consider the following.

The Eucharist acknowledges Jesus Christ to be the Lord, the master who commands the disciples and contemporary Christians to remember him in the liturgy. "Lord" is a political symbol, defining relations of allegiance and justice, and stands as a counterbalance to the bloody atonement symbols. "The Lord Jesus Christ" is a common expression in Paul's letters, and the title has resonances with Jesus' coming kingdom. Identifying the divinity as king or lord was almost as common among the Axial Age religions as the concept of creator. Those two symbols set up special resonances with one another in Israelite religion in which God creates by speaking like a king (Genesis 1). Yahweh leads His people out of Egypt as a warrior king; the Israelites do no fighting against the Egyptians themselves. In the histories, God rules as king over Israel, working through the judges as his representatives, until the anointing of Saul as king; 1 Samuel 8 makes clear just what a change this is, and not at all for the better. Nonetheless, "messiah" means anointed king; when Saul did not work out, David was anointed messiah; Cyrus of Persia was called messiah (Isaiah 45:1) for exercising God's kingship in Israel's behalf. That Jesus was called messiah meant first that he was the Davidic king who would deliver Israel from her enemies and establish justice and order in the land. That Jesus seemed so little like such a king was the reason the non-Christian Jews dismissed him. That he seemed as if he might be a political insurrectionist, elevated by popular fantasies of the restoration of the Davidic kingdom, is what concerned Pilate about him.[17]

The significance of kingship in ancient societies lay in the sudden increase in population that new agricultural methods made possible. Family, clan, and tribal systems could not bring order to such dense populations, and the political form of the king was invented.[18] A king is someone with the martial power to impose order on a large population in which people relate as citizens and not kin. Justice is defined in primitive levels as the defense of the rights of the weak against the clan-strength of the strong. At the very least, the king prevents blood violence and cannibalism. The king stands for higher order and the power to impose that on social processes that would reduce the city to feuds and violence if left to their own.

The "Lord Jesus" is such a king, armed with the power of God and set in place to impose the divine order of the Kingdom of God. The symbol of Jesus as Lord of Creation and King of Heaven and Earth, discussed in the next chapter, is set alongside the cannibalistic symbols of Jesus as the sufferer whose death substitutes for ours when we consume his dead flesh and blood. That juxtaposition modifies both symbols in their indexical reference. The suffering crucified Christ makes sense of the fact that Jesus surely does not seem to be a king by ordinary standards. The Lordship of Christ defangs the criminality of cannibalism and turns it into a just and merciful divine command. The symbols obviously are not consistent or harmonized within a higher-level pattern. Rather the harmonies are discordant, finding a higher meaning in their contradiction. The Eucharist exercises both symbols at once, sets both tones to vibrating.

A third symbol rings through the Eucharist, modifying the others, namely, that the eucharistic community has all the tightness of a family gathered for a festive meal. This partly reflects a deep social transformation beyond kingship, in fact, to empire. Put crudely, an empire unites people of different nationalities and imposes at least some elements of a common law and language. As Han language was imposed on all the peoples of China, so the many peoples of the Roman empire spoke Koine Greek, and the upper classes Latin. Most also spoke a native language or dialect. Personal identity was thus divided, or torn, between

---

[17] Fredriksen's *Jesus of Nazareth, King of the Jews* develops this point in detail.
[18] See the marvelous discussion in Jared Diamond's *Guns, Germs, and Steel*, chapter 14, "From Egalitarianism to Kleptocracy."

kinship identifications oriented to a particular place with a local language and cosmopolitan identifications oriented to being able to move about the empire and communicate along all the lines of its international body. Although we do not know how well Jesus spoke Greek in addition to Aramaic, Paul was a proud citizen of the empire, moving from capital to capital as if at home in all. Christianity became a religion of empire or, as we would say today, of a multicultural world.

One aspect of this imperial internationalization was the relegation of kinship relations to much less importance for identity than they would have in a tribal or even national society ("national" defines the group in terms of birth, *natus*). With loosened kinship identifications, and loosened loyalties to a king of one's place of birth, people became more "individualistic." Hence it was possible, if not easy, to identify oneself with the Creator God of the universe who is no closer to any one nation than to another. As early as Paul (indeed Isaiah 2), Jesus was King of the Universe for everyone, not just Israel, and God the Creator was both the interior source of the law in each individual and the common judge. Whereas Paul also held to the special status of Israel, the tension between divine closeness to Israel and divine closeness to everyone, including all Gentiles, remained problematic for him. The inclusion of Gentiles as well as Jews in the New Israel was not the only distinction Paul noted. He also enumerated the Greeks, Romans, Scythians, and unnamed barbarians, all brought into the Eucharistic community. This cosmopolitan distance from tribalism was also at a distance from conditions in which cannibalism might be practiced. The Eucharistic community would be sophisticated in the ways of the world, even when dominated by the lower classes, so long as the people identified with others across national and ethnic boundaries.

Another aspect of this symbol of cosmopolitanism in the Eucharistic community is the transformation of kinship symbols. They were not suppressed, but rather displaced to treat the multicultural community as the family of God. We have already noted that the Creator God is Father of all, making all human beings brothers and sisters. As mentioned above, Jesus explicitly created an artificial family for his mother and beloved disciple when they both had perfectly good kinship families in proximity. Jesus was also quoted as somewhat negative about actual kinship demands, denying his own family as not as real as his universal brothers and sisters (Mark 3:31–35), claiming to bring not peace but a sword to households (Matt. 10:34), and commanding the abandonment of filial burial obligations (Matt. 8:21–22). In primitive societies, the worst taboo violence against one's kinship family is fratricide and incest, and against those outside that family, ritual cannibalism. The universalization of the symbols of kinship undoes both of those. Violence and rape of other nations becomes fratricide and incest, and there is no one outside one's community whose body can be cannibalized.

A fourth symbol system in the Eucharist is that of the table fellowship itself, what went on at the table. That was where Jesus taught his disciples, where they shared experiences of success and failure, came to bear one another's burdens, defined their roles, and learned to love each other. The Farewell Discourses in John not only illustrate that fellowship but explicitly characterize it as a group of friends. The disciples become friends of one another, and Jesus ceases to be the master and becomes a friend as well. Even God, united to Jesus and the disciples by love, becomes a friend in some sense. Here it is enough to note that the relation of Christians at the Eucharistic table to Jesus is that of loving friends, which puts symbolic cannibalism in yet a new perspective, at once more radical than and subordinated to more concrete and non-symbolic relations.

A fifth symbol is the call to remember Jesus, which puts the Eucharistic community in direct historical continuity with Jesus and his own friends. Historical identity is clear and modern, not at all the murky dream stuff of eating the Lord's body and drinking his blood. Given the inclusiveness of the Eucharistic community over all the nations to which Christianity has gone, and the solidarity of friendship and love across that, Christians define themselves to one another across the world and down through time when they remember the historical Jesus. Remembering Jesus establishes distance and finite connections, countering, or at least counterbalancing, metabolic merging. Christians are connected to the historical Jesus by the intervening history. Historical consciousness in addition calls to mind those aspects of history for which people are indeed personally responsible. When Christians reflect on the historical Jesus, they also reflect on their own historical identities. Their particular missions, and the particular sins for which they individually or as a community are responsible, are part of their remembrance of Jesus. Although these are not matters of blood-guilt as defined above, and therefore not a function of the atonement, they are indeed matters of the responsibilities that accrue to living the new life in Christ, the life of holiness. Chapter 5 will discuss this in more detail. The point here is that the symbol of remembrance means that the members of the Eucharistic community not only are participants in Jesus' crucifixion and resurrection but also have historical responsibilities.

A sixth symbol or symbol system in the Eucharist is a reversal of the broken-body, spilt-blood atonement images, namely, that the elements nourish the communicants as healthy food and drink. This is cannibalistic in a sense, but not for the sake of participating redemptively in Jesus' death and resurrection. It is rather like being fed with his spirit, akin to taking on the mind of Christ, or becoming his continuing body in the world to continue his ministries. Contemporary Eucharistic observances most often focus on being nourished as the body of Christ. Here the communion elements are literally memorials of Jesus, and as such feed the Church with information and spirit, recalling what Jesus was like and what he might be like today. The bread and wine remember his love in laying down his life for his friends, and that memory feeds the Church.

Many other symbol systems are to be found in the Eucharist, of course, and some will be examined later. These are sufficient to make the point, however, that the cannibalistic symbols of eating Jesus' body and drinking his blood are not alone, but are set in motion to engage God along with those other symbols and symbol systems that engage God in other respects. Perhaps none of those symbol systems can stand alone. Perhaps most or all are needed. Christian engagement of God is not by any symbol system alone, but by these and more working together. Three points remain to be made in this chapter.

First, none of these symbol systems surrounding atonement symbols is incompatible with the world-view of late modernity; every one resonates with problems of the day. The contemporary world has deep concerns for political authority, for authentic kingship, though commitments to democracy call for deep rethinking of Lordship even in personal meditations about Jesus. The contemporary world is multicultural and international; Christianity is present and often flourishing in every nation of the world and ecclesiastical politics are filled with real concerns about universal and local languages; how can that multicultural church be regarded as an integrated family? Given cultural diversity and the skepticism of the European Enlightenment, can Christian communities have table fellowship that serves the ancient educational purpose and also results in a group of actual friends? What is the place of each Christian and congregation in the historical panoply of Christians since Jesus, rightly related to Jesus' ministries that fall to our contemporaries around the globe? How can the contemporary Church be nourished by the memory of the historical Jesus and all the symbols of Christ that engage people with God? How does that engagement take place, which is to say, how can the Holy Spirit be identified today? These

Eucharistic symbols are directly relevant to contemporary, late-modern life. Nothing in the symbol system of atonement by the blood of Jesus, not even the cannibalism when put in context of the other symbols, requires commitments that are incompatible with the metaphysics of late modernity.

Second, Christian engagement with God, through these or other symbols, takes place not on an individual basis alone but as acts of members of the Church. The Church is the context in which the symbols are real and are exercised, even when a Christian is closeted in private meditation. The prayers of a Christian are acts of the Church, a point especially true of the symbols involved in the Eucharistic liturgy, the central defining act of Christian worship as a community. Those symbols have their meaning always contextualized in part by their communal use. Therefore the extremity and fantasticalness of meditative identification with the blood of Christ have a communal context that integrates them with many other practices.

Of course, most actual Christian communities are not ideal. Most would not be explicitly conscious of the extremity of the atonement symbol system, or of much of the corrective character of other symbol systems in the Eucharist except perhaps those having to do with nourishment. Many Christian communities would deny blood-guilt, abuse authority, exclude people different from themselves from their fellowship, cultivate prejudice and backbiting rather than Christian learning and friendship, misunderstand their historical position, and prefer nourishment from popular culture to the embarrassing memory of Jesus. So participation in a Christian community as part of the Church needs to be in a critical mode as well as in a mode of integration into the Body of Christ. Where does that criticism come from? In very large part, it comes from the central symbols of worship itself, especially the Eucharistic liturgy. Those symbols, even the few just enumerated, lift up judgment on corruption. What better wake-up call could there be than sudden recognition that communion is not fuzzy fellow feeling but the symbolic cannibal eating of a fellow? What fellow? For what purpose? What purpose could possibly justify such a symbolic rite?

Third and finally, after all the qualifications and contextualizations of the symbol systems of atonement in the blood of Jesus, the atonement remains the dramatic historical center of Christian history and life. It is anchored in the Levitical problematic of sin as impurity that disqualifies one from the presence of God. But it transforms that problematic by radicalizing the sense of sin to what is here called blood-guilt, by extending sin's problem from the people of Israel to all people, by requiring not a goat but an innocent man for a scapegoat, by not sending him away into the wilderness but rather internalizing him so radically as to eat him, and by conceiving the proper relation to God as a rising from the dead to new life, a symbol of abomination in Leviticus for which even the touch of a corpse makes one impure. Jesus as celebrated in the Eucharist is what first and most dramatically set Christians off from other forms of Second Temple Judaism.

We live very far from the cultural world of the Levitical temple rites. But an account has been given here of blood-guilt as the price paid for human life and civilization, an account that is sharpened on late-modern sensibilities. The remedy for blood-guilt, making possible a genuine engagement of the Ultimate, God the Creator, is not a form of ancient animal sacrifice, meaningless in our world, but identification with a person like ourselves who suffered the punishment for blood-guilt that we deserve, an identification as primal as cannibal ingestion and as cosmopolitan as the Eucharistic table. The atonement so understood makes sense in late-modern culture.

The truth of this symbol system is not much in iconic description of the historical Jesus. The truth of the atonement symbol system rather is in its indexical reference that transforms sinners being alienated from God by blood-guilt to redeemed sinners who can embrace God, even move to friendship with God and one another, reconciled to God despite blood-guilt. The empirical question is whether people are so transformed. The symbols of the atonement schematize the transcendent creator to the human condition of blood-guilt.

CHAPTER THREE

Jesus the Cosmic Christ

The symbol of the Cosmic Christ is about as far from the depictions of the historical Jesus as one can imagine. Compare the Cosmic Christ Pantokrators of figure 1 (p. 19 above) and figure 7 (next page) with Sallman's personal Jesus in figure 14 (p. 211 below): the Pantokrators bear the creative power of the Father whereas Sallman's Jesus merely reflects the Father's blessing as we all might. Western mainline Christianity's preoccupations for the last two centuries with the historical Jesus have led to its almost total neglect of interpretations of Jesus as the Cosmic Christ although the symbol has remained central in Eastern Orthodoxy and some evangelical Christianity.[1] The Cosmic Christ is an ancient symbol in the Church, going back at least to Paul and finding classic expression in the Prologue to John (1:1–18) in which Jesus is called the incarnation of the Word. The theme, moreover, is closely related to the realized eschatology evident in the atonement symbols analyzed in the previous chapter, as for instance in Colossians 1:15–20.[2]

What is at stake in the symbol systems of the Cosmic Christ? The underlying problem being addressed is how human beings can be at home in the cosmos. The conception of the cosmos in the first century was radically different from our current conceptions. But the problem of cosmic hospitality is intensified for us, not lessened. The argument of this chapter is that the symbol systems of the Cosmic Christ schematize God understood as Creator *ex nihilo* to the human condition in respect of the problems of being at home in, or alienated from, the universe.

The first section here will explore some biblical roots of the symbol system of the Cosmic Christ, finding within it five sub-systems of symbols. The second will turn to the question of human habitation in

---

[1] For exceptions regarding mainly Christianity, see Matthew Fox's *The Coming of the Cosmic Christ* and Raimundo Panikkar's *The Hidden Christ of Hinduism* and other items in the bibliography.

[2] For a brief history of the symbol of the Cosmic Christ as symbol, not so much as doctrine, see Jaroslav Pelikan's *The Illustrated Jesus through the Centuries*, chapter 5.

Figure 7. *Christ Pantokrator*, apse mosaic, Duomo, Cefalu, Italy

the cosmos in its ancient and contemporary expressions. The third will develop a conception of the Logos as a metaphysical ground for engaging the religious dimension of human habitation today, developing the discussion begun in chapter 1. The concluding section will explore that engagement.

THE COSMIC CHRIST: BIBLICAL ROOTS

The author of Colossians, Paul or someone close to him, describes Christ this way (Col. 1:15–20):

He is the image of the invisible God, the firstborn of all creation; for in him all things in heaven and on earth were created, things visible and invisible, whether thrones or dominions or rulers or powers – all things have been created through him and for him. He himself is before all things, and in him all things hold together. He is the head of the body, the church; he is the beginning, the first-born from the dead, so that he might come to have first place in everything. For in him all the fullness of God was pleased to dwell, and through him God was pleased to reconcile to himself all things, whether on earth or in heaven, by making peace through the blood of his cross.

There are a number of themes, or symbolic sub-systems, that can be singled out. The first two symbol systems that define the Cosmic Christ are the ground of all the others.

The first is that Christ is the visible image of the invisible God, a theme also in Paul's earlier writings (2 Cor. 4:4). The Letter to the Hebrews (1:3) says Christ (the Son of God) "is the reflection of God's glory and the exact imprint of God's very being. . ." Concerning the relation of the invisible God to Christ his visible image, John wrote (John 1:18), "No one has ever seen God. It is God the only Son, who is close to the Father's ear, who has made him known." Later (14:9) John quotes Jesus: "Whoever has seen me has seen the Father." Note that the sense in which Christ is the image of the Father is different from the sense in which all human beings are created in the image of God (Gen. 1:26–27). Christ is the unique cosmic image through which all things are created, not like any other person. Yet there might be continuity between the senses of imaging God. The Genesis sense of divine image can be interpreted on the analogy of children representing their parents (see Gen. 5:2–3 where the line about humankind being created in the image of God is repeated and Adam hands on that image to Seth). Similarly, Jesus Christ can be called Son in the sense of representing the invisible Father within creation, although what Christ does as representative has a scale far beyond what any other person is called upon to do. The point of the symbol of the Cosmic Christ as the original image of the invisible God is that without the Cosmic Christ God cannot be known. This is perfectly compatible with the metaphysical position in chapter 1 which says that God is not determinate in any way apart from creation, and gains determinateness, even the nature of being God, only in the creating. The visible Christ as image of God is what does this. Any other revelations or characterizations of God, therefore, have to express the Cosmic Christ. In this sense, the Cosmic Christ is not limited to Jesus of Nazareth but is the principle of creation itself, which is the second defining theme.

The second defining symbol system is that Christ is the one in whom all other things are created. John 1:3a says "All things came into being through him, and without him not one thing came into being." Rev. 3:14 calls Christ "the origin of God's creation." All the imagery of the Divine Word, from Genesis 1 to John 1, is devoted to specifying the sense of Christ as Creator. This will be analyzed in terms of a contemporary theory of Logos in the third section below.

But in addition feminists have rightly pointed out the similarity of the claims that the creation took place through Christ with the role ascribed to Wisdom in Prov. 8:22–31:

The Lord created me at the beginning of his work, the first of his acts of long ago. Ages ago I was set up, at the first, before the beginning of the earth. When there were no depths I was brought forth, when there were no springs abounding with water. Before the mountains had been shaped, before the hills, I was brought forth – when he had not yet made earth and fields, or the world's first bit of soil. When he established the heavens, I was there, when he drew a circle on the face of the deep, when he made firm the skies above, when he established the fountains of the deep, when he assigned to the sea its limit, so that the waters might not transgress his command, when he marked out the foundations of the earth, then I was beside him, like a master worker; and I was daily his delight, rejoicing before him always, rejoicing in his inhabited world and delighting in the human race.

Wisdom in Proverbs 1:20–21 and throughout is personified as a prophetess, a female image. This is continued in the apocryphal Wisdom of Solomon 7:26 that says "she is a reflection of eternal light, a spotless mirror of the working of God, and an image of his goodness." See also Sirach 24:9 where wisdom says of herself, "Before the ages, in the beginning, he created me, and for all the ages I shall not cease to be" and (24:21) "Those who eat of me will hunger for more, and those who drink of me will thirst for more," a line on which Jesus was likely playing in John 4:13–14. For reasons feminists have brought forward, and perhaps more, the early Church suppressed the feminine imagery despite what they might have heard in it and applied the masculine imagery to Jesus.[3] The Pantokrator of late antiquity and the Byzantine period is solidly male.

Two more things are worth noting here about the symbol system of the Cosmic Christ as creator. On the one hand, the cosmos created goes far beyond the ordinary human world to include the invisible as well as the visible. The "thrones, dominions, rulers, and powers" listed in Colossians 1:16 are ranks of angels. As pointed out in chapter 1, these other dimensions of the cosmos are part of creation, not supernatural except that they generally are higher up than the plane of human affairs. These ranks of angels are not always beneficial; they are sometimes "the cosmic powers of this present darkness" (see Rom. 8:38), though still part of creation. The sense of the extension of the cosmos beyond the human sphere is an important corrective to the tendency to limit Christ's significance to human salvation history, or the cosmos itself to the sphere in which Jesus of Nazareth is meaningful. The cosmic imagination of the first century was not rivaled again until the twentieth!

On the other hand, in the creation symbols of the Cosmic Christ, Christ is not aboriginal in God apart from creation but is rather the first Creature and agent of creation. On the surface at least, this subordinationism is not consistent with the claims that Christ is the Second Person of the Trinity and thus prior to creation. That Trinitarian conception, chapter 4 will argue, belongs to a different system of symbols. The reality of the Cosmic Christ in creation, as a function of creation itself, is crucial for the theory of the Logos to be developed here.

A third subsystem of symbols for the Cosmic Christ is that Christ bounds and integrates the plurality of things in the cosmos. He is the Alpha and the Omega, as in Revelation 21:6. "He himself is before all things, and in him all things hold together" (Col. 1:17). Hebrews 1:3 says "he sustains all things by his powerful word." Furthermore, there is a kind of cosmic purposiveness to Christ such that all things are for the sake of the Cosmic Christ – "all things have been created through him

---

[3] The feminist discussion of Sophia and God or Christ as feminine is extensive. Good introductions are Cady, Ronan, and Taussig's *Sophia: The Future of Feminist Spirituality* and Mollenkott's *The Divine Feminine*. See also Elisabeth Schuessler Fiorenza's *In Memory of Her*, especially chapter 4, and *Jesus, Miriam's Child, Sophia's Prophet*. For a womanist's perspective see Jacquelyn Grant's *White Women's Christ and Black Women's Jesus*. For a more general treatment focusing on the Hebrew scriptures, see Frymer-Kensky's *In the Wake of the Goddesses*.

and *for* him" (Col. 1:16). The cosmic scope of the purposiveness of creation makes it a mystery, but it includes, pertaining to the human scale,
the reconciliation of people with God; so, Ephesians 1:8b–12:

> With all wisdom and insight he has made known to us the mystery of his will,
> according to his good pleasure that he set forth in Christ, as a plan for the full-
> ness of time, to gather up all things in him, things in heaven and things on earth.
> In Christ we have also obtained an inheritance, having been destined accord-
> ing to the purpose of him who accomplishes all things according to his counsel
> and will, so that we, who were the first to set our hope on Christ, might live for
> the praise of his glory.

This cosmic purposiveness, of all things being gathered up in Christ, is
very different from a kind of historical purpose sometimes attributed to
God. Beth Neville's *From Caves to Cosmos* (plates 1–7, between pp. 158 and
159 below) displays the purposiveness of an Alpha-to-Omega summing
up, but not a historical purposiveness except for the local human adventure.

   A fourth and related system of symbols for the Cosmic Christ has to
do with Christ reigning over the cosmos, not just over Israel as an
expected messiah might, but over the entire cosmos. This is symbolized
in many ways such as the position of the ascended Christ in Heaven
(Eph. 1:20, Col. 3:1 and many other places), the direction of the
Ascension (Acts 1:9–10) and Jesus' leaving the disciples (John 14). The
realized eschatology of John and Colossians emphasizes Christ drawing
all to himself; the historical eschatology of much of Paul and Revelation
emphasizes the Second Coming in judgment. Hebrews 1:8–12 says:

> But of the Son he says, "Your throne, O God, is forever and ever, and the right-
> eous scepter is the scepter of your kingdom. You have loved righteousness and
> hated wickedness; therefore God, your God, has anointed you with the oil of
> gladness beyond your companions." And "In the beginning, Lord, you founded
> the earth, and the heavens are the work of your hands; they will perish, but you
> remain; they will all wear out like clothing; like a cloak you will roll them up,
> and like clothing they will be changed. But you are the same and your years will
> never end."

These are quotations from Psalms 45 and 102 applied to Christ.

   The symbol of the Cosmic Christ as heavenly ruler is juxtaposed with
that of Christ as the Head of the Church (Col. 1:18). As Christ is the
head, the Church is his body. But the Church in this sense itself has a
cosmic dimension: "And he has put all things under his feet and has
made him the head over all things for the church, which is his body, the

fullness of him who fills all in all." The relation of Christ to the Church is in itself a whole set of symbol systems that will be explored in chapter 5. The point here is that at least in some respects in which Christ is Head of the Church that is his body, he is the Cosmic Christ, and hence it is a cosmic Church. For those such as Panikkar who are interested in the symbol of the Cosmic Christ for purposes of interfaith ecumenism, the cosmic Church requires interpretation beyond membership in the Jesus movement!

A final theme of the Cosmic Christ is that of the divine cosmic agent who comes down from Heaven to effect the reconciliation, not only of humanity, but of the entire cosmos, moving from heavenly state to human flesh and back again. The initially quoted passage from Colossians continues (Col. 1:19–22) in this way:

> For in him all the fullness of God was pleased to dwell, and through him God was pleased to reconcile to himself all things, whether on earth or in heaven, by making peace through the blood of the cross. And you who were once estranged and hostile in mind, doing evil deeds, he has now reconciled in his fleshly body through death, so as to present you holy and blameless and irreproachable before him…"

The reference to the blood of the cross of course connects with the atonement symbols discussed in the previous chapter. But it is also larger in scope, reconciling all things in Earth and Heaven. Perhaps the most telling passage on this theme for recent Christian writers is the Kenosis Hymn in Philippians 2: 6–11, speaking of Christ Jesus:

> who, though he was in the form of God, did not regard equality with God as something to be exploited, but emptied himself (kenosis), taking the form of a slave, being born in human likeness. And being found in human form, he humbled himself and became obedient to the point of death – even death on a cross. Therefore God also highly exalted him and gave him the name that is above every name, so that at the name of Jesus every knee should bend, in heaven and on earth and under the earth, and every tongue should confess that Jesus Christ is Lord, to the glory of God the Father.

Though some thinkers like to emphasize the humility of Jesus in this passage, and indeed that is part of its point, the main point is that the agent is the Cosmic Christ, descending from heaven to the form of a slave, suffering an insurrectionist's death, and returning to glory and reign as Lord of Heaven.

Perhaps the most telling passage on this theme comes in Ephesians 4:4–7 where Paul (or someone like Paul if he is not the author) is trying

Figure 8. *Resurrection*, fresco, Church of the Savior in Chora, Istanbul

to harmonize differences within the Church as different gifts – apostles, prophets, evangelists, pastors, teachers (see also 1 Cor. 12) – by saying "there is one body and one Spirit, just as you were called to the one hope of your calling, one Lord, one faith, one baptism, one God and Father of all, who is above all and through all and in all. But each of us was given grace according to the measure of Christ's gift." The image Paul uses to describe this (Eph. 4:8–10) bursts beyond the ligatures of Church politics:

> "When he ascended on high he made captivity itself a captive; he gave gifts to his people." (When it says, "He ascended," what does it mean but that he had also descended into the lower parts of the earth? He who descended is the same one who ascended far above all the heavens, so that he might fill all things.)[4]

Christ here becomes like a shuttle on a loom, weaving back and forth between Heaven and Hell, descending from the heights to the depths of the Earth and back beyond the highest Heavens to bind the world together. This stands behind the ancient Church tradition that between the crucifixion and resurrection Jesus broke down the gates of Hell or Limbo and brought the souls of the righteous to Heaven. Figure 8, a fourteenth-century Byzantine fresco, shows Jesus bestriding the smashed gates of Hell, surrounded by the broken hardware of bondage, with Satan bound beneath the gates, hauling Adam and Eve from their graves so forcefully they fly through the air. Eve looks as if she would rather not. The dynamism of Christ is so great that it torques his gloriole – no place is so far, no corner so dark, no sin so foul that Christ cannot draw it into his unity.

The various systems of symbols that flesh out the great symbol of the Cosmic Christ are not all coherent with one another. Together, however, they set up a powerful resonance that has come down strongly through Christian history. What is the fundamental problem that rings these systems of symbols? Why interpret the short but inspiring life of a rural Galilean rabbi to be the Cosmic Christ? If the atonement symbols ring in response to the human alienation from God in blood-guilt, what rings the symbols of the Cosmic Christ?

---

[4] The first line of this quotation is from Psalm 68:18. The translation in the Anglican Book of Common Prayer is: "Thou art gone up on high, thou has led captivity captive, and received gifts for men, yea, even for thine enemies, that the Lord God might dwell among them." This describes God going up to the Temple in Jerusalem. The New Revised Standard Version, however, significantly alters the meaning: "You ascended the high mount, leading captives in your train and receiving gifts from people, even from those who rebel against the Lord God's abiding there." It is possible that David is the subject of the line, bringing captives and tribute to the Temple. Paul, of course, considered the subject of the line to be Christ.

The answer must lie in the relation of human beings to the cosmos. The imagery of the atonement symbols comes mainly from the Levitical tradition that was concerned with the people of Israel relative to their God and their land. Jesus the Lamb of God in the first instance reconciles individuals in their specific communities to God. The Cosmic Christ, however, confronts people in cosmic perspective, as the Pantokrator in figure 7 organizes the world.

Because of the early admission of Gentiles to the Christian communities, Christianity let slip its identification with Jerusalem fairly easily, with the great cities of the Roman Empire, Rome, Antioch, Alexandria, and Constantinople, becoming as or more important. Persian cosmic apocalypticism had entered Hellenistic Judaism during the Exile (see, for instance, Isa. 24–27) and it was prominent in Christian cosmic apocalypticism (for instance, 2 Peter 3:10). Greek philosophy, present in Philo, also gave Christians a cosmic perspective. Culturally and often physically dislocated, Christians asked what it means to be at home in the cosmos.

In the ancient world that question had at least four dimensions: What is cosmic justice? What goes into making up the individual? What is the meaning of existing in this place and time? And what is the purpose of it all? The distinctions among these follow from the components of the Logos examined in chapter 1: right form, right deference to components formed, right existential location, and right value. Those dimensions remain lively with burning issues for our own time.

The concerns for cosmic justice were perhaps best articulated in ancient Stoic philosophy which, on the one hand, conceived the cosmos to be vast and impersonal and, on the other hand, conceived justice to be related to the abstract rationality of the cosmos and also to be written in the human conscience. Paul recognized this in Romans 1:18–20:

For the wrath of God is revealed from heaven against all ungodliness and wickedness of those who by their wickedness suppress the truth. For what can be known about God is plain to them, because God has shown it to them. Ever since the creation of the world his eternal power and divine nature, invisible though they are, have been understood and seen through the things he has made. So they are without excuse.

See also Romans 2: 14–16. Although first-generation Christians such as Paul struggled mightily to reconcile universal justice with the observance of Torah, Christianity quickly developed an ethic it thought of as universal, that is, one which applies to all people Christian or not and to which Christians are obligated in addition out of deference to God, the source of the principles of justice.

In our own time, however, we have become conscious of how ethics that seem universal can still be parochial. Kantian ethics, that Western ethical theory which most clearly and intensely grounds itself in universality, is viewed by Confucians as advocating inhumane equality and by feminists as slightly absurd masculine aggressive objectification. Moreover, the mistaken belief that some parochial sense of justice is in fact universal has reinforced colonialism and rendered the moral perspectives of others impotent. The Western conception of a just society is simply not universally persuasive; but neither is any other. So contemporary Christians (and Buddhists, Confucians, Saivites, and so forth) look for new and persuasive principles of universal justice. Without them in a world society, we are not morally at home.

In addition, there are pressing practical problems of justice that demand religious response. Christianity has long had carefully honed conceptions of distributive justice. But they never applied beyond a national or, at largest, imperial locale. Now, however, through the social sciences we have developed some decent conceptions of how the world economy works, how practices in one country affect life in another, how money supply shifts economies globally. In particular, we have learned how some people live in oppressive conditions because of the causal connections between their situation and the situations of other, more favored, people. The global causal structure of distributive injustice cannot easily be correlated to retributive justice: rarely is it the deliberate willed fault of rich countries that other countries are poor. The structures of wealth are at fault nonetheless because they also cause the structures of poverty. Contemporary questions of distributive justice have to do with determining what changes should be made to effect a globally just distribution of the world's wealth, and all answers seem problematic.

The contemporary questions of justice are not merely instrumental ones of achieving equality. They are fundamental questions of what it means to be at home in the universe, to own things, to have responsibilities to others, some of whom are close and others remote but still connected by economic and other causes. What obligations does the luck of birth have? What rights are there of inheritance? Does it make sense at all to identify oneself with a place to which one has a right, since nearly all places have been the historic homes of other people at one time or another (poor Jerusalem!). Has anyone's ancestral line failed to be oppressors at some times and oppressed at others? Has anyone only one historical ancestral line? These questions go to defining what it is to be human in a larger environment with other people. What does it mean to be in Christ so that God is all in all (1 Cor. 15:28), with everyone reconciled? Paul, in Philemon, thought that condition perfectly compatible with slavery. All the issues of justice have to do with how to order the many components of human life as means and ends.

The second dimension for the problem of homelessness is what goes into making up the human. Just what are our crucial components? This question will be asked in cosmological ways here, in biographical ways in chapter 5, and in psychological ways in chapter 6. The ancient world supposed one component was to have a home at the center of the cosmos. Since the rise of early-modern science, however, we have known that our cosmos is far vaster and older than anyone imagined in the ancient world and that it has no natural "center," now a problematic component.

In the ancient world many people conceived their bodies to be like those of animals but their souls, their centers of consciousness and subjectivity, to be immaterial. Not everyone agreed with this, of course, for instance the Chinese. But that view had wide currency in South and West Asia. Now most late moderns have come to think of their personal subjectivity as an extension of their biological make-up. How can we relate to our bodies and also to our souls?

In the ancient Christian world there was considerable deference to various things making up the human environment, even when that environment was humanly organized for the sake of social or religious prosperity. Jesus could cite the animals as objects of God's care. The components of life were seen to be all equally creatures of God. At the same time, Christian thinking was hierarchical in its assumption that all creation adds up to the creation and salvation of human beings. That assumption is harmless where people cannot do anything about subordinating nature to human interests. But as humans develop technologies to enforce their hierarchical dominance, the sense of deference to the components of nature is lost. In our time the sudden appearance of catastrophic ecological devolution has shaken apart older conceptions of how to relate to nature and the other components organized within human life.

The third dimension to the question of home is the meaning of being in this place and time. There is an absurdity to being thrown into this situation, especially if it is not related to a beginning or end, or center.

What can the meaning of life be? Paul Tillich took this to be the central question of twentieth-century Christianity.[5] The question of salvation in the ancient world, he noted, centered around life and death, and the classical symbolism of resurrection, immortality, and eternal life was taken to address this question. By the late middle ages and the time of the Reformation, he said, the question had shifted to moral justification or condemnation which, practically, meant going to Heaven or Hell. Luther's preoccupation with justification by faith reflects this shifting of the question. By late-modern times, said Tillich, the question had turned to whether life has any meaning at all. The question of faith for Tillich and his generation of existential theologians, including even Barth, was whether we have the grace or courage to embrace our historical situation with authenticity. Or do we live in denial, bad faith? If life is not meaningful, we are homeless in yet another sense.

The fourth dimension of the question of homelessness is whether its relation to the ultimate defines human life in any significant way, or whether instead it takes all its definition from the connections of nature, society, and culture. In the latter case human life quickly becomes defined by consumerism. What Paul could complain about as being "conformed to this world" can now be achieved with a credit card. No one, not even Paul, denies that we have to live in this world. In fact, the third dimension of the question of homelessness is whether we can embrace the specifics of the world we have. But is there also an ultimate dimension to life? Is there anything ultimate at all? Perhaps in the long run this is to ask whether there is any home at all.

In ancient Christianity the questions of cosmic justice, proper deference to the components of creation, faith to engage the day, and hope for an ultimate place in things were summed up, organized, and addressed in the symbols of the Cosmic Christ. Those questions are as burning today as in the ancient world. Yet can the symbols of the Cosmic Christ be plausible or potent now? Can we justify a contemporary conception of the Logos that might undergird a contemporary engagement of those questions with the symbols of the Cosmic Christ?

LOGOS

Recall the discussion of the Logos in chapter 1. There it was argued that every created thing has four features: a form, components formed, an existential location, and a value resulting from getting these components harmonized with this form in this place and time. These four are transcendentals in the sense that they are to be found in every determinate thing. Determinateness itself requires them. They always go together and thus form a unity or harmony of conditions for determinate being. They are plural and cannot be defined exclusively in terms of one another. Each has a metaphysical problematic of its own, that is, the nature of form, the nature of being related and contained, the nature of space-time and eternity, and the nature of value. The accounts given here of the transcendentals comes from a contemporary metaphysics.[6] They of course have antecedents.[7] There also have been other lists of transcendentals, for instance the medieval Unity, Truth, Goodness, and Beauty, which might not be too different from those defended here.

The point to stress here about the transcendentals is that they go together and form a harmony themselves. I suggested in chapter 1 that this harmony is love, but in a metaphoric sense somewhat distant from ordinary notions of human love. The classic discussion of love as creativity was in Plato's *Symposium*, where *eros* is described as having many levels, each of which in its exercise excites and brings into existence the next higher. Eros in the physical sense is lust aroused by sensual beauty. The exercise of lust gives rise to care and desire for the best for the beloved. That in turn gives rise to the desire to create a home with progeny,[8] which gives rise to the desire to create a community and finally a civilization in which one's highest aspirations can be embodied and made immortal beyond one's lifetime. Plato himself did not apply that dialectic of eros to ontological creation, though he did say that the ontological Creator is the Form of the Good which gives rise to good things and to the human capacities to know and appreciate them.[9] Early Christian theologians did apply that Platonic idea to interpret the claim that God is love.

---

[6] I have elaborated theories of form, of being contained of existential location, and of value, in *Recovery of the Measure*, chapters 5–12.

[7] This list of four transcendentals is a development of Plato's list in the *Philebus*: the limit, the unlimited, the mixture, and the cause of mixture.

[8] Or at least to cultivate students in the case of Socrates' gay companions at the symposium. See Diotema's speech in the *Symposium*, 201d ff.

[9] See Plato's "Analogy of the Sun" for explaining the Good in *Republic* 507–09. "In like manner, then, you are to say that the objects of knowledge not only receive from the presence of the good their being known, but their very existence and essence is derived to them from it, though the good itself is not essence but still transcends essence in dignity and surpassing power" (509b, Shorey translation, Loeb Classics).

That the Logos is the first image or character of God the Creator was already remarked in chapter 1. What kind of creator is God? One whose creation is of determinate things with at least the transcendental characteristics described and whose creation therefore is an act of love in the ontological sense defined. With this we can interpret the claim that Christ is the visible image of the invisible God: God apart from creating has no features or determinateness at all, and hence is invisible, though in creating has the determinate structure of ontological love in the Logos. What is needed to make full sense of this claim is a way of identifying the Logos with Jesus Christ. The Cosmic Christ is not merely the abstract Logos, but a symbolic expansion of Jesus of Nazareth to cosmic proportions.

The connection, of course, is in the notion of the incarnation. How is the Logos incarnate in Jesus, as John claimed in the Prologue to his gospel? In a transcendental sense, everything expresses the Logos, that in and by which every thing that is made is made. But in a special sense Jesus expresses or embodies the Logos. What is that sense?

To answer this question it is necessary to recall from chapter 1 the significance of the Logos on the human level. Human beings have some control over what they do and who they become. Therefore human beings always have the question of what form to strive for, what things to include in their lives, how to engage their existential context, and in the long run what value to achieve. We have seen in the previous section that these four questions define whether and how human beings relate to the universe as their home. We late moderns are shocked into a confusing homelessness because we suddenly must deal with global distributive justice to achieve right form, with the problematical environment to have proper deference to the components of our existence, with the question of the meaningfulness of human existence itself, and with whether there is anything ultimate in relation to which we can conceive our worth.

Christianity from the beginning has said that these are not only problematic elements, but problems beyond ordinary human solving. Not only is there blood-guilt as discussed in chapter 2, but people's rebound from blood-guilt is to alienate themselves from God by turning the good parts of life into sin for which they are responsible. Paul's pre-eminent metaphor for this is sex which, when pursued out of harmony with a life lived before God, becomes a lust that binds the soul (for instance, Rom. 7, and elsewhere where "flesh," whose metaphoric root is sex, itself becomes a metaphor for all the sins of unloving selfishness). Similarly, a right pursuit of wealth can turn to greed. Enjoyment of the good things of life turns to gluttony, and so on. Once we turn to these things for fulfillment, rather than to God, we are in bondage to them. This is another dimension of meaning to Paul's admission (Rom. 7:14–25) that the good he would do, he did not and the evil he would avoid, that he did. Not only was the snake of primitive passions bursting through his deliberate will, but he was committed to his sins. The classic analysis of this bondage is in Augustine's *Confessions*, whose conversion (in book 8, chapter 29) turns on reading Romans 13:14: "Instead, put on the Lord Jesus Christ, and make no provision for the flesh, to gratify its desires."

So the human condition, on the Christian analysis, is to be *unable* to be just or attain the right form, to be *unable* to be properly pious or deferential to the components of life, to be *unable* to engage our existential situation, and to be *unable* to relate to the Ultimate in terms of which we have some absolute value. The human condition is alienated from the Logos, existing by it and normed by it, but wrongly, and impotent to do anything about that.

Salvation from this condition would be whatever overcomes the alienation in some appropriate sense of overcoming. The Christian claim is that Jesus is the incarnation of the Logos in a sense that did overcome this alienation and did so in ways that make it possible for others to do so too. The Light that has been overcome by darkness in ordinary people was not overcome in Jesus, so said John in his Prologue. Is there something in the person of Jesus that repairs or completes the work of creation in the human sphere so that human beings need not be in bondage to sin and alienated from their Creator, but reconciled to God and God's creation? To answer this question we will have to look more deeply, not only at Jesus, but at the problem of sin.

One of the contributions of twentieth-century existential philosophy and theology was to show that a dimension of the human predicament lies simply in being finite creatures. As finite creatures, it is impossible to be fully just, fully deferential, fully engaged, and fully present before God as worth something, which is to say that there is no perfect global distributive justice, no way to defer properly to all the components of life, no way to engage our situation fully, and no way to present ourselves fully before the ultimate. On the one hand we lie under the obligations of justice, pious deference, the need to engage our situation, and the religious quest to present ourselves in ultimate perspective before God. On the other hand there is no way we can do any of this perfectly. Whereas in the previous section I said these areas of human habitation are problematic, I now say they are impossible to fulfill perfectly. And the common human response to this inevitable failure is alienation. How is this so?

Consider justice. In the most comprehensive sense, to be just is to influence for the better all the dimensions of order in which we live. For many others and myself the most important orders are my family and my job. The latter in my case has three distinguishable orders: academic administration, teaching, and scholarship, which in turn has three parts: study, thinking, and writing. Hardly less important are the public roles associated with my job, work in the church, and community obligations. Then there are the great issues of our time to which I might make some small difference: poverty, racism, ecological concerns, and (albeit remotely) the world economic order insofar as I have some control over the investment of retirement funds.

Every reader can write a personalized version of the previous paragraph and this one. I cannot do the best that I possibly can for the good ordering of my family because I have to go to work. At work as dean of a theological school I can never do enough for the faculty or the university, and never raise enough money, because I have to spend too much time teaching. The students assure me that they do not get enough attention and that my classes are not student-friendly enough because I feel pressed to do the scholarship that justifies the teaching. But as a scholar I never have read enough of the right books, have never thought through the ideas to sufficient clarity, and have never rewritten enough times to present the ideas with proper respect for readers, as is self-evident here. As a churchman I serve on various committees, but never with enough preparation and follow-through to do what I really could to help. Because of the travel associated with that, I support my local church with monthly deposits from electronic banking and attend when I can. I simply excuse myself, that is, fail utterly, in the matter of supporting my community, hoping that my wife's good works there will be enough. I've been favored to associate with people who have made significant differences to the large social issues, but I am not one of them; the best I do is stay informed to vote intelligently, and even there some of the issues are so complex that my votes might do more harm than good so far as I really know. So I am a failure in every sphere of life to which I might have made a contribution to justice had I given it my full devotion. For me to be just everywhere is intrinsically impossible, and because I participate necessarily in all those orders of life, and would have just as many different orders were I to change my life, I am unjust in all of them.

Kantians would say that, where it is not possible to do a thing, there is no obligation to do it: ought implies can. Therefore no obligation obtains to be just in all of the orders of my life, they would say, only in some single order that does not compete with others. The world is filled with Kantians, according to academic reports. But there certainly are none in my family, or on my faculty or in the university administration, or among my students, or among reviewers. No church bureaucrats are Kantians, surely not the pastor of my church, and there are none among the people who come to the house wanting support for this or that good cause. Each points out that I could have done more for them and have simply failed. Could I have focused on one order of life, say family, and deliberately neglected the others? Of course I could have made that choice but would still be guilty of neglecting the others where in each it would have been possible to do much better.

In practice I do what everyone else does. I establish a shifting pattern of my life in which I compromise every set of demands and try to serve them all a bit in turn. Though a moral failure in each, I try to do some good in all, and on good days think this works. But then it appears that in nearly all these orders of life sometimes I do things that make the situation worse rather than better, and I would not have done those things if I had given them sufficient attention and energy.

With regard to the pattern or order of my own life, therefore, I simply have to give up on the hope for integrity and settle for the task of harmonizing things as best as possible, shifting the patterns in opportunistic ways, trying not to let everyone get unhappy at once, cutting losses, and hoping to do more good than harm in the long run.

Although this is not the place to attempt any precise definition of justice, it vaguely means an ordering of things so that all things flourish. But ordering means that things are ordered as means to ends. No matter what the scheme of justice, some people are circumscribed in their flourishing by having to serve in some respects as means to the flourishing of others. Is it just to have to work to supply others, go to war to defend others, suffer to care for others? Society is a net of dependency relations in which the dependent are the ends for which the providers are means. Ideally we compromise as best we can so that dependency is reciprocal, or passed from one generation to the next, or compensated for in some other way. But there is no possible pattern for the whole of society that optimizes everyone and every group; the best is a compromise. And should we attempt to include the environment within the bounds of the ends that justice should serve, how much more complicated! Nature is organized on principles of consumption and metabolism: lambs are food for lions and it is "unjust" for one or the other no matter what happens.

Nature without the human sphere is a variety of processes with hierarchical organization such that the higher feed off the lower. Higher orders regiment and use the lower orders insofar as they are able. Add the human sphere and the organic and social hierarchies are all the more obvious, as we saw in the previous chapter. Acknowledging this, can we still not have proper deference and piety toward the components of life that we suborn to our purposes and needs? It is said that the Native Americans reverenced the buffalo before killing it, and used every part they could in recognition that the animal had paid a price for their lives. If so, that was true courtesy but I doubt it made a difference in the buffalo's perspective. Can we behave deferentially to those we need as components of our order? Does it help to preserve a few samples of the smallpox or HIV viruses before we attempt to stamp out the rest? Does it help to sympathize with the raging blood hatreds between the Hutus and Tutsis, or the Catholics and Protestants in Northern Ireland, and let them go on killing for generations? That would be deference to love of tribe and faction, but it would be unjust. Shall we therefore work toward the justice of imposing civil peace through force? That would be undeferential toward the components of civilization.

Perhaps a truly deferential way of life would be to scale back the human population itself to a limit that could support itself in complete harmony with the natural environment, with no tilled fields to be defended and no need to kill off predators. Hunter-gatherer societies live close to the earth, doing little damage except for immediate need and being regulated in population by the limits of food, disease, and steady ritualized tribal warfare.[10] But then we would be unjust to our families not to provide better, to let our children starve when we could garden for them, to let people die of diseases that could easily be treated with modern medicine, to let our friends die needlessly in the tribal warfare characteristic of such primitive social organization. In point of fact, to be as deferential as human beings might be to the conditions of existence would be to give up all the higher orders that constitute justice, all the way up to civilization itself. The best we can do is to attempt to compromise justice and deference.

Now it is becoming apparent why the impossibility of complete justice

---

[10] Daniel Quinn advocates this scenario in his popular *Ishmael: An Adventure of the Mind and Spirit.*

and the impossibility of complete deference are matters of how to be at home in the world. If we were to work by analogy with common ways of thinking about a human home, we might look for ways we all could fit in, doing the jobs defined by the domestic roles. But if the analysis in the previous chapter was on the mark, then even those roles are constrictive of the lives of the people who play them, and their individual interests pay a price. If being at home in the cosmos is defined as having obliged positions that it is possible to fulfill, then we are not at home. The cosmos is filled with normative obligations; everywhere we can affect things for better or worse. And yet it is not possible to fulfill them perfectly, nor even particularly well. We are unjust by necessity. And we are impious, undeferential, by necessity. No matter how we live, we compromise both justice and deference.

Paul Tillich described this situation as follows.[11] Human beings have an essential nature, by which he meant the ideals or obligations that define what we ought to be. But under the conditions of finite existence it is not possible to realize our essential nature. His word for the character of finite existence relative to essential human nature was fragmentation. We live fragmentary lives at best, being a little just here but unjust there, a little deferential where it doesn't cost much and wholly undeferential when our lives depend on it.

The ideal of fragmentation brings out a special problem not yet mentioned with the ideals of integrity, of ordering one's own life justly. Ordinarily we do not conceive the order of our lives mainly as a pattern of daily existence, though that is part of it. Rather, we think of our lives as stories. We employ a narrative form to think about how we respond to our changing environments and the events of our lives, and these responses are hopefully turned into a meaningful story, a "life." But most personal narratives are fictions and self-deceptions, are they not? We start projects but someone else has to finish them. We develop relationships but most get cut off or sidetracked by events. Only a very lucky person has a dramatic story with a good beginning, middle, and end. And even then, the single-line "life" narrative is a distortion. At every event in a person's life, others are involved with their stories. Any event is infinitely dense with the trajectories of its various natural, social, and personal participants, and to abstract out the role that event plays in the life of an individual is grossly to distort it. For it leaves out the implications of that individual for all the others. The story of the Exodus, God's

---

[11] See the analysis in his *Systematic Theology*, volume II.

electing Israel to be saved, favored, and given a promised land, is not how the Egyptians and Canaanites would think about what happened. How has Israel distorted what happened to get a story out of it? The Egyptians, good record-keepers, did not record even the death of all the firstborn of their children, flocks, and herds. The narrative form is a very great abstraction that invites lying and self-deception. At best, a "life" is a chronicle, not a story, but a record of where we lived, what we did, and how we end. The units of narrative meaning are fragmentary.

What do we do with this fragmentariness, this necessary failure to fulfill the obligations of justice and deference and have singular stories that add up to heroic lives? This is the existential question of how to engage our time and place. Tillich and other existential theologians said that we ordinarily live in alienation or estrangement. That is, we reject the ground that gives us lives obligated by norms that we cannot fulfill. And in rejecting that ground, we also reject ourselves as normed creatures. Thus we live in many forms of denial. Sometimes we deny that we are under genuine obligation. Other times we deny our roles as actors, never investing ourselves in the affairs of our time and place. We live in what the existentialists called "bad faith," refusing to engage the realities of our existential situation. Obsession with material things, with blending in to the herd of mass culture, is a form of denial. Obsession with existential analysis, with detailing how and why we deny our engagement, is also a form of denial. The narcissism of the wild swings from grandiosity to affectless boredom so characteristic of many groups in society is a form of denial.[12] All these denials constitute alienation.

The existential theologians rightly saw that the true problem of human will is not what we choose among options but whether we engage.[13] Shall we engage life fully, knowing that we shall be normative failures, or shall we deny life and choose alienation? That choice is not between two competing options on the same level. It is more like having the courage to choose life or the weakness that slips to alienation.

Whether to engage is not a single commitment, but something that has to be faced in nearly all life's choices, and every day. Who has not experienced emotional withdrawal in family life, or sleepwalking through the job? With regard to the norms for engaging life, the specific choices, say affecting justice, are not as important as the lifelong existential choice to engage the struggle for justice and stay engaged. The

---

[12] See Lawrence E. Cahoone's *The Dilemma of Modernity* for an analysis of cultural narcissism.
[13] Tillich's discussion is the best, in *The Courage to Be*. See also Rudolf Bultmann's "The Historicity of Man and Faith" in his *Existence and Faith*.

existential theologians were one-sided. They took the issues of justice
for granted and produced little of a social ethics. They overlooked the
issues of the environment, or of piety relating to nature and the components of society, and assumed that morality and art are the highest
human achievements. But they were right about the importance of
engagement.

Now we grasp the question of home. Can we engage the cosmos as
our home, or shall we fall into alienation? Tillich and Bultmann said that
to engage our situation we need faith. The alienated do not have faith.
Faith, Tillich said, is the acceptance of our selves as ultimately and
unconditionally accepted. But how do we know that we are ultimately
and unconditionally accepted? His answer was that Jesus appeared in
history as one who was perfectly reconciled to the life of obligation in
which we necessarily fail because Jesus was confident of the loving mercy
of God. Jesus' God was the righteous king, yes, otherwise justice would
not be an issue. But Jesus' God also forgives the sins of those who
embrace him. Because it was possible for Jesus to live without alienation,
and we have his picture, we too as disciples can live without alienation.[14]

The truth of this Tillichian argument will be discussed in the next
section. But the argument itself leaves a great hole that must be mentioned here. Who loves us with justice and mercy? Jesus could take for
granted the God of his culture and the themes of justice and mercy were
ancient in the religion he knew. In our more skeptical age we ask whether
anything is ultimate. If so, can it bear the personifications of an accepting lover? The Christian existential proclamation that human beings are
unconditionally accepted requires conviction about that which unconditionally accepts, which leads to the fourth kind of obligation.

The fourth kind of obligation, beyond those of justice, deference, and
engagement, is to find the ultimate before which we have meaning and
value. This is the religious quest and different religious cultures shape it
different ways. Tillich expressed the point in terms of ultimate
concern.[15] He claimed that everyone has an ultimate concern, a concern
that remains even when all proximate concerns are given up. Much of
the religious task is to identify and eliminate false contenders for the
legitimate object of ultimate concern, the idols and demons. Tillich's
own answer was that the Ground of Being, his secular language for God
the Creator, is the legitimate object of ultimate concern and that,

[14] Tillich argues this in his *Systematic Theology*, volume II, as well as many sermons.
[15] Ultimate concern is a pervasive theme of ibid., volume I, but especially at pp. 211ff, where he
relates it to God as the ultimate.

because of the historical fact of Jesus and the availability of his model, our understanding of that object is that it accepts us unconditionally. The power of the Spirit, in Tillich's analysis, gives us the faith to accept that unconditional acceptance even when we reject ourselves.

Tillich surely was wrong, however, to think that everyone has an ultimate concern. Is not ultimate concern the first thing to go when we acquiesce into alienation? We think we are engaged when we throw ourselves into proximate concerns, for family, justice, saving the environment. As alienation deepens, the proximate concerns soften into desires, and even inconstant desires at that. The people who live "lives of quiet desperation" have no ultimate concern. Ultimate concern means hope, and the alienated have no hope.

So the situation is that we have obligations to seek the ultimate, to have an ultimate concern, but no guarantee that we have that concern. In fact, many people in our culture just want to get through life, to be not concerned for anything ultimately. Many cannot even imagine the ultimate. Even many who profess belief in God have such domesticated notions of God as the Fellow-sufferer, the nice Provider who will answer prayers, that there is nothing ultimate in their belief. Tame religion prevents ultimate concern more satanically than atheistic secularism.

COMING HOME

So here is the situation. The question is not mainly to find intelligible symbol systems of the Cosmic Christ. These systems are intelligible enough. They do not fit together into a single larger univocal system, but they do overlie and reinforce one another. The symbol systems explored in section 1 above are the Cosmic Christ as: (1) the first visible image of the invisible God, (2) the one in and by whom all things are created, (3) the Alpha and Omega who integrates the plurality of created things, (4) the King of the Universe, and (5) the heavenly agent who comes to the human sphere and reconciles it with God.

Rather, the main question is whether the symbols of the Cosmic Christ can serve truthfully to engage people with God in respect of the issues of homelessness, analyzed as alienation. Our theory of religious symbols provides a structural clue. We need to ask about the primary referent of these symbols – God in Christ as Ultimate – and also about the secondary referents – the kind of people who can relate to the primary referent through these symbols, that is, find them meaningful. We also need to ask whether the interpretation of the primary referent by means of these symbols is true in our contexts of life. These are intertwined questions and cannot be answered singly. The following attempts to pursue their complications.

Consider the last issue treated in the previous section, whether there are grounds for an ultimate concern. I observed that, contrary to Tillich's contention, people with genuine ultimate concern are rare and that existential alienation undermines such concern. What can the symbols of the Cosmic Christ do to address this failure of ultimate concern?

For the secondary referents who can use them, that is, the people for whom they are meaningful, the first three symbol systems listed above can present the Ultimate as having overwhelming beauty, glory, awesomeness, holiness, and loveliness, so as to elicit concern or desire for the ultimate. Because they are so overwhelming, that concern can take on an ultimate commitment. This is Plato's point, that the attractiveness of the object arouses desire for it, which is capable of desiring a more worthy object which elicits even greater desires. The Ultimate, apprehended in overwhelming beauty, glory, awesomeness, holiness, and loveliness, elicits and creates in certain people (the ready secondary referents) an appropriately overwhelming concern and desire for the Ultimate. "Beauty, glory, awesomeness, holiness, and loveliness" are not intended here in ways that technically distinguish them, only as a group of metaphors that get at the overwhelmingly attractive.

What do concern and desire for the Ultimate mean? Many symbol systems, not only in Christianity, have been elaborated to express this. Kenneth Kirk (1931) has written an extraordinary study of the symbol of the desire for a Vision of God.[16] Mystics such as Eckhart and Boehme have developed the notion of return to and absorption into God.[17] For the less spiritually athletic more common symbols have to do with Heaven as a place to meet God, to journey toward, to enter the divine throne-room, to join in the eschatological banquet.[18] I have used the symbol of "presenting oneself before the Ultimate" as the object of this ultimate concern.

That a person is aroused with an ultimate desire for God means that the person is bent to a spiritual question, to be ultimately serious about religion. But it does not mean that the desire for God can be fulfilled.

[16] See Kirk's encyclopedic *The Vision of God.*
[17] See Bernard McGinn's magisterial series on mysticism, *The Presence of God.* See also Berdyaev's *The Beginning and the End.*
[18] See McDannell and Lang's *Heaven: A History.*

The issues of blood-guilt explored in the previous chapter center around the Levitical claim that unholy people cannot enter into the presence of the holiness of God. Similarly with the injustice, impiety, and profound existential alienation analyzed here. All of these prevent the fulfillment of the ultimate desire for the Ultimate. Augustine's analysis of his own case on the brink of his conversion is a classical statement of the ultimate pitch of desire for God frustrated by an irreconcilable alienation.[19]

How do the symbols of the visible image of the invisible God, of that in and by which all things are created, and the Alpha and Omega, present the Ultimate as overwhelmingly, that is, ultimately, desirable, to be desired beyond all things? Consider first the last of those three.

The Cosmic Christ presents the Ultimate as the ground and goal of the cosmos, including the human sphere, and somehow as containing all things within the divine life. This symbol system is powerful for what it does not say as well as for what it says. The Cosmic Christ as ground, as Alpha, is not about some specific creation, say of the people by the water hole and in the garden (Gen. 2), or even of the evolution of the cosmos from an initial burst of energy against darkness (Gen. 1). Alpha is just radical beginning, whatever we might hypothesize that to be in our small ways. Beth Neville (plate 1, between pp. 158 and 159 below) symbolizes the Alpha as the interior of a dream-cave. Similarly the Cosmic Christ as Omega is simply radical ending and consummation, which she symbolizes (plate 7) with the straight-line order and increasing darkness of cosmic expansion to irrelevance. The Book of Revelation has been read variously as a specific depiction of what that consummation will consist in, but the book itself deconstructs those readings. It can be about the violent triumph of righteousness over evil and the destruction of all opposition to God. But the violence is beyond whatever might justify it, and the symbols are ironic and two-faced – the Blood of the Lamb becomes the warrior Lamb with seven horns and eyes (Rev. 5:6) and then a mounted warrior from whose mouth comes a sharp sword (Rev. 19:11–16). The consummation is inconceivable, and all we know is that the religious quest shall be over: there is no temple in the New Jerusalem (Rev. 21:22). Between the Alpha and the Omega the Cosmic Christ contains all things within the divine life. There may be no visible meaning or connection that we can make out. But somehow all things are contained within that great arc from Alpha to Omega. At one level, this is

[19] See Augustine's Confessions, book 8. For a brilliant analysis of Augustine on this, see Carl G. Vaught's "Theft and Conversion."

attractive because it promises some kind of context and meaning for human life, or for the cosmos, that is invisible to human thinking. But at the human level, the arc from Alpha to Omega has no specific content; see Beth Neville's plates 2 and 3 in which the rainbow arc goes from what we think is our own home to the cosmic place from which "home" is objectified as an Other. At another level this symbol makes the Ultimate attractive as being that in which the entire cosmos and the human sphere have their home. However absurd and fragmentary our lives might be, however entropic the universe might be, fading out to a final dissolution where nothing is related in any way to anything else and hence completely indeterminate, nothing: that still lies within the Alpha and Omega.

Closely related is the system of symbols of the Cosmic Christ as that in and by which all things are created, most clearly schematizing creation. However far the arc from Alpha to Omega stretches beyond the imagination of beginnings and endings, beyond time and space, beyond the indefinitely large and indefinitely small, each part exists because of the creativity in the Cosmic Christ. The analysis I have given is that everything has transcendental form, components formed, existential location, and ultimate value; this only shows the conception of the creative Logos "in and by which" things are created to be possible. Another analysis might be more plausible. Whatever the analysis, the symbol of the Cosmic Christ as that in and by which things are created presents the Ultimate as immanent in and intimate to every thing, to every starburst and to every human being, to every sinner, to every sin. Nothing exists save by the creative presence of the Cosmic Christ and nothing hides behind the gates of Hell (figure 8, p. 100 above).

The resonance of these two symbol systems, the utterly transcendent arc from Alpha to Omega and the intimate presence of the Cosmic Christ in each creature, is extraordinary. Together they present the Ultimate as our infinite home and as more at home in us than we are in ourselves. What could be more fascinating, lovely, awe-inspiring, or desirable to attend to properly?

The symbol system of the Cosmic Christ as the prime visible image of the invisible God conveys the heart of glory and holiness, that is, the juxtaposition and oscillation of the knowable and unknowable God. If God were wholly unknowable, that is, wholly indeterminate, nothing, there would be no point. Yet if God were something knowable, some very large but determinate and therefore finite Being or Principle, God might be admirable and respected but not worshipped as ultimately beautiful, glorious, awesome, holy, and lovely. In fact, looking at the world we see around us, a God who is just maker of this is of dubious character, siding with Israel sometimes, Canaan or Egypt at other times, despite what Israel likes to say.

But the symbol of the Cosmic Christ as visible image of the invisible Creator denies both sides, that God is wholly unknowable and that God is plainly knowable. It also unites both sides in saying that in the Cosmic Christ God is knowable both as the Logos of creation and as the arc from Alpha to Omega, and yet this is but the visible image of the invisible God who is not this. The invisible is constructed in the visible, as all kataphatic theology says. And the visible is deconstructed in the invisible, as all apophatic theology says. The theory of creation *ex nihilo* in chapter 1 models just why this is so, and the symbol of the Cosmic Christ, with these three systems of symbols, presents a vivid engagement of the Ultimate as the ultimately beautiful, arousing, object of ultimate concern.

For what people might these symbols be meaningful? This is to ask, what are the secondary referents for these symbols of the Cosmic Christ? In the first place, they must be people for whom some version of the metaphysics of creation *ex nihilo* is amenable. They do not have to be metaphysicians, of course, but they do have to accept the sense of the underlying logic, namely, the bringing of determinate being into existence, moving from the indeterminate to the determinate. This is what is symbolized in the Cosmic Christ being the visible image of the invisible Creator, and it lies behind the symbols of the Cosmic Christ as Logos in each thing and as the encompassing Alpha and Omega. For these symbols to be meaningful, people need to have a large sense of the cosmos in order to see beyond interpretations of boundaries and presence that are too limited and determinate. A late-modern scientific imagination is helpful here, and nothing in these symbols in respect of the metaphysics of creation needs to be "broken" for that imagination.

What is more limiting with regard to the people for whom these symbols might be meaningful is the connection of the Cosmic Christ with Jesus. However exalted the symbols of the Cosmic Christ, the symbols still relate to Jesus. Perhaps in comparative perspective it is possible to liken the Cosmic Christ to the Dao, or to Isvara the visible image of Brahman. But for the purposes of engaging the ultimate with the symbols of the Cosmic Christ, the imagery of Jesus, and beyond Jesus of the religion of Israel, must be acceptable. There must be some willingness to take on those specific symbols that personify the Ultimate as imaged in Christ. Note that it is Christ the image that is personified, not the invisible God. But the invisible God must be accepted as imaged in the personifying symbols of the Cosmic Christ. We shall return to this shortly in dealing with the symbol systems of the Cosmic King and Agent of Reconciliation.

First, however, we can make a preliminary assay of the truth of the first three symbols insofar as they are interpreted by the appropriate people to engage the Ultimate. Suppose that, by both the iconic and indexical dimensions of reference, living with the symbols of the Cosmic Christ as visible image of the invisible God, as Logos, and as Alpha to Omega, arouses an ultimate passion and desire for the Ultimate: is this right and true? Is there something so worthy in the Ultimate that an appropriate response would be to desire it ultimately? Or is it the case that the Ultimate as creator *ex nihilo* is a mere matter of fact, a cosmic accident of creation that might be either noted or ignored?

How can this question of truth be answered? The most real and important answer lies in living long with the symbols as one's life is engaged in its totality, connecting these symbols to others, and finding them either reinforced or undermined in the pivotal experiences of living. A briefer answer to the question, however, can be given from the standpoint of a metaphysics of value compatible with late-modern thinking. Of course people do not have to accept the metaphysics of value to engage the Ultimate as worthy of ultimate desire. But in asking whether their elicited passion for God is true in respect of a worthy object, the intelligibility of the metaphysics of value shows that their ultimate passion might be true. And if the metaphysics of value is itself true, at least as far as it goes, then their passion is also true that far.

The metaphysics of value I presented in chapter 1 hypothesizes that value consists in characterizing harmonies that have both complexity and simplicity, and that the more both are optimized, the greater the value.[20] Complexity is the difference among the kinds of components in the harmony and simplicity refers to the unity in the form by which the complex things are harmonized. Pure complexity would consist in everything being different from and unrelated to everything else; pure simplicity would be homogeneity. Every harmony has a mixture of complexity and simplicity, and hence some value. The greater values are those in which sharply contrasting things are harmonized, each of which has a great density of complexity and simplicity different from the

---

[20] See the discussion in my *The Cosmology of Freedom*, chapter 3, and *Recovery of the Measure*, chapter 7.

other and yet harmonized with it. The contrasts involved in human beings, where individuated persons live in social relations and consciousness distinguishes subjects from objects, are of high development and value.

But the greatest contrast is between the visible and the invisible so that the highest value lies in the act of creation *ex nihilo* itself. Without the visible, that is, without the creation, the invisible would be nothing, and worthless. Without the invisible, the visible would not exist. The contrast of the two is the greatest of all value and the ground of all other values. Similarly, with reference to the created world the contrast between the Logos intimate in each thing and the arc from Alpha to Omega constitutes the harmony of inner density and outer embracing infinitude. *The contrast between those two contrasts contains all the value that might be.*

Therefore, insofar as the symbols of the Cosmic Christ as visible image of the invisible Creator, as Logos in and by which created things are made, and as the Alpha and Omega engage the Ultimate so as to articulate these contrasts, they reveal a beauty, glory, awesomeness, holiness, and loveliness that are truly engaged and interpreted by an ultimate concern of worship and desire.

The argument should recall that these symbols represent the Ultimate, not in all respects, but primarily in respect of how the creation is home for us. What these symbols say is that the cosmos is our home in the sense that we have something of ultimate beauty, glory, awesomeness, holiness, and loveliness to love, desire, and worship with all our heart, mind, soul, and strength.

Given this ultimate passion, however, can we fulfill it? For this we need to turn to the two other symbol systems of the Cosmic Christ, that of King of the Universe and that of Agent of Reconciliation.

The symbol of Christ the King needs to be understood in light of a kind of unsteady progression from ancient Israelite conceptions of kingship to the Christian notion of the messiah. For the ancient Israelites, the first and foremost king is God who promises to protect Israel from her enemies and to execute justice within the nation, on the condition that Israel remain faithful in fealty through obedience to the law and divine word. When Israel was not faithful in fealty, God as King punished her but still loved her and would take her back when her crimes were atoned. Human kings, beginning with Saul and David, were also expected to defend the nation and to execute justice, paying special attention to the widows, orphans, and foreigners who did not have families and clans to press for their interests. Perhaps the single most dominant image of God in the Psalms is that of the righteous king. What is so striking about the Psalms, however, is that despite firm adherence to and affirmation of the righteousness of God as King, there are steady laments that God does not protect His people as He ought, that He is absent when needed, and that He lets the unrighteous flourish while the righteous suffer.

When the earliest Christians proclaimed Jesus to be messiah, Lord, and King, the notion of kingship was radically changed. Jesus did not drive out the Romans and as to justice he himself was crucified for no relevant cause. His kingdom surely was not of this world. But then, of what world? Several symbol systems give answers to that question. For some it is a world to come later in history. For others it is a world to come that ends history. For yet others it is the kingdom of God that is real now despite the continuance of the kingdom of this world. For the symbols of the Cosmic Christ, however, Jesus is king of the entire creation, the Cosmic King. That Jesus Christ is symbolized as Cosmic King is obviously compatible with the injustices and failures of human history. What does tiny human history have to do with the Lordship of the entire cosmos?

Is there any content at all to the symbol of Christ the King? The clear answer, coming from the words and ministry of Jesus and repeated in the early Church, is that the rule of Christ the King is characterized by justice and mercy. What do these mean in contemporary terms?

The justice of the Christ the Cosmic King means that the obligations under which our lives lie are all in fact ultimate and normative. How we fare with respect to those obligations defines who we are in ultimate perspective. Our absolute, ultimate, and eternal identity consists in more than our placement and resources: it consists with what we do with who we are and what we have, as normed by our obligations. This is symbolized by our relation to Christ the King as Judge. Our deepest identity is who we are as we stand before the Judge.

A problematic part of the symbolism of Christ as ultimate Judge is the inference many have made that people will be rewarded according to what they deserve. This obviously does not happen much in ordinary history. Many have conceived Heaven and Hell as final rewarding fields where justice is finally meted out. That is likely not to be plausible to the late-modern imagination in any literal sense: our cosmic geography is different. In fact, the business of divine rewards and punishments is in direct conflict with the second element in the symbolism of Christ the King, namely the divine mercy. The mercy symbolism says that, despite standing under judgment as such failures as we are, we are at home in

God's love. We are accepted as sinners. The sins are not denied; they are part of our eternal identity. But they are forgiven and not held against us, and the good harmony we have achieved is accepted for what it is. This is precisely the answer to alienation that we sought: unconditional acceptance as sinners. Christ the King judges us and thus takes us as seriously as we would take ourselves in our most serious moments. Only by being taken so seriously can we accept our own identity. Only when we are mercifully accepted, sinners that we are, can we be at home in the universe where we so deeply fail our obligations. Only when there is cosmic mercy as well as justice can we be at home in a universe where it is impossible to be. The point of the divine mercy is that there is judgment and acceptance but no rewards and punishments: we are who we are before God.

To overcome actual alienation, judgment and mercy must be internalized so that we act as people at home in this universe, this kingdom. As the Words of Absolution in the old Book of Common Prayer put it:

He pardoneth and absolveth all them that truly repent and unfeignedly believe his holy Gospel. Wherefore let us beseech him to grant us true repentance and his Holy Spirit, that those things may please him which we do at this present, and that the rest of our life hereafter may be pure and holy . . .

Divine acceptance has no meaning or power to overcome alienation if we do not first recognize sins, accept the divine judgment, and repent. Only then can mercy be significant. Christ the King might be universally merciful; but that will not cure anyone's alienation and estrangement from engaging life unless the person first has some inkling of the sorry truth of his or her absolute identity and makes the appropriate response. Repentance is the human mirror of divine judgment. The point of the prayer of absolution is not to say everything is forgiven but rather to petition for true repentance. True repentance is the work of the Holy Spirit that leads us to the judgment seat. From there we can accept ourselves as unconditionally accepted and get on with living without alienation. No longer alienated, we still will find it impossible to be perfect because this is the kind of world we have. But we will not have the compounding of failure that results from failing to engage our situation with full faith and good will. Sanctification is learning to be at home in a cosmos where we inevitably fail but are accepted nonetheless and can thus get on with life.

With regard to the primary reference of the symbols of Christ the King, is it the case that we are both judged and mercifully accepted? Yes,

for the world does indeed have obligations in it – that is part of the creation, and they are impossible to fulfill together so that we stand obliged
and yet are failures. As to the merciful acceptance, that too is just part of
creation: we are created to be obliged and yet cannot fulfill those obligations together. What more could acceptance be? The only way to
demand more would be if we assumed the role of the Creator ourselves
and insisted that perfect fulfillment of obligation should be possible.

What about the secondary referents? For what kinds of people can the
symbols of the Cosmic Christ as King of the Universe serve to overcome
alienation? Certainly these symbols cannot be meaningful for people
who do not take sin seriously, for those who believe "nobody's perfect so
don't sweat." The symbols also cannot be meaningful for people who
insist on iconic descriptive reference for a Judge with interior subjectivity thinking condemning thoughts. Not only is that kind of Cosmic
Being implausible in our time, but the causal power of the symbolism
would be ruined. If divine judgment means a divine being thinking
judging thoughts, how is that to be causally connected back to the judged
person so as to make a difference, to aid in overcoming alienation?
Unless there were some super-human reading of divine thoughts, it
would have to be through the causal administration of rewards and punishments. This is the logic of the old conception that if people suffer,
they must deserve it; and if they flourish, they must deserve that too.
That logic was rejected in Job as well as elsewhere. If there were subjective divine judgmental thinking, it would be wholly irrelevant, causally,
to the transformation of people regarding alienation. Finally, the symbol
of Christ as Cosmic King would not be meaningful to people whose
political sensibilities are so offended by kingship that its metaphors of
judgment and mercy are a priori impossible. I have argued here,
however, for a conception of a divine ruler of the universe that does not
come by analogy from the human political realm but is defined by the
Logos; perhaps the analogy could work the other way, from the conception of the divine judge and mercy-giver to appropriate forms of government that do the same, forms that might not be on the kingship model.

The people for whom the symbols of the Cosmic Christ as King are
meaningful are those who can refer with the symbols indexically so as to
be reoriented as sinful but accepted people. For these people, the truth
of engaging the Ultimate with these symbols is that they truly become
at home in this universe.

But what is the content of living at home in the cosmos as forgiven
sinners, and how is this connected with any content to the symbols of

Christ the King? For this we must turn briefly to the last set of symbols for the Cosmic Christ, the Agent of Reconciliation.

Christ the Agent of Reconciliation comes from Heaven, taking on the form of a slave (Jesus), and returns to Heaven with his people reconciled; that is, he takes them to heaven with him. This is an enormously complex set of different systems of symbols. Some have to do with how the Agent is properly part of Heaven. That is the topic of chapter 4 on Christ as the Second Person of the Trinity. Other systems of symbols in this complex have to do with Jesus' own life and how this is reconciling. This is the topic of chapter 5 on the historical Jesus. Suffice it for now to say that *how* to be at home in the cosmic kingdom of Christ the King is closely associated with how to be a follower of Jesus of Nazareth.

CHAPTER FOUR

Jesus Christ the Trinitarian Person

This chapter stands in something of a pivotal relation to the ones immediately preceding and succeeding. For the sake of keeping some sense of
balance among the rather extreme and controversial symbols of the
Cosmic Christ, the Trinitarian Second Person, and the historical Jesus,
it is worth while to step back and look at some structural considerations
for handling them. These are not structural considerations of doctrine
in any usual sense – these symbols overlap, resonate with, and pass
through one another while being used in several heavy-duty doctrines.
Rather, the structure has to do with symbolic themes.

The historical locus of the symbol of Jesus Christ as a Trinitarian
Person is not the Bible or early Christian community but the Church in
Patristic times, mainly in the Roman Empire. The Trinity is indeed a
heavy-duty doctrine, and one of its main functions is to give definitive
interpretations to the limits for using such symbols as the Cosmic Christ
and Jesus of Nazareth, the human person. The phrase "the historical
Jesus" is loaded with connotations from the last two centuries' "quests
for the historical Jesus," and is anachronistic in reference to the Patristic
discussions. Nevertheless, the Patristic Church was aware of the tension
between Jesus conceived as a divine heavenly being and Jesus the man
whose life was reported in the gospels, whom we can refer to as the historical Jesus. The doctrine of the Trinity, and this chapter about it, are
the pivot between the Cosmic Christ and the historical Jesus.

The scheme of my analysis of the Christological symbols has been to
relate them to some fundamental human religious problem, some very
important aspect of the religious dimension of the human condition,
and show that they can be schematizations of the Creator God to that
religious problem. The symbol systems concerning the Cosmic Christ
were related to the issues of whether human beings can be at home in
the universe. Those of the historical Jesus will be related to whether God
can be present in and with us, in our historical circumstances, and what

this means for shaping life. The pivot question between whether we can be at home in creation and whether God can be at home in us is whether we can be at home in God, finding our connection through the Second and Third Persons of the Trinity. The metaphor of "home" is dangerous in the last case, treading as it does on idolatry and over-familiarity with God. Perhaps at this point it is safer to ask the question, can we be properly related to God? Is there a connection, such that we can become fulfilled in God? Murillo's *The Heavenly and Earthly Trinities* (figure 4, p. 28 above) invites the viewer into connections with both heavenly and earthly deity.

Because of its pivotal place, the problematic of Jesus Christ the Trinitarian Person is curiously abstract and incomplete. Restating and reformulating some of the symbol systems of the Cosmic Christ, it is a proleptic anticipation of some of the issues of historical involvement in the symbols of the historical Jesus. In an abstract but rough sense, the way to be properly connected with God and fulfilled in that connection is, on the one hand, to be made to be at home in the cosmos as a creature and, on the other, to have God be at home in us and our world as Murillo demonstrates.

Given the puzzlements over the doctrine of the Trinity, not all of which reflect well on the Christian intellect, I fear, why not simply abandon those symbols and divide the work between the symbols of the Cosmic Christ and the historical Jesus? The reason, of course, is that we need to face straight on, as the European Church did in its first five centuries, the questions about how Jesus is to be understood in relation to God and in relation to us, and how that affects our relation to God. The trajectory of the symbol systems of the Cosmic Christ moves away from human things to the divine. The trajectory of symbols of the historical Jesus not only moves from the divine to the human but, as we have seen in the last two centuries of quest for the historical Jesus, it might be disconnected from any anchor in the divine whatsoever. The doctrine of the Trinity needs to interweave these trajectories. The doctrine of the Trinity also needs to deal with the Holy Spirit, historically a late consideration to be given importance but, as we shall see, crucial for Christ and creation. In the *Heavenly and Earthly Trinities*, the Holy Spirit is just a little bird.

The doctrine of the Trinity is important here as a problematic, as a locus to engage crucial issues of Christian theology. It is not so important as the orthodox answer in Chalcedonian form to those issues. Indeed, the Patristic discussion must be viewed as a particular inculturation of

Christian life and theology in the Greek and Latin forms of late antiquity. The two great heresies excluded by the Patristic discussion, Arianism and Nestorianism, had the effect of separating the "Catholic and orthodox" Church from the Christian inculturations in other groups. The Arians were mainly Goths and the Nestorians mainly lived under the Persian emperors and nations farther east in Asia. One cannot help suspecting that the dynamic of the Patristic discussion (with several of the councils either presided over or superintended by the Roman Emperor) had to do in some measure with drawing safe boundaries around a political unit of Christianity. This suspicion is doubled when one examines the arguments for the various sides from our twenty-first-century perspective. If anything, the Arian and Nestorian positions, in different ways and for different reasons, look better than Catholic orthodoxy in some respects from our perspective in which we are anxious to maintain continuity with the historical Jesus. In other respects, the orthodox Chalcedonian position is well taken. The point is that our context is vastly different from that of the Patristic discussion and we need to sort things appropriately. The discussion of Jesus Christ as a Trinitarian Person needs to begin with historical considerations.

TRINITARIAN SYMBOLS

The Trinity is not an explicit idea in the New Testament, despite the fact there are a number of passages associating the Father, the Son, and the Holy Spirit, especially in benedictions and in baptismal formulas. Matthew 28:19 says, "Go therefore and make disciples of all nations, baptizing them in the name of the Father and of the Son and of the Holy Spirit." Nevertheless, the issues that gave rise to the doctrine of the Trinity very early in the Church were manifest in the New Testament.

The God of Jesus' Judaism was explicitly identified as Father, by Jesus and the writers of the New Testament texts, as noted in chapter 1. Paul was explicit in saying that it was the God of Abraham, Isaac, and Jacob, and of the Gentiles too, who sent Jesus to extend the promises made to the Jews on to the Gentiles. Jesus was different from God the Father, and was sent. And yet Jesus himself was claimed to be divine in some sense, or senses. What sense or senses?

Jesus was called the Son of God in at least three senses. First, it is commonly observed that, whereas Matthew (1:1–16) traces Jesus' lineage back to Abraham, patriarch of the covenant of Israel, Luke (3:23–38) traces it back to Adam, the first man. But the end of Luke's text on this reads "son of Enoch, son of Jared, son of Mahalaleel, son of Cainan, son of Enos, son of Seth, son of Adam, son of God." In this sense, every person is a son or daughter of Adam and Eve and also of God; Luke calls explicit attention to Jesus being in the lineage of God. As noted earlier, being a son of God in the Levitical tradition meant to inherit the work of the divine parent, caring for the Earth. Jesus, in Luke's account, bears the great weight of that inheritance beyond that of others. For, as Paul put it (1 Cor. 15), Jesus was a new Adam; see figure 3, p. 27 above.

A second sense of being Son of God appears in the Johannine writings. The Prologue of John's Gospel begins with the statement of the incarnation of the pre-existent and transcendent Logos, which is then identified with Jesus Christ, the Son of God (1:18). The phrase is quickly repeated in a citation of the testimony of John the Baptist (1:34), who also calls Jesus the Lamb of God. John cites Jesus' frequent use of that title for himself, as, for instance in the famous passage at 3:16: "For God so loved the world that he gave his only Son, so that everyone who believes in him may have eternal life." In John 8 Jesus discusses the senses in which he was sent by and from the Father. Much of the Farewell Discourses, John 14–17, has to do with Jesus explicating the senses in which God is his Father, he does the Father's work, and returns to the Father. That Discourse also elaborates the connection between Jesus, the Father, and the Holy Spirit or Advocate. The first two letters attributed to John regularly refer to God as the Father and to Jesus Christ as his Son.

A third and related sense of being Son of God, although without the explicit language, is in Paul's claim in Philippians 2 that Christ Jesus had a pre-existent form as a God, was equal to God but did not "regard that equality as something to be exploited" (2:6), descended and then re-ascended to be exalted with God. The phrase, son of God, had been used in the Hebrew Bible to mean heavenly beings in the divine court (Job 1:6, 2:1). It was transformed in the Christian scriptures to indicate a unique Son of God who was a heavenly being. The author of Hebrews speaks of the Son as a heavenly being higher than angels (Heb. 1).

The title, Son of Man, has many meanings in the New Testament, some perhaps no more elevated than being an indirect form of first-person reference.[1] But it might also refer to the heavenly being, "like a Son of Man," who appeared before the Ancient One in Daniel 7 and who was given eternal dominion over the nations, a claim made for Jesus

[1] See Vermes, *The Changing Faces of Jesus*, pp. 38–41, 175–76.

as we saw in discussing the Cosmic King in connection with the Cosmic Christ (see Rev. 1:12–16).[2] In John 8:28 Jesus refers to himself as Son of Man in claiming to have come from and to be about to return to the Father. Other symbols of Jesus claim that he uniquely does the work of God in redeeming the people and reigning over the divine kingdom. Many of these have been discussed in connection with the symbols of the Cosmic Christ.

Much less is said about the Holy Spirit in the New Testament, although it is claimed to be the divine agency, to be Jesus' substitute in presiding over and leading the fellowship (John 14:18–26), to be the agent who transformed the gathered believers into a Church with a mission (Acts 2:1–5), to be the divine baptizer with fire (Luke 3:16), and in the letters of Paul to be the agent of ecstatic confirmation of new life, the inspirer of Christians with divine speech, and the creator.[3]

Although the New Testament ascribed divinity in a variety of senses to both Jesus and the Holy Spirit, it generally was clear about the priority of God the Father and the subordination of the Son and Spirit, however coeternal with God they might be and instrumental in the creation. Nevertheless, the clarification of the relation of Jesus Christ and the Spirit to God the Father was necessary for the early Christians, especially in light of the emerging practice of worshipping Christ as Lord and also the Holy Spirit, something that looked idolatrous to other forms of Second Temple Judaism.

For that clarification the early Church turned to Greek philosophy. Some thinkers of the twentieth century thought this was a great mistake, contrasting Athens (bad) with Jerusalem (good). Christianity was alleged to be a Semitic religion. In fact, the situation was far more complex. The Jews in exile had already appropriate motifs of Persian apocalyptic religion. Second Temple Judaism struggled with Hellenism from the Alexandrian conquest onward, and Philo, the great scholar contemporary with the first generation of Christians, employed themes of Greek philosophy. Christianity from the beginning had Semitic, but

---

[2] The imagery in Daniel is particularly complex. The one like the "Son of Man" is most likely the archangel Michael who is the patron angelic defender of Israel (Dan. 10:13, 12:1) and might represent Israel in righteous rule over the nations. Daniel 12:2–3 contains the first biblical reference to resurrection to everlasting life or everlasting contempt, a theme important for early Christianity and very different from earlier Israelite "resurrection" images such as that of Ezekiel's "dry bones" returning to life as a reconstituted army and symbolizing a regathered Israel from exile.

[3] See the fine discussion of the Holy Spirit as more than just the communications facilitator in Rowan Williams' *On Christian Theology*, pp. 110–27.

also Persian and Greek roots, and Paul in Romans appealed to Stoic ideas.

One of the chief features of the Semitic root was the understanding of God in terms of the history of Israel. That is, God was understood through the narrative of Israel, and this in two senses. In one sense, God was known as a Person who interacted with Israel (and other nations) over the centuries, from the Patriarchs through Exodus to the establishment and ruin of the Davidic Kingdom, the Exile and the return. In another sense, the story of Israel itself is a narrative of the emergence of a knowledge of God through the interaction and mutual correction of strains of interpretation through Israel's history.

By the time of the Christian era, however, there was a special problem. Early Christianity was clear in claiming that God created the world *ex nihilo*, a theme as old as Isaiah 40–55. If God creates everything, even space-time, then God cannot be a player of roles within an historical narrative. There might be a narrative of the coming to understand this, but not of divine identity itself. So on the one hand this high view of divine transcendence as creator *ex nihilo* called for intermediaries that are not so transcendent – indeed, for a visible image of the invisible God, as discussed in the previous chapter. On the other hand something must be said of the transcendent creator. For it was assumed that this Creator has to have a reality apart from creation if the creation depends on God wholly. I argued in chapter 1 that this assumption is not necessary. But it was made progressively inevitable as the dramatic quasi-personal character of Yahweh was conceived to be more and more transcendent.

Here Greek philosophy came to the rescue and provided a conception of God as divine substance, a being with properties, a subject that can be given predicates independent of relational predication to the created order. Two virtues, at least, lay in adopting this philosophy. First, it responded conceptually to the issues of absolute transcendence that were fueled by the anti-idolatry dialectic of Jewish thought. Second, it was the native thought of many in the Gentile Hellenistic world, and therefore explicated much of the Gospel for them.

The notion of a divine substance and its variants provided the terms with which the Hellenistic and Late Antique world of Christianity attempted to understand the relation of the Father to Jesus Christ and the Holy Spirit. This conceptual repertoire led to some debates that look rather silly from our perspective. For instance, was the Trinity to be conceived as three different but related beings that have the same essence? Or as one Being with three different though related natures? Or three beings that are so internally defined in terms of one another (*perichoresis*) that they really are one being? The three-in-one, one-in-three debate prompted Pseudo-Dionysius to warn that those numbers regarding the Trinity do not mean what the numbers mean anywhere else.[4] This attempt to define a three-in-one substance is driven by the concern to make sense of the philosophical concept of substance once the labels of Father, Son, and Holy Spirit have been attached, but it makes no sense of those particular labels. Indeed, it almost precludes being an interpretive tool of the God of Abraham, Isaac, and Jacob, Jesus of Nazareth, and the Holy Spirit known at Pentecost.

An equally spurious debate arose from the concept of substance when the Arians and Athanasians attempted to talk about the relation of the First and Second Persons. The orthodox position turned out to be that the Second Person is exactly identical to the First Person except that it is generated whereas the First Person is original and not generated. The assertion of identity in all things except generation makes it impossible to relate the Second Person to Jesus of Nazareth. And because the First Person was held to be perfect and simple, the Second Person likewise can have no finite determinate features! The day might be saved by sharply distinguishing the Second Person as the discarnate Logos from Jesus of Nazareth as the incarnate one, a supposition underlying the outcome of that discussion. But that then would frame the question of the relation between the heavenly and earthly Jesus in an insoluble way, as having two natures defined over against each other (or alternatively being a mishmash that attains neither divine or human nature properly). Moreover, that substantizing of the categories of the discussion ruined the great truth in the distinction between ungenerated creativity and generated creativity, namely, that the absolute and original act of creation by God the Creator is continued or brought to some further fulfillment by the human generated but also generating creativity of Jesus.[5]

Another aspect of the problem of substantizing God is in the distinction between immanent and economic conceptions of the Trinity. The economic conception of the Trinity says that God is Three Persons in relation to the created world, and says nothing about God apart from

---

[4] Cited in ibid., p. xv, to make a similar point.

[5] This is the heart of Rowan Williams' argument for the divinity of Jesus. See ibid., pp. 137–42. He writes, on p. 140, "So Jesus shares the creativity of God, yet not as a 'second God,' a separate *individual*: he is God *as* dependent – for whom the metaphors of Word, Image, Son, are appropriate. What I am suggesting is a tentative sketch of what might be meant by ascribing 'divinity' to Jesus without simply walking into the logical absurdity of saying that Jesus 'is' the creator of the world, *tout court*."

the world. Every biblical reference to God as Creator, Holy One of Israel, Father, Son, and Holy Spirit is economic by definition. The immanent conception claims that God is complete in the divine self without the world and that the divine self includes the Three Persons. The immanent conception has no religious interest unless it is entailed by the economic conception. But it would not be entailed unless it is supposed that divine (economic) agency requires a substance (immanent in itself) in order to act, the supposition of Greek substance philosophy. I argued in chapter 1 that this supposition is *not* required because the conception of God as creator *ex nihilo* is a clear alternative.

What then shall we say about the Trinity so as to locate Jesus properly as the Second Person? Instead of the categories of Greek philosophy, whatever their virtue for inculturating the gospel in that context, we need categories appropriate to our own context. In this instance we should recur to the theory of creation *ex nihilo*.

Recall that this theory says the singular divine act of creation itself constitutes the divine nature to be (1) the source of the created world, (2) the created world, and (3) the act creating the world. With regard to the created world, we have distinguished the ongoing temporal world of finite things from the transcendental principles that need to be expressed in every thing, which we called the Logos. The Logos is that by virtue of which everything that is, is, without which nothing can be. The Logos can be called "begotten, not made" (the Nicene formula) in the sense that it is the condition for any and all finite things, all of which can therefore said to be made and not begotten. The Logos does not arise in time, as temporal things do, but is the condition for time and temporal things. Therefore the Arians were wrong in one sense to say that there was a time when the Second Person of the Trinity was not, the sense, namely that identifies the Second Person exclusively with the Logos and not with temporal Jesus of Nazareth. By the same token, there never was a time when the Second Person existed and the temporal world did not yet, for temporality itself supposes temporal things, that is, made things. The begotten Logos/Son and the made temporal world arise together in the eternal act of creation.

From within the temporal world two elements of creatureliness are crucial to distinguish. One is the presence of the Logos as the harmonized form, components formed, existential location, and value of each thing, and their interconnections. The other is the act of creativity itself laid out in temporal process. Creativity within temporal process is the power and inertia of existence in past things, spontaneity in present things, and the dynamic adjustment of pure form to relevant form in future things, all as discussed in chapter 1. So the presence of God the Creator in the world is not merely in the Logos, although with that harmony of form, things formed, existential location, and value, this Logos-presence is the outcome of divine love in lovely things. The presence of God in the world is also in the dynamics of creativity, pushing to novelty, exchanging these harmonies for others, opening up processes, entropically loosening harmonies so that other harmonies result. *Because of the Logos, the results of creativity will always be harmonies, though perhaps not better harmonies. Because of creativity, the Logos can never be fully fixed and satisfied in any one harmony, with any one form, with one set of contents, with any one achievement. God in the world is wild as well as loving.*

If it were possible to separate the harmonizing Logos from the temporal divine creativity, we might have two competing principles. Some thinkers like to characterize God as principles of order and creative chaos. But those are not separate. Creativity in the world is determinate because of the symmetrical Logos and yet always changing determinations because of the asymmetrical spontaneity in creativity.

This is not yet a full doctrine of the Trinity because the Logos has not been related particularly to Jesus, nor temporal creativity to the saving activity of God. Before these ideas can be developed, we should reflect on two symbol systems that have to do with the image of God: that already examined in which Jesus Christ is the visible image of the invisible God, and that in which people are created in the image of God, the next topic. Together these show the senses in which Jesus can be divine, and people too.

THE IMAGE OF GOD

That human beings are created in the image of God is one of the fundamental affirmations of the biblical religions, almost on a par with the conception of creation itself, indeed part of it. The critical biblical passage is Genesis 1:26–27:

Then God said, "Let us make humankind [Heb. *adam*] in our image, according to our likeness; and let them have dominion over the fish of the sea, and over the birds of the air, and over the cattle, and over all the wild animals of the earth, and over every creeping thing that creeps upon the earth." So God created humankind in his image, in the image of God he created them; male and female he created them.

The overall force of that passage is to affirm a divine kinship or likeness to human beings so that people are created as better than good. Everything God created in the first six days of the Genesis account turns out upon divine inspection to be good, but people have something of God in them as well. This affirmation stands as a limit to all doctrines of sin and depravity: though the divine image can be blurred, distorted, and maimed, it remains and is the first thing to be said about human beings in their creation. In this very positive affirmation of goodness or divinity at the heart of human beings, the biblical religions stand with the strong Confucian claim that human nature is derived from Heaven (a close Confucian parallel to the biblical God). The Confucian *Doctrine of the Mean* (attributed to Confucius' grandson, Tzu-ssu, 492–431 BCE, but perhaps as late as 200 BCE) begins:

What Heaven (*T'ien*, Nature) imparts to man is called human nature. To follow our nature is called the Way (Tao). Cultivating the Way is called education. The Way cannot be separated from us for a moment. What can be separated from us is not the Way.[6]

The affinity of the biblical religions (and also Greek paganism with different motifs) with Chinese religion in affirming the essential defining goodness of human beings stands in some stark opposition to Buddhism and some forms of Hinduism.[7] Of the biblical religions, Christianity goes the farthest in pushing the limits of sin in destroying the image of God.[8] Even Augustine, however, who is notorious for interpreting sin as a genetic condition inherited from birth, notes that this is a condition laid upon inheritance by Adam and Eve who are already created in the image of God.[9]

Within Christianity, the image of God has been interpreted in a great many ways, perhaps most often in terms of traits or psychological faculties such as reason, will, or love. Augustine used a version of faculty psychology in his interpretation of the Trinity. The European Enlightenment particularly liked cognitive reason, will, and love or appreciation because those were the traits it singled out as defining the human as such, for instance as the topics of Kant's three Critiques

---

[6] The translation by Wing-tsit Chan in his *Source Book of Chinese Philosophy*, p. 98.
[7] For detailed comparisons of Confucianism with Christianity on this and other topics, see my *Boston Confucianism*, especially chapters 5–10.
[8] For comparative studies of the Jewish and Muslim interpretations of the image of God and how it is affected by sin, see the essays by Anthony Saldarini and S. Nomanul Haq respectively in my *The Human Condition*.   [9] See the essay by Paula Fredriksen in my *The Human Condition*.

respectively. John Wesley, the paradigmatic Enlightenment Enthusiast, interpreted the image of God in Adam to be perfect knowledge of everything that came to his attention (whereas God knows everything without qualification), perfect moral affection for everything that came to his attention (whereas God loves everything without qualification), and perfect indifferent freedom to choose among the options presented him (whereas God freely makes everything).[10]

For a contemporary reading of the image of God, however, we can begin with the original text in its context. The first thing to notice is the point mentioned before that being "sons of God," or more graciously "children of God," means that people inherit the work of God. That in fact is what is described in the Genesis passage: humankind are to exercise dominion over the things in their world. In the other creation story in Genesis 2, God is more explicit about the work, namely caring for the garden. Expelled from the garden, Adam and Eve did not have an easy time exercising dominion, were at odds with at least some of the animals and had to scrabble in the earth to eke out a living (Gen. 3:14–19). The theme of somewhat wayward children of God is developed throughout the Hebrew Bible as a call to exercise divine justice and mercy. Paul interpreted Christian redemption as the restoration of people to their divine heritage as children of God, not slaves (for instance, Rom. 8:14–29).

A second point to notice in the Genesis 1:26–27 passage is the plurals. Not only is humankind, *adam*, created plural, "them," "male and female," but God is referred to as plural: "Let *us* make humankind in *our* image, according to *our* likeness." Scholars suggest that the plural divinity originally referred to a heavenly court; some Christian theologians have interpreted this as a reference to the plurality of Trinitarian Persons. The point with regard to the image of God in humanity is that people are essentially social (and sexual), and the image of God has to do with human relations. This point is also reflected in the second creation story (Gen. 2:4–25) in which Adam is created in successive steps. First he is a clay doll made at the oasis, and second God breathes life into him. Third, the living being is moved into the Garden of Eden to have a home and work. Fourth, the being learns language, naming the

---

[10] See, for instance, *The Works of John Wesley*, volume II, pp. 293–94. See also the Ph.D. dissertation of Philip R. Meadows, *Sadhana and Salvation*; Ramanuja holds to a Vedanta view of human nature as good in the sense that people and the entire world are the body of God. My discussion of this is in *Boston Confucianism*, pp. 161–64, which compares Wesley's view with the Neo-Confucian position of Wang Yangming.

animals, which is to say that human reality requires conventions of language and society. Fifth, God lays a special convention on Adam, not to eat of the tree of the knowledge of good and evil, with a covenantal penalty: eat and die. Sixth, the being is provided a companion, of its own species when the animals won't do. The creation of humankind is finally complete – Adam is fully human (taking into account the biblical double play on *adam* as an individual as well as humankind) – when Adam and Eve cling together as if reuniting separated flesh.

The essentially social definition of the image of God is thus a question of how people can live together, with a distinction between ideals and actual states of affairs. One of the chief symbolic systems for developing this theme in the Bible is the idea of covenant. The first covenant was God's with Adam to provide life in the Garden of Eden for obedience not to eat the apple. The second was with Noah (Gen. 9:1–17), the third with Abraham (Gen. 15:1–21, 17:1–27), the fourth with Moses (Exodus, Numbers, Leviticus, Deuteronomy), the fifth with David (2 Samuel 7), a sixth promised by Jeremiah (31:31–34) and claimed by various New Testament (New Covenant) authors, for instance those of Hebrews 8 and of the Eucharistic references to the blood of the new covenant cited near the beginning of chapter 2 above.

At least part of what the image of God means, therefore, is to live as God's children and heirs in the creative process under the conditions of covenant. What does this mean today? Two answers can be given. One addresses the shape covenant life should have in our historical circumstances, our specific obligations and conditions, the topic of chapter 5. The other addresses the generalization of the idea of covenant beyond the historical trajectory of Israel's covenants so as to be seen as normative for humanity as such, since the image of God is so universally normative. In the next chapter it will be argued that Christians find their particular covenantal conditions as part of self-identity in a continuation of the covenantal history begun with Israel and decisively shaped for Christians by Jesus Christ. But the image of God, and hence covenantal identity, applies to all humans, not just Jews and Christians.

For a general theory of covenant, we can recall the doctrine of the Logos developed earlier and note that there are four kinds of obligations: to act so as to establish the right form (justice), the right deference to the components formed (piety), right relation to existential location (faith), and right pursuit of ultimate value and meaning (hope). These are integrated in the creative processes of life in the obligation to love. The first condition of covenant, then, is that people all live under obligation, and the obligations are of at least these kinds.[11]

But as was argued in the previous chapter, the perfect fulfillment of these covenantal conditions is impossible. Therefore the second condition of covenant is to accept this fact as the situation of human life, repent failure, and continue to strive to fulfill the obligations as best as possible. Whereas the Levitical dimension of the Mosaic covenant prescribed divinely ordained sacrificial remedies for covering sin (sacrificial atonement), the more general covenant requires acceptance of being accepted as covenantal failures, as discussed in the previous chapter. The Christian New Covenant version of this is to live in the world as governed by Christ the Cosmic King who exercises both justice and mercy.

Actually, the New Covenant version is far more specific for Christians than simply being at home in a cosmos normed by justice and mercy. It means living out the extended life of Jesus in our time, as will be discussed shortly and in the next chapter. But that will make sense only when we see how the symbols of the Logos as covenant relate to Jesus.

Breaking the covenant, as can be inferred from the previous chapter, requires at least two things. One is to fail the covenant's obligations, which is inevitable and is in itself not sin, on my interpretation. The second is to be alienated from God because of broken pride at that failure, alienation that we can choose, habituate into the way we structure our society, and teach our children with our earliest coos and cuddles. That alienation is the standard condition of human life, built into our social structures and learned personalities. At least this is the way Christians have come to read the human condition.

Redemption, therefore, would consist in whatever would allow us to release the alienation and return to God who rules with justice and also with the mercy that allows us to go on living as good children and heirs of God, and to exercise in our turn both justice (along with piety, faith, hope, and love) and mercy. What can redeem us from our standard and deeply socialized condition of alienation from God and rejection of the covenant as binding and defining us? The previous chapter argued that the beauty of holiness in the Cosmic Christ might elicit acceptance of the divine mercy so as to accomplish that. But it did not say much about the content of the beauty, holiness, awesomeness, glory, and so forth, except to give a metaphysical argument that the Creator is the source of the greatest good. In fact, the cosmic divine justice combined with mercy

---

[11] For a more elaborate discussion of this, see my *A Theology Primer*, chapter 5.

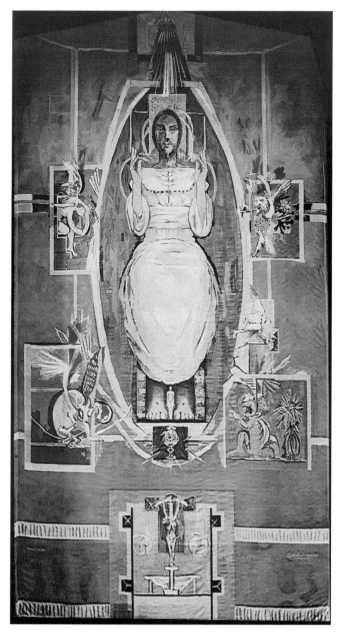

Figure 9. Graham Sutherland, *Christ in Glory*, tapestry,
Coventry Cathedral

attributed to the Cosmic Christ is not different from what the biblical Jewish tradition attributes to Yahweh.[12] The prophetic books – thoroughly mined by Christian writers – push the limits of language to express both judgment and wrath on the one hand and mercy and restitution on the other. But the Deuteronomic writings are also clear in emphasizing both divine judgment and loving mercy. Christians have claimed since early on that Yahweh's judgment and mercy as expressed in the covenant and lived out in Israel are not enough to overcome alienation. Paul, in making the Christian point (for instance, Rom. 4, 9–11), downplayed divine mercy in Jewish tradition. Whatever would make the symbols of the Cosmic Christ an advance upon the symbols of Yahweh as judging and merciful would have to be some connection with Jesus of Nazareth. The Cosmic Christ has to be some extrapolation of Jesus.

So we return to look at Jesus' life to discern redemption, including in that life how he was received (for good and ill). From a formal point of view we look to Jesus to see just how to live a covenantal life under the condition of its inevitable failure of obligation.[13] This means, at least, seeing from Jesus how to be just when we are inevitably unjust, how to be pious when our deference is compromised, how to be faithful when our existential location betrays us with alienation, and how to live in hope of the Ultimate whose apophasis is like the Cheshire Cat. More prosaically, what does Jesus show us about how we can love, where love has the social covenantal shape?

Jesus' redemption, however, is not his living the proper covenantal life. It is his transformation of others so that their alienation is released and they too can live the proper covenantal life. Redemption is not of Jesus but of others. The Christian claim is that the early disciples so responded to Jesus that their alienation was overcome and the blessing of the Holy Spirit frequently rested upon them. They came to live out a community in their own lives that was a (more or less) successful covenant. The Church's claim is that others, including ourselves, can live out Jesus' redeeming life in our own circumstances. Now the rub is that the redeeming qualities of Jesus' life are not in his specifics as a moral leader, a teacher of piety, a critic of existential hypocrisy, or antidote to despair, not even in his facility at teaching friendship and love. The redeeming qualities had to do with his response to his social culture including its religion, the fact that he was crucified remaining faithful to a God who

[12] See Saldarini's essay in my *Ultimate Realities*.
[13] This point is the center of Paul Tillich's Christology.

was revealed in the last moments to have forsaken him, and the fact that he was perceived by his followers as resurrected from the dead, first in a personal sense and then in the sense that the community itself could become his body, extending his story. To be more blunt, his redeeming qualities have to do with his prophetic criticism, his death by crucifixion, and resurrection, all as taken to heart by the disciples.

What is the image of God, then, according to Christianity? It is: to be bound by the covenant whether people accept it or not, to be measured in it as failures, to be generally unable to accept vague promises of mercy and thus to be alienated, and to be susceptible of redemption by participating in the redeeming life of Jesus (including the crucifixion part). The divine image is in everyone, and everyone is susceptible of redemption by participating in the redeeming life of Jesus. There may be other paths to redemption than the Christian one, and Christians can acknowledge that. Those other paths might add extra and alternative elements to the image of God. But the way through Jesus is the one that Christians walk. The content of this will be explored shortly.

One more dimension of the image of God needs to be added to this discussion. We noted above that two interwoven traits of the divine Creator are pervasive throughout nature and history, namely the structure of the Logos in ordered determinateness and the spontaneous creativity and fecundity that expands beyond any determinate order. Thus we can have two special images *for* God within the created world. On the one hand God is the maker of lovely harmonies, of determinate things each of which achieves a value. In this sense God is love. On the other hand God is the destroyer of harmonies to make more, a little chaotic, the force of fertility and fecundity, the dangerous pressure that with respect to any ordered harmony whatsoever is wild.[14] God is love, and God is wild. The latter trait is not always welcome to those protective of some order, especially those orders that embody great value. Their wild destruction might not lead to improvement. We know from the theory of creation *ex nihilo* that these two traits go together and cannot be separated, however separately we notice the achievement of harmony now, its dismissal like a straw dog later.

Human beings are images of God in this sense too, being both loving achievers of goods in life and wild creators who risk that for something different. Again, those who protect achieved orders are suspicious of the

---

[14] I learned this expression from a sermon by Wesley J. Wildman, "God the Destroyer," which is paired with his sermon "God the Friend."

creative, rebellious, artistic streak in people. But with regard to redemption, the wild side is absolutely crucial. The divine image in us means
that we need not be stuck in alienation or be in bondage to anything.
Human freedom has many dimensions, some of which are the fragile
and delicate achievements of subtle civilized harmonious order. But the
dimension of sheer spontaneity is freedom at the heart of the divine
image. The divine wildness in us gets bored easily, even with the high
achievements of life. This can lead to great evil. But it also means that
we can get bored with alienation and sin, bored with organized oppression and suppression.

God's love and wildness go together in the created order, and so they
should as elements of the divine image in human beings. The explosion
of given harmonies ought to be guided by love of greater ones. The
loving enjoyment of given harmonies ought to anticipate greater glories.
Insofar as the Divine Logos is creative love in the world, it cannot be separated from the Spirit as the creative act's energy working through temporal process. The Spirit cannot make anything that does not have the
Logos as its condition for determinateness. The Logos cannot be in anything lovely save by the spontaneous creativity of the Spirit. The Spirit
always creates with the form of the Logos and the Logos is never real in
things save by the creative Spirit. Both are elements within the temporal
order of the eternal act of the Creator. The classic Trinitarian principle
that the act of any one Person of the Trinity is the act of the other two
also is thus valid in this contemporary sense.

In human beings that principle is true but not always optimal. The
wild spirit can destroy something resulting in some other harmony, but
it might be a disastrous change. The covenant expresses the abstract
obligations. In respect of redemption, there needs to be a special integration of Logos and Spirit. Without taking Jesus to be the incarnation
of the Logos, the Logos could be any old harmony, a demon with seven
colleagues returning to a swept house (Luke 11:24–26). The spirit in a
person could be any old change. But with Jesus as the Logos, embodying a way to live rightly in covenant, and with the Holy Spirit guiding
what that means for particular people in particular circumstances,
redemption is possible.

GROWING INTO GOD

The discussions of the previous chapter and the previous two sections of
this one were controlled by the universality of people before the Cosmic

Christ and the universality of the divine image in humankind. Everyone can be understood as a child of God, defined by the obliging covenant, and participating in the divine creativity that is loving and wild with no automatic coordination. Of course not everyone accepts these symbols for understanding themselves, but they could be applied to everyone universally.

The Christian claims that give distinguishing sense to the Cosmic Christ and deal with redemption, however, are particular. They have to do with the historical Jesus of Nazareth and with how the historical groups of early Christians could construe that person to have redemptive power for them. Although redemption was local to them, so far as they knew, it had to have divine origin. Insofar as they took Jesus to be the redeemer, he had to have some divine connection, and the extension of the understanding of him to the Cosmic Christ (in the first generation of disciples!) is not unexpected.

But how is this to be understood in our time? To symbolize the cosmic Logos as the Cosmic Christ and King, in respect to the question of whether human beings are at home in the universe, is one thing. For us to relate humanly and historically to the historical figure of Jesus of Nazareth is another thing. How can they be connected? The Earth with its human history is a tiny speck in space, a blink of an eye in cosmic time. What does the Earthly history of redemption mean for rational sinners on planets in other galaxies? They have no identification whatsoever with Israel. For that matter, what does redemption in Israel's terms have to do with the Chinese, Indians, and Native Americans before any contact with Israel or Christian culture?

We have the records in the New Testament and early Christian writers of their attempts to understand all this. Clearly, even in the earliest records we see a growing understanding, even a representation of that growth, in what the disciples could understand only after the crucifixion and resurrection. We will discuss the open-ended and historically changing understanding of the New Testament Christian community in the next chapter. Here we can be satisfied to note that different writers, addressing perhaps overlapping but different communities employed many different symbol systems. What follows is a reading of these sources designed to connect with contemporary imagination.

The first thing to note is that the New Testament writers took Jesus and their new community to be all about God. The concerns for justice, for healing, for the poor, all were set in the context of right or wrong relation to God. The new community constituted around Jesus stood in some

Figure 10. Titian, *Noli me tangere*, detail, National Gallery, London

critical theological relation to the old situation within which they had lived
and out from which the new life in Christ brought them. For Jesus and the
original disciples (not only the Twelve), this was the life of Israel as it had
worked out its history in reference to God down to the days of the Roman
occupation. This original community, including Jesus, saw itself as the
continuation and rectification of Israel's history, a rectification even more
momentous, though continuous with, those associated with Abraham,
Moses, David, Josiah, and the post-exilic re-establishment of the Temple
community.

The addition of Gentiles to the Christian community was problematic
on many fronts. As already noted, the background from which they were
called out and that needed rectification was not Israel but Hellenistic
pagan culture. They associated themselves with Israel, and the New
Israel, and took the Septuagint to be their first scripture. But their past
was not that of Israel, and their evolving discovery of what the Christian
life meant for them was thus involved in complicated and confusing ways

with the rhetoric of Jesus himself and that of the Jewish Christians. These concerns were a constant theme in Paul's writings and the gospels of Luke and John were addressed to Christian communities with large Gentile populations. This meant that these writers' representations of Jesus' and the first disciples' relation to the history of God with Israel picked up on the elements that could be recognized and identified with by Gentiles. For us in the twenty-first century to participate in the audience of the New Testament authors is for us to be able to see ourselves, with our background world, as registered in the new community established by Jesus.[15] The Christian community in our time is supposed to be a rectification of *our* history's relation to God.

The second thing to note is that Jesus and his first community retained the covenant understanding of the relation of people to God, and of Israel's history. The community called itself a New Covenant, as fulfilling the promise in Jeremiah cited earlier. Because of this we can employ the ideas of our abstract conception of covenant to help understand Jesus and his covenant. Those notions come from the conception of the Logos, namely obligations to foster right form or justice, right deference to components of life or piety, right relation to existential location or faith, and right address of the ultimate or hope.

With regard to justice, Jesus is to be read as affirming the strong tradition of the moral commandments (for instance, in Matt. 19, against murder, adultery, stealing, false witness, and so forth). He criticized the Pharisees for using obedience to certain Torah prescriptions as excuses not to be just (Mark 7:6–13). Gerd Theissen points out that Jesus in fact had a kind of dual teaching about justice.[16] On the one hand there is a radicalizing of Torah: from the commandment not to kill Jesus moved to command not even being angry (Matt. 5:21–26); from the commandment against adultery Jesus moved to forbid lust (Matt. 5:27–30); and so on with divorce, swearing, retribution, etc. On the other hand there is recognition of realism and tolerance of human weakness that might be understood and even justified in a narrative that goes beyond the commandment-form (that Theissen calls "logia"). So, with regard to non-anger, Jesus lost his temper in chasing the money-changers from the Temple, a pique he took out the next day on a fig tree (Matt. 21:12–22). With regard to adultery, he is recorded (John 8:1–11) as defending an adulteress about to be stoned by saying that only the sinless could

[15] For a splendid elaboration of this point see Rowan Williams' *On Christian Theology*, especially pp. 63–92.   [16] See his *A Theory of Primitive Christian Religion*, pp. 27–31.

condemn her, and accepted the adoration of a "woman who was a sinner" (Luke 7:36–50), forgiving her sins and holding her up as a model to the more cautiously righteous. From these and many other teachings, Christians on the one hand have affirmed a very high standard of justice, even an ethics of perfectionism, and on the other hand have recognized the inability of people in their life's narratives to perform this, hence needing continual forgiveness and further work of sanctification. Both the content of justice and its forms, for instance in rules, policies, or goals, have been much debated, and are currently under debate. But surely Jesus did teach and exemplify the obligations of the covenant for right form, or justice.

With regard to piety, no clear line was drawn in ancient times between what I have distinguished as the obligations of justice – right form – and the obligations of piety – deference to the integrity of the components of our world. But some of the commandments surely fall into the kind of obligation appropriate for deference. For instance, the honoring of father and mother is deference to origins and can stand in considerable tension with obligations of justice when father or mother is unjust. Here too Jesus radicalized the commandment, banning Corban (Mark 7:9–13), which is the giving to God of what otherwise was due to parents. But in his realism he told a disciple who wanted to bury his father that he should let the dead bury the dead (Matt. 8:21–22), said he came to set children against parents, especially in-laws, was distinctly resistant to honoring his mother and other family members (except when he made wine at his mother's request, John 2:1–22), and at his death put her into the hands of his friend John rather than her other children, a very non-Jewish form of honor (John 19:26–27). The commandments about the observance of the Sabbath also might be construed according to the logic of deference. Jesus faithfully attended the Sabbath services in synagogues and the Temple, teaching at them. And yet he famously relaxed the Sabbath requirements, saying that the Sabbath was made for human beings, not the other way around (Mark 2:27; not the view of Gen. 2:2–3 or Ex. 20:8–10). Here again Jesus recognized the fierceness of the obligation and the realistic tolerance of what that obligation might be in human life. Jesus expressed even deeper observations about deference. The rain, he said, falls on the just and unjust alike, and the sun too shines on both. Nature has its own operations and rhythms that do not respect the human moral universe. God cares for birds as well as people. Especially in the last decades Christians have become aware of the vast practical consequences that fall from whether human beings respect the integrity of God's creation. Moreover, we have come to a consciousness that in the vastness of the created cosmos the issues of human justice and injustice are very small indeed, however important to us. Part of proper piety to the world in which we live is deference to its immense indifference, like the sun and rain (Matt. 5:45).

With regard to existential location and the faith to embrace it, again the ancient world did not treat this as a separate kind of obligation. As an existentialist theme tout court, it is anachronistic when applied to the first century. But it is implicit in Jesus' critique of hypocrisy, for instance. A hypocrite is someone who pretends, at least to the outer world, that the situation is something other than it is, for instance regarding prayer and fasting (Matt. 6:1–21) and the "woes" in Matthew 23. The bite of Jesus' teaching on existential location and faith, however, has to do with himself and the kingdom of heaven. John's (8:14–17) Jesus says that the world is in deep delusion if it does not recognize who he is, coming from God and going to God, and that true knowledge comes only with faith in him. Many of the parables (for instance in Matt. 21, 22) about the kingdom of God take the form of "people think this is not the kingdom of God when it really is, so wake up!" Faith was most thematized by Paul, of course (in letters written before the Gospels); for him (for instance, Rom. 7, 8) the existential situation might seem (falsely) to be living sinfully to the law, whereas the reality is the possibility to be living in Christ by faith which makes people really children and heirs of God and genuinely free. The early Christians interpreted Jesus to be the object of faith that provides realism for what their situation is, without which there is delusion and bondage.

With regard to that part of the Logos having to do with one's ultimate value before God, Jesus was eminently clear in affirming Israel's monotheistic commitment to the One God who should be the object of all possible love.[17] The orientation of his entire teaching and cultivated community was to address God faithfully. John (John 17) symbolizes this by citing Jesus to say that he himself is returning to the Father and bringing his community. The ultimate aim of all of life is the religious quest, which is to give glory to God and participate in God's glory (John 17:1–5). What glorifies God, according to John and others (for instance, Paul in Rom. 15:1–13), is the complication of living in a community of love, loving the world so as to make it more loving, loving Jesus as the revelation of the

---

[17] Gerd Theissen takes this to be one of Jesus' two "basic axioms," one that is perfectly continuous with Judaism. The other basic early Christian axiom was faith in a redeemer. See ibid., p. 13.

Father, and loving the Father as the source of the grace to love.[18] The poignancy of Jesus' presentation of himself to God was that he was abandoned: "My God, my God, why have you forsaken me?" (Matt. 27:46). His resurrection was not of this world but consists in being at the right hand of God in heaven. Jesus' presence in the world as glorifying God is only in the Church.

The Logos is four principles harmonized to make a fifth, creative love, I have argued here. Love, of course, is one of the main themes of Jesus' preaching, and I have frequently cited the crucial texts in the Farewell Discourses of John (14–17). Love requires justice but forgives injustice, requires piety but accepts sacrilege, demands faith but offers the grace to have it to those who do not, and demands perfection before God but is willing to present miserable sinners before the throne of grace. Consider Luke's two great parables of love. The Good Samaritan undertakes common justice to the Jewish roadside victim which higher justice dictated that other Jews should administer; he defers to the Jew's different identity, not engaging him in theological debate or even expecting him to repay a Samaritan; he surely finds the situation to be both a religious offense and a dreadful bother, but accepts it and takes care of things; there is no fancy ultimate or divine love in what he does, just fundamental kindness. The father of the Prodigal Son was scrupulous in justice and obligatory generosity to both his sons, welcoming the prodigal with love that was totally undeserved and reaching out to the elder brother who resented that love. Jesus' love set itself on creating perfection, and yet was at its truest when it accepted imperfection.

Taken collectively, these traits of Jesus' life and teaching spell out, at least for his circumstance, how to live before God obligated by the strictest demands and yet to be made acceptable by love's mercy. The early Church did not have these neat distinctions, but it recognized all the points. The Logos does not merely define the obligations for individuals, but in fact obligates individuals to live in covenanted community. The Logos obliges the community and its structures. The response of the earliest Christians was to form a community modeled on what Jesus had started to develop with them, but vastly expanded. Of course there were many circumstances, for instance the entrance of Gentiles into the community, for which Jesus had provided no explicit model or teaching. So the Church worked through the tension of elaborating a developing con-

[18] For an elaboration of this sense of glory, see Rowan Williams' *On Christian Theology*, pp. 254–61.

tinuation of what Jesus had started. To use the metaphor of the Church as the Body of Christ, that body was growing very fast.

The Church was supposed to be the ideal community that embodies the New Covenant. The New Covenant should express all the obligations – of justice, piety, faith, hope, and love – but under conditions of steady and forceful expressions of forgiveness, mercy, tolerance, and support. Part of doing this requires faith that Jesus, the initiator of this community, in fact is the revelation of God and that this community is a true religious reality. Therefore the heart of the community is the remembrance of Jesus and worship of him as the agent who makes the community possible. Another part, however, is the struggle to determine just what the community should be and do, under changed conditions. For this the early Church conceived its work to be under the guidance of the Holy Spirit which interprets Jesus, completes the teachings he lacked time to give, and directs the Church in its responses. At least this is the way the early Church, as recorded by John and Paul, understood things.

In this understanding, Jesus is both in the Church and out of it. He is in the Church as its initiating cause, through the Church's regular memory of him and its progressive interpretations of his teachings. The Eucharist especially is a place of the presence of Christ. To shift the symbol only slightly, the Church itself becomes the Body of Christ by means of which he lives in historical resurrection. So one meaning of an individual's being "in Christ" is to be in the Church as a part of Christ's body with a continuing mission that is also the glorification of God.

In another sense the risen Christ is not exhausted in the Church but stands above it as a judge, as symbolized in the Ascension and the Second Coming. Because of the discontinuities of historical existence, the Church is never complete at any time. It is always fair to ask, as the Church's leaders must, whether the Church's internal forms and external addresses to the world are properly just, properly deferential, properly faithful to the existential situation, and properly hopeful in bringing all things home to God. And to ask this is to imagine Jesus as judge. In this sense, for an individual to be "in Christ" might well mean standing in some kind of external creative opposition to the Church, or at least to a part of it. *Because the Church does not exhaust Jesus Christ, neither does the Church exhaust life in Christ.* The relevant identity of Jesus Christ for individuals in this circumstance is not his first-century image but whatever would be the personification of justice, piety, faith, hope, and love in the individuals' situation. As Matthew 25:31–46 put it, "Truly I tell you, just as you did it to one of the least of these who are members of my family, you did it to me." To be "in Christ" in this sense is to relate to Jesus as the incarnation of the Logos as it applies to one's own circumstances.

Therefore, growing into Christ means not imitation of Jesus' first-century life per se but proper imitation of how the Logos he incarnated in his circumstances should be incarnated in one's own. This is impossible without the creativity the early Church knew as the Holy Spirit. The Holy Spirit is the creativity of God creating harmonies that embody the Logos. The relevance of that creativity for personal and communal life is the finding of the right structures of justice for one's circumstances, the right forms of piety for the human, social, and natural world, the right kinds of engagements of the natural, social, and human world, and the right kinds of religious quest for one's time.

Why associate this "growing into Christ" with the person of Jesus rather than with some universal "social ethic" of Jesus? The answer lies in the person of Jesus apprehended as the continuing revelation of God, with the historical significance of creating a new reality. The answer lies also with the continuity of personification of the Logos in Jesus from one historical circumstance to all others. The answer in addition has to do with the role of the Holy Spirit to interpret Jesus as both person and divine revelation. These are the topics of the next section. Such metaphysical questions, however, should not deflect attention from the concrete questions of what particular individuals should do to be in Jesus, the topic of the next chapter.

JESUS CHRIST OUR COMMUNION WITH GOD

In what sense can Jesus be considered divine and how, as divine, does he relate to the Father, the Creator? The question can be asked in two connected contexts. The bottom-line context for this study of Christological symbols is our own: how in our time and cultural situation might we think of Jesus as divine, and how does this fit into contemporary Trinitarian thinking? But before that we need at least to acknowledge the question in terms that address the context of the first-century Christians who established the symbols with which Christianity still expresses itself. Then of course we need to ask how to get from the latter to the former in normative ways.

How can we make sense of the deification of the historical Jesus in the first generation or two after his death? Gerd Theissen asks the question in terms of how the cultural sign system of the early Christians moved from the Jewish religion of Jesus, however he pushed its margins, to the extraordinarily un-Jewish view that a man "whose family we know" could be a heavenly resident at the right hand of God, a Son of God. Theissen points out, for instance, that Judaism would abhor the sexual union of divine and human beings, as in the birth narratives in Matthew and Luke, because such congress between the Sons of God and the daughters of men gave rise to the violence occasioning Noah's flood (Gen. 6:1–8); it is an improper mixture of kinds.[19] Much of the transformation would be due to the incorporation of Gentiles into the Church, which explains how the new deifying signs could be acceptable in Christianity. But that does not explain why the Christian movement changed so as to have such signs that would appeal to Gentiles in the first place.

In this regard, Theissen suggests that the development of the Christian sign system deifying Jesus was itself a continuation and intensification of the development of Jewish monotheism itself, paradoxical as that might seem in light of the addition of Jesus Christ and the Holy Spirit as deities. Theissen looks first at the development of monotheism, which he says became clear and central to Israel only during the Exile.[20] Prior to that Israel's religion had been generally monolatrous: that is, the Israelites assumed that there is one God which is theirs, by the adoption and covenant stories of Exodus, but also that there are many other Gods, worshipped by other nations, as well as a fairly well-populated heavenly court with Sons of Gods, angels (messengers to humanity), and other ranks of beings, for instance cherubim and seraphim. Yahweh did well during the Exodus, the conquest of Canaan, and the establishment of the extensive kingdom of David and Solomon. Political troubles of subsequent kings might be explained for a while in terms of the apostasy of Israel serving, and perhaps strengthening, other Gods. But the total defeat of first Israel in the north and then Judah in the south, with the removal of the people from the land onto which they had been moved by Yahweh back to where they were nothing was intolerable cognitive dissonance with the monolatrous worship of Yahweh. The Jewish response was not to abandon Yahweh, as might be expected, but rather to intensify devotion to him so as to claim that the other Gods did not exist and that what was claimed about Yahweh was a "competitive outdoing of the other gods and the

---

[19] See his *A Theory of Primitive Christian Religion*, p. 56.   [20] Ibid., pp. 41–60.

peoples who worship them. In the face of the one and only God they all become ridiculous 'nothings.'"[21]

The dynamic sign world of the earliest Jewish Christians, according to Theissen, continued this "dynamism of monotheism":

> The *experience of crisis* here is the crucifixion as the refutation of the expectations attached to Jesus. The Easter appearances made it possible to transform this defeat into a victory of the exalted one over his judges and the world. The deepest humiliation could be compensated for only by an exaltation which outdid everything. The dissonance of the cross was got over by elevating the crucified Jesus to a status equal to God.[22]

This elevation confirmed an existing belief (at least among Pharisees) that God could raise the dead to new life *ex nihilo* (Rom. 4:17) and the new symbol systems for Jesus competitively outbid all rivals, either in the authority structure of Temple Judaism or in that of Rome, both of which had judged and condemned Jesus. Isaiah 45:22–23 had sung the monotheistic principle: "Turn to me and be saved, all the ends of the earth! For I am God, and there is no other. By myself I have sworn, from my mouth has gone forth in righteousness a word that shall not return: 'To me every knee shall bow, every tongue shall swear.'" Paul quotes the quote in his Philippians hymn (2:6–11) discussed in the previous chapter, but applies it to Jesus as Lord, not to God. Paul quotes it again in Romans 14:11 where the referent is ambiguous, either God or Christ the Lord of the dead and the living.

Though much recommends Theissen's scheme, there are other considerations as well. Israel from much earlier had affirmed that God was the creator of the world but perhaps had not reflected on how that might be, particularly on the problems of creating by Committee. During the exile they were among an extraordinarily cosmopolitan people at the western end of the Silk Road, and participated in the greatest court in the world of that day (the Zhou Dynasty being in disastrous decline, as their contemporary Confucius complained, and India not yet having been unified). Moreover they were among people, the Persians, whose own religion, Zoroastrianism, was forming into one of the great Axial Age cultures, for the first time conceiving of the universe as a whole and the human individual as one who could relate to the principles of the universe in some disconnection from broken identifications with place and tribe. The genius of the Exilic prophets was to bring into tension the universalizing and totalizing elements of cosmopolitan Axial Age relig-

---

[21] Ibid., p. 43.   [22] Ibid.

ion with the tribal particularity of the earlier religion of Israel. Isaiah pushed the former and Ezekiel the latter, but each held both sides together: Yahweh created the entire vast physical cosmos and is Lord of all nations, and his earthly residence is in Jerusalem where he has a tribal nation of priests who had better be pure (as Ezra-Nehemiah said). The dynamic of changing conceptions of the creator God operated as much through the dialectic of the unity of the act of creation and the vast diversity of what is created (as I argued in chapter 1) as on psycho-social reaction to the dissonance of defeat (that Theissen lifts up). The former dialectic in fact served the psycho-social purpose by providing a transformed, ready, monotheistic model.

Cognitive dissonance and compensation by elevating the signs for Jesus to deity may well be a persuasive explanatory principle for the earliest Christians who had known Jesus personally. But it would merely have been a puzzle to those who had not previously known and identified with Jesus, who would have to be attracted to Jesus as deity for reasons having to do with their own situation. In point of fact, in the not very long run, perhaps not much longer than the generation who had known Jesus personally and the next generation or two who talked with them, Christianity ceased to be a form of Judaism. The Christian symbols of Jesus were not easily taken to be an extension of Jewish monotheism, and the Church became overwhelmingly Gentile. So we have a complicated situation, with a Gentile reinterpretation of the heritage of Israel giving meanings to Jesus that address existential situations largely different from those of Israel. What were these religious existential situations? It is hard to tell from such distance. We have few records from any but the literate classes. But they include at least the following.

First, with the breakdown of local and tribal identifications for people, and recognition of how vast the world is with so many nations and cultures, there was a need for a conception of a Creator who is equally God for all people and places, not a God tied to a particular place or nation.

Second, with the breakdown of local sacrifices in the creation of Empire and the compromising of local religions with cosmopolitan visions and imperial religions, there was a need for genuine and effective new symbols of sacrificial atonement. Sacrificial religions and mystery cults were rife in the first century, and the Christian symbol system was more potent, at least for many, than the Roman family rituals, Mithraism, the Roman version of Isis and Osiris, and other pagan rites and imported religions (of which Second Temple Judaism was one).

Third, with the breakdown of localism there was a deep anxiety about homelessness, or about how to find a home in a cosmos represented by an alien Empire. The Cosmic Christ responded to that need for those who could relate in a personal way to Jesus who is that Cosmic Christ.

Fourth, or perhaps part of the third, was the situation of dubious divinity in government. The Flavian emperors were declaring themselves divine, but their rule was not regarded as divinely just. Jesus as the Cosmic King was the proper image of divine rule.

Fifth, as the conception of God as creator became more and more transcendent, divinity seemed farther and farther from the human. Conceptions of intermediate heavenly beings flourished in the Roman world, as illustrated in the New Testament writings. Symbolized as at once human and divine, Jesus economized neatly in that mediation. Although the doctrinal symbol of the two natures was long in coming, its roots are in the New Testament, for instance, in the Philippians passage quoted.

Sixth, with the imperial dislocation, people lacked not only a sense of home but also of history. How can people have an identity in history without a history of their own? Their own family history was often forgotten in the dislocations or, worse, was remembered as a disaster. With Christianity the Gentiles could buy into a people-making history by adopting that of Israel as leading to Christ and the Church. The more typical first- and second-century rabbinic understanding of the history of Israel was very different from the Christian one. The rabbinic understanding was not easily available to Gentiles, however, because they were not part of its history of Israel, indeed were distinguished from Israel precisely as Gentiles. Gentile Christians could be the "new Israel" because the "old Israel" from which they were excluded had been extended to include them. So they could adopt the history of the "old covenant" at a second remove from real identification, all the while coping with their own pagan past. The exaltation of Jesus as a cosmic priest after the order of Melchizedek in Hebrews picks a Gentile Canaanite as model, and develops Jesus' priestly service in terms of the Mosaic tent of the tabernacle, which was not attached to any place, rather than of the Temple in Jerusalem; the same book (Heb. 8:8–13) cites Jeremiah's promise of a new covenant, not an entirely attractive passage for other Second Temple Jews.

Seventh, also because of the imperial dislocation and the abundance of attractive but alien religious cultures, many people in the first century were profoundly lonely. Not only feeling deeply stained, or cosmically homeless, or in a chaotic ungoverned world, or cut off from identifying tradition, they had to face the singular God alone. Jesus was promised as friend.

Eighth, and finally for this list, the first century was a time of deep skepticism about whether life mattered. "What is truth?" Sometimes this was expressed in terms of questions about whether there was an after-life that mattered; other times it was expressed in various forms of phil-osophical nihilism or Stoicism. Christianity answered with a schematization of the Creator that affirms that, yes, there is a Judge, Jesus, who calls everyone to a personal and communal life of love and kindness. What matters is not winning or losing but being Jesus' person.

These eight, of course, are the symbols under investigation in this book (distinguishing the Cosmic Christ from the Cosmic King and Judge). The first century as characterized here is not unlike the twenty-first.

But what truth is there in these symbols that deify the historical Jesus? Is there any way by which we twenty-first century people can receive true, valid, existentially powerful answers to our versions of these ques-tions by engaging God with the symbols of Jesus deified? Three positive responses are possible, the first of which will be made here, the second in the next chapter, and the third in chapter 7.

The first is that it is legitimate, from our perspective as well as that of the first and intervening centuries, to symbolize Jesus as God in the fol-lowing sense. God the Creator, according to the metaphysical argument in chapter 1, creates the world as expressing the harmony of the Logos principles of form, contents to be formed, existential location, and ulti-mate value. This is complicated in the human sphere by the fact that those principles are norms for ideal life as well as expressed in whatever actually happens, and that people are created under obligation. The obligations are both personal and social, for few things people do are not functions of conjoint actions. Moreover, because it is impossible to be perfect according to the norms, people find ways of rejecting their created status and project, denying the norms of any or all sorts, and the creation is frustrated or incomplete.

Jesus came into the public world and showed how to live as a proper creature in the cultural terms of Israel in his time, obligated by the norms, accepting them and the negative judgments of failure, and living in the mercy of the Creator with love. He began a small community that, after his crucifixion, reformed so as to continue and expand the Way of Jesus. In this community, individuals could find a New Being (2 Cor. 5:17) of creative life as redeemed sinners, and the community itself, to the extent it continues to re-embody the nature and work of Jesus, is a New Covenant. The Way in which individuals and the community itself could participate in the ongoing life of Jesus, now resurrected in at least this sense, is very complicated as indicated above. It requires the Holy Spirit because the Way always needs to be creative, as God is creative, both bringing things to new harmonies in the Logos and breaking out of those boundaries to extend the life of Jesus in individuals and their community. The New Being and the New Covenant are advances in creation.

Jesus is divine in the historical sense of overcoming the block to the continued creation of the human according to the ideals of the Logos by establishing and actually being (raised) in New Beings and the New Covenant community. He himself in life was only human and offered a way of living with sin and obligations in love of the just and merciful God. That Way is available to anyone who understands the cultural definitions of the terms. If Jesus' humanity did not have the integrity of the human, neither his personal behavior nor the community of kind friends that he founded would be a Way others could enter. But having entered it, sinning redeemed people constitute Jesus as the Creator of the New Being and New Covenant within history. This was light not being overcome by darkness. Jesus did not redeem because he was divine but was divine because he redeems.

Participating in Jesus, in the senses discussed above, is a condition for the actuality of this New Being and New Covenant. Participation requires attending to the norms of the Logos, not as they might have been relevant in Jesus' time and place but as relevant to the time and place of any contemporary person or community. For our time, the living reality of Jesus can only be found in addressing the twenty-first-century needs for justice, pious deference, existential faith, and religious hope. A similar issue faced the Gentile Christians of the first and second centuries whose covenantal conditions were not those of Galilee or even Israel. Because it is Jesus' historical work that makes him God, he is God in history, and that history is limited. Jesus is not God in this sense outside the history of earth. Indeed he is not God outside the historical conditions in which people can adopt the history of Israel that makes Christian sense of these matters. So he is not God for other cultures. But he is God wherever people can "put him on," as Paul puts it (Rom. 13:14), wherever people can be New Beings in a New Covenant because of faith that his life, and their participation in it, is God's revealed way forward.

Jesus thus is God in yet another sense, namely, that he is the special embodiment or incarnation of the divine Logos that is made relevant for the redemption or continued creation of the human. That Logos is indeed the character of the eternal and universal Creator. Jesus Christ is the Logos made relevant for the salvation of human beings, taking "salvation" to cover the answering of the existential issues listed above and more. This does have cosmic significance for humans: it is the divine Logos relevant and working to create properly kind and free human beings in community. The transcendental principles of supernovae and the evolution of slime-molds are those that become norms with judgment and forgiveness within the human sphere. Therefore Jesus is for humans the Cosmic Christ. Insofar as the symbol of kingship is relevant to human judgment and mercy, Jesus as king is the Cosmic King. Were it not for the Logos there would be no obvious way to connect Jesus and his community of kind friends, telling themselves and others about the judgment and mercy of God, with God the Creator. But the Logos is the transcendental form of all creation, that in and by which all things are made that are made, and the mediator of the Creator to the human condition. This is what Jesus makes constitutive of the new creation.

These claims about the divinity of Jesus are by no means exclusivistic. Other religions might express the human predicament differently, perhaps not as universally as Christians. Judaism, for instance, expresses the predicament less as a universally human one than as a predicament special to Israel (though Enlightenment Judaism does universalize the matter). East Asian, South Asian, and traditional religions also have different expressions. They might pick up on aspects of religious predicament Christianity misses, or miss some that Christianity gets. They might have very different solutions to the predicament. Whether they do is a matter for comparative theology to study. These claims about the divinity of Jesus are indeed claimed to be true for those who enter into the life of Jesus in the ways described (and soon to be discussed in more detail). Anyone, even those who do not enter into Jesus and his Way, should be able to understand why that Way is valid for Christians and why it is true for them to say that Jesus is divine in the senses mentioned.

How does this interpretation of the symbol of Jesus as Second Person of the Trinity stand with regard to the historical expressions of that doctrine? It is a solid Logos Christology, with a metaphysical understanding of the inter-definition of the Logos, Spirit, and Father-source that is similar in spirit to, if different in metaphysics from, the thinking in the fourth- and fifth-century debates. In terms of those debates it is an economic Trinitarianism in that all the Persons of the Trinity are defined in terms of creation, not apart from creation. But also, in that it claims that the creation is contained within God and is not external, it is also an immanent Trinitarianism.[23] It affirms that the act of any one Person of the Trinity is the act of the other two also. With respect to the Logos, this theory is anti-Arian in affirming the eternity of the Logos: time itself is created with the Logos. With respect to Jesus Christ being historical, and incarnating the Logos only in time, it is Arian: there was a time before the Logos was incarnate in Jesus and his ongoing living body. With respect to the two natures of Christ, it is thoroughly Chalcedonian in affirming that Jesus was fully and only a human being, like us, and that he also incarnated the Logos so as fully to be God working with human beings in history to redeem them and establish the New Being and New Covenant: God could not be more God than Jesus to be historically located and working redemptively as Creator in the human sphere. With regard to the real agenda of Chalcedon, it is Nestorian and anti-Chalcedonian in emphasizing the human side of Jesus as the key to understanding God-for-human-beings in Jesus Christ.

The issue here is not historical orthodoxy as defined by the councils, however, but whether the symbols of Jesus as divine are true for those who put them on. They cannot be put on in ways that are insensitive to their symbolic character. They are indexical in their claims to truth, not metaphysically iconic, to use the earlier distinction. The question of truth is not a matter of whether people decide to believe in Jesus as the symbols say. It is rather that, when they do decide so to believe, the true nature of God is carried over into them in the respects in which their needs for salvation in Christ interpret God. The criteria for judging that case, in part, depend on the validity of the symbols of the historical Jesus, Jesus as friend, and Jesus the Eschatological Savior, topics of the following chapters.

---

[23] On this point, see Hermann Deuser's "Neville's Theology of Creation, Covenant, and Trinity."

Plate One: The lines of dreams

These seven canvases trace three evolutions: of the human spirit, of the cosmos, and of human understanding of the cosmos. The perspective of The *lines of dreams* looks out on the sharply edged clear mountain/seascape (a view of California's Big Sur) from within a cave-womb on which are etched chthonic figures from many cultures, "dream time" icons as the Native Australians call them. Both as primitive responses to nature and deep psychic images stretching toward the ego's consciousness, these figures line a womb-wall that explodes outward in light across the next two canvases. Each canvas shifts perspective until perspective itself dissolves in ambiguity in plates 6 and 7.

Plate Two: Having arrived, we planted and the earth was fertile

With horizontal perspective on the earth's surface and organized like a first-person narrative, this canvas quotes Millet's *Angelus for Adam and Eve* figures, with golden apples (the artist's parents were apple farmers) in the basket with a serpent; Millet's *The Sower* is quoted as the grim reaper walking with shears through a rose ranch (in Petaluma, California). Christo's umbrellas are sited among the succulents that live on blown spray along the coast, among the many artistic works quoted and commented on in these seven canvases. The rainbow of fiery colors begins from the pot of gold of human work and arcs across the sky, breaking the boundaries of an earth-bound narrative of birth, hope for prosperity, work, imposition of human order, and judgment.

Plate Three: God's rainbow's really fire, not light and water

Noah's rainbow separates the plane of earth from the heavens, marking God's promise not to open again the gates of heaven's waters that would undo created order. The heavens, drawn from patterns in Tlinget Indian featherwork, look on the one hand like the roiling waters of the pre-creation chaos, now held back by the divine word of promise. On the other hand they seductively beckon like Northern Lights. The rainbow's swoop of color rises in plate two, plunges forward and down in plate 3, disappearing beneath the subject in 4 to emerge lower right, rising to a new crest in 5 in the form of a celestial river on which space-craft sail in 6 where the colors explode again, there and in 7.

Plate Four: Behold the past, a place we knew not when we dwelt there

From high orbit plate 4 looks down at the earth from the perspective of space-travellers who have left it, glancing back in wonder before turning spaceward. But it appears concave like the Pantokrator's dome of some great cathedral (see figure 7), and the earth is circled with Byzantine tesserae, a pattern from Ravenna. The flow of the rainbow and river moving against the mosaic halo spins the earth around a center-point from which much of its landmass can be seen, though the view is exaggerated here. The earth is not the center or source of life, but a brief clump of gases spun by vaster currents. Though the apparent center of the seven-canvas painting, the centrality the ancients accorded the earth is represented here as only human artifice now objectified and transcended.

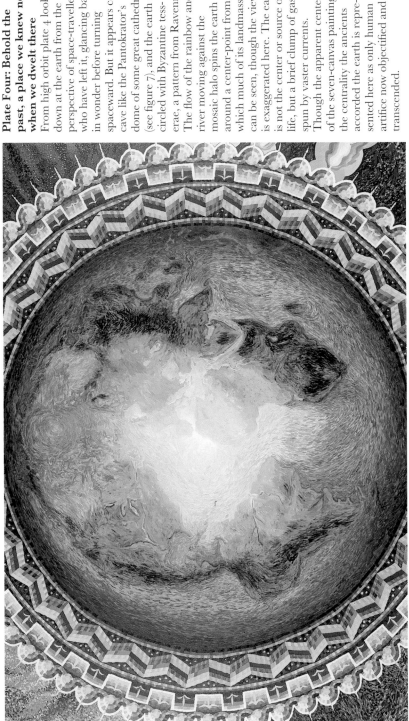

Plate Five: What lines are there in the ether?

The ancient and most modern visions characterize the outward look toward the cosmos, the direction of human longing and adventure. In the upper left are Near Eastern constellations with the narrative lines drawn in, the imaginative icons of the ancient world. Through the center curve two motifs. One is a representation of the "river of time," comprised of blood-red arrows, extrapolated from a schematic diagram of the expansion of matter from the Big Bang published by some cosmologists from MIT. The other is a fairly literal copy of photographs of gamma radiation from the Big Bang taken by the COBE telescope and supplied by NASA scientists. The sensuous globular egg-forms of the gamma rays entwine with the sperm-like arrows to place the source of cosmic fertility in the blast of gasses rather than the anthropocentric human habitat.

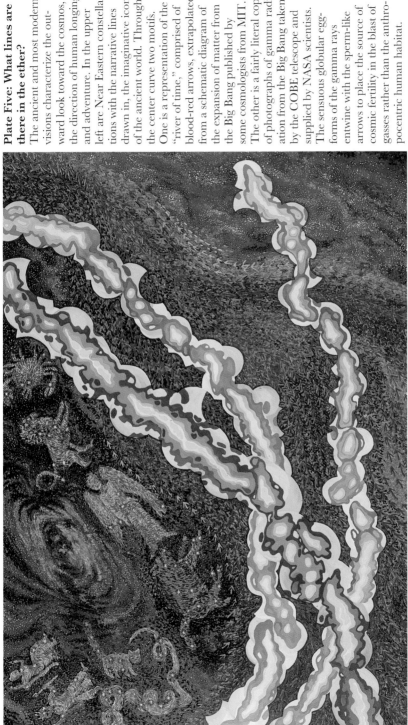

Plate Six: O what deaths are these, the supernovas?

Two answers are given to the question. One is the price in blood, which the arrows of time's river come to signify, paid by the space explorers of our generation. An armada of telescopes (COBE, the Hubble, etc.) flies off along the river. The supernovas themselves are the deaths of stars imploding, marking at once their ending and the fertilization of further space with their radiant remains. At the bottom center is a portrait in radio waves of Cassiopeia A, which exploded in 1667 CE; in the upper right and in plate 7 is a portrait in visible light of supernova 1987A. Fixed-point perspective is wholly lost in this canvas: are we looking back toward the Big Bang, toward the galactic core, or out toward the future of our place of origin?

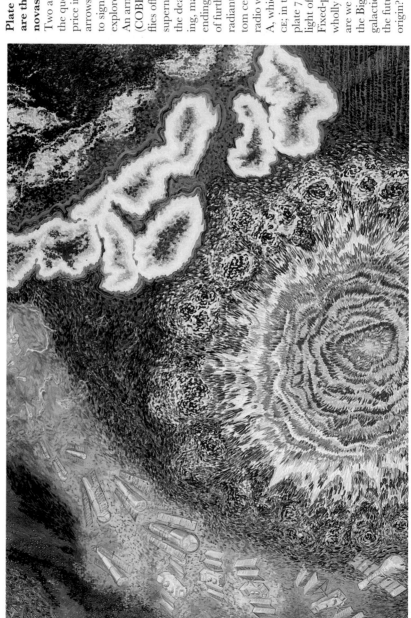

Plate Seven: In the end

The supernovas are crises of order and entropy. Begun as a depiction of the background radiation from the Big Bang, this canvas came to foreshadow ultimate entropy. In the end, the rounds and curves of living forms, the corners and compartments of our works, the talk, the trade, the learning and the loving of our cities, turn to straight line order, simple inertia, things moving without touching, farther and less relevant. Geometry simplifies and colors fade toward black. Time runs out to stillness and the dark. This book argues that creating time's arc from Alpha to Omega, God's eternal fire burns hot and timeless, birthing dreamlines, heaven's icons in the cosmos's cave.

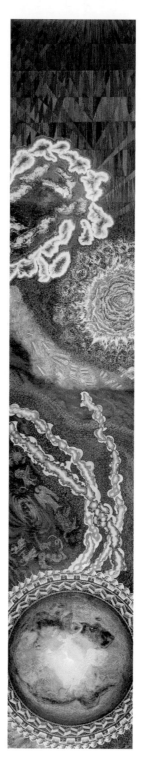

CHAPTER FIVE

The historical Jesus and the Incarnate Word

THE HISTORICAL JESUS AND THE CHRIST OF FAITH

Much of the history of Christian theology in Europe and its colonies has consisted in efforts to clarify and establish theoretical doctrines, from the early Apologists through the Patristic debates, the great Orthodox and Western medieval systems, the Protestant reformers and Counter-Reformation thinkers, down to great twentieth-century systematic theologians such as Barth, Rahner, Tillich, and Zizioulis. In the last two hundred or more years, however, great Christological interest has focused on what could be known historically about Jesus, with deliberate separation of that inquiry from the critical elaboration of doctrine. The series of "quests for the historical Jesus" have had the great advantage of associating Christian theological interests with the leading theory and practice in contemporary historical and social sciences.[1] At the same

[1] *The Quest for the Historical Jesus* was the title of Albert Schweitzer's classic (first edition, 1906) study that summarized and evaluated the nineteenth-century work. The rise of Neo-Orthodoxy in the third decade of the twentieth century distracted much attention from the quest. Then in the mid-century interest in the historical Jesus was revived by a synergistic confluence of the demythologizing strategy of Rudolf Bultmann with the hermeneutics of Heidegger and Gadamer, as illustrated, say, in the work of Schubert Ogden and Ray L. Hart. See James M. Robinson's *New Quest for the Historical Jesus*. The social revolutions in America and Europe of the 1960s sparked interests, first, in applying social scientific knowledge to the understanding of the biblical texts, as in the work of Howard Clark Kee, and then in using contemporary cultural-political categories to reinterpret Jesus, as in the studies of John Dominic Crossan, Richard Horsley, and Marcus Borg. Somewhat in reaction to the study of Jesus as an ideological ally is the deliberately more skeptical historical work of scholars such as E. P. Sanders, Paula Fredriksen, and Geza Vermes. For a comprehensive analysis of the theological problems in Christology occasioned by the quests for the historical Jesus, see Wesley J. Wildman's *Fidelity with Plausibility*, chapters 1–2. See that book also for the connections with the sciences, in chapter 3. The remaining chapters of Wildman's book analyze options for Christology in light of the failure of the quest for the historical Jesus to provide a grounding for classical doctrines asserting absolutistic claims for Jesus, in Troeltsch's meaning of that term. Wildman treats all the options, like the absolutistic Christologies, as sets of doctrines, not symbols to be understood in terms of their functions in engagement. My own position is that doctrine emerges from a dialectical relation between the symbols used in faith and the metaphysics or philosophy that sets their bounds, and most of the alleged Christological doctrines are the symbols understood in naive disjunction from their philosophical ground.

time, the "quests" have the advantage of being of interest to Christians across a wide spectrum of theological commitments, from conservative to liberal, especially within Protestantism.

The theology of symbolic engagement is different from both the doctrinal and the historical approaches, as will be discussed in this section, although there have been overlapping concerns. The quests for the historical Jesus have had to work with great ingenuity to decipher how the symbols for Jesus arose and what they meant at various times. In particular, they have had to discover through careful historiography how so many of the symbols of the long-developing religion of Israel were transformed to Christian meanings that were referential to mainly Gentile congregations, as discussed in the previous chapter. Many of the doctrinal discussions as well, though couched in the form of attempting to establish descriptions of Jesus as Lord and Savior (or whatever), in fact make more sense when interpreted as symbols that are true through indexical reference rather than iconic. Tillich went so far as to treat other people's doctrines as symbols, and sometimes his own as well.[2] This is especially true of theological traditions such as the Orthodox, Roman, and Anglican that arise more out of liturgy where the symbols are used and performed than out of biblical studies or metaphysics where they are read as elements in narrative or theory.

The argument of the previous chapter produced the claim that the symbols of deity for Jesus revolve around his historical person and the continuity of that person in and above the Church, a conclusion of the chapter before that as well. Therefore we must relate the symbols to the historical Jesus. Indeed, in our time, "the historical Jesus" has itself become a powerful Christological symbol.

The scrupulous effort in the eighteenth- and nineteenth-century quests for the historical Jesus to prescind from theological and symbolic construals of Jesus was based on new conceptions of history as a science. Other social sciences such as sociology, psychology, and archeology have been added to historical science in the twentieth century, as well as theory-laden literary critical methods such as reader-response and genre analysis, all aiming to understand the first-century documents about Jesus in their historical setting. For many of the early historical scholars, the quest was itself a theologically driven act of piety. The European Enlightenment skepticism about anything that could not be proved by science, most especially miracles and such that seemed directly to

---

[2] He did this throughout his work, but especially in the third volume of the *Systematic Theology*.

contradict scientific explanation, had moved into historical research itself. Given a strong hermeneutical suspicion about any ancient source that had an interest in the story it told, nearly everything could be doubted. We delight to discover that Homer, the alleged author of the Iliad and the Odyssey, never really existed, and those texts were in fact the editing together of many different strands of poetic legend by a much later redactor, himself a bard, likely blind, and probably also named Homer. The legends of Christianity suffered mightily from such debunking.

The quest for the historical Jesus, at least for many scholars, aimed to prove that there was in fact good scientific historical evidence to support the foundational Christian claims about Jesus. The research turned out otherwise, however. Very little could be established with skeptical rigor about Jesus. Some German theologians quickly turned to redefine Christianity in moral terms rather than doctrinal claims about Jesus: Christianity defines the moral life of high civilization. Much of later theological liberalism continues this response. Other thinkers simply gave up on Christianity. Yet others sharply distinguished the historical Jesus from the Christ of faith, the Christ described in classical doctrines and represented in classical symbols. For them, Christianity did not care about the historical Jesus but only about the Christ of faith. The Christ of faith is known by faith. For some, this meant faith in an authority such as the Bible or the magisterium of the Roman Catholic Church. Evangelical Protestant fundamentalism is one extreme of this reaction. For others, the Christ of faith is known in the Church's direct encounter in faith with the Word of God, to which the Bible is a witness, the position of Neo-Orthodoxy so magnificently expressed by Karl Barth. Meanwhile, what little could be known by scientific history, according to Albert Schweitzer, for instance, who summed up the nineteenth century's quest, was that Jesus was something of an embarrassing apocalyptic extremist, believing sincerely but falsely in the very close end of the world. The Jesus known by scientific history was demonstrated by that same empirical history to have been mistaken. So Schweitzer turned to music and good works in Africa, art and moral fervor being the only good things left in Christianity.

What a great relief then when Rudolf Bultmann in the first half of the twentieth century refocused the question of biblical theology from the scientific history of Jesus to the translating of the ancient symbols into the existential truths of late modernity. Bultmann could treat the representations of Jesus and other matters of early Christian doctrine as myths, thereby evading the criticism of scientific history that treated them as bad science. He demythologized those myths with the language of existentialism that had its own authoritative truth in his time, and the existentialists concepts of faith and authenticity served to remythologize the early Christological claims in a late-modern symbol system that could undergird the practice of Christianity. In many respects, although not all, Paul Tillich can be read as developing Bultmann's demythologized biblical theology into a full-scale systematic theology. A striking characteristic of this movement was a concentration on the writings of Paul, rather than the synoptic gospels, as the proper expression of faith interpreted by Augustine, Luther, and Kierkegaard. The synoptic gospels were thought to be tainted as unreliable by the quest for the historical Jesus, and also were associated with social gospel liberalism that was perceived to have sacrificed Christianity for an ethical program of progress itself given the lie by the World Wars.

By the 1970s or even a little earlier the quest for the historical Jesus was renewed with somewhat different impulses. One was the enthusiasm of the social revolutionary movements in America and Europe that rejected existentialism, individualism, and Paul in favor of a radical, not progressive, social gospel supposedly found in the gospels. Perhaps reading in an unfair amount of proleptic Marxism, thinkers from the radical social movement such as Crossan interpreted Jesus as less an apocalyptic extremist than a social revolutionary. Yet another impulse came from the interest in Jesus on the part of Jewish scholars, an impulse itself fed by the extraordinary convulsions in Jewish theology after the Holocaust and also in Christian theology regarding how to interpret the Jewish people. Geza Vermes and Paula Fredriksen represent this impulse. Finally, in many important universities there was a relocation of the quest for the historical Jesus from divinity schools with a theological orientation to history departments where it was part of the historical and social scientific study of late antiquity. In this context "Christian Origins," as the study of New Testament is now called, is intimately and intrinsically tied with developing Judaism and interactions with other religions of the period. The results of the latest quest for the historical Jesus are extraordinarily rich, and laced with the showbiz humor of the Jesus Seminar voting on which sayings of Jesus are authentic.[3]

[3] A solid and very helpful summary of current biblical resources for Christology is in Roger Haight's *Jesus: Symbol of God*, especially chapter 3.

In a few respects, the theology of symbolic engagement is a continuation of Bultmann's project. Surely its discussion of existential location and faith is a direct derivative of that by way of Tillich. But in many respects, it is very different from Bultmann's project. To begin with, the discussion of existential location is located within the larger discussion of the obligations imposed by the Logos, which has three other equally basic terms. The concern for justice, or right form, was an important dimension of culture, for Tillich for instance, but it was not put at the heart of his theology. Instead, it was important mainly because of how it bears upon the authentic will, the reconciled spirit. The concern for deference or piety hardly registered at all in existential theology. Partly this was because the insistent demands of coping with ecological degradation had not reached crisis consciousness, in the heyday of Christian existentialism. But more it was because the considerable aesthetic consciousness of the existential theologians was turned to matters of the inward heart, not to external and objective matters to which the inward human heart could be a clear and present danger. The heart of existential theology, of course, is the presentation of the self before the Ultimate; in this respect its emphasis on defining the human through the religious quest is developed by the theology of symbolic engagement. But it had no tolerance for notions of value in any objective or genuinely aesthetic (perceptive) sense; existentialism largely displaced objective value with the subjective problematic of the inauthentic or authentic will. In this respect, the theology of symbolic engagement introduces an alien element.

With its emphasis on faith and the authenticity of the interior will, existential theology has an ineluctably individualistic cast quite at odds with the cultural semiotic orientation of the theology of symbolic engagement. The individualism has roots in Luther's nominalism and insistence that justification is by faith alone and not by works. The juxtaposition of faith and works makes the theological action turn very centrally on the interior will, not on whether what Christians do actually leads to more just conditions, more careful deference to nature, or even to presenting something good to God.

With respect to the historical Jesus, the positions I develop in this volume are not reducible to demythologizing the ancient texts and re-expressing them in the language of current imagination, although at least the latter is part of the project. Rather, I claimed at the conclusion of the previous chapter that contemporary Christians can participate in the historical Jesus and by means of that engage God truly in respect of the issues involved in Christian salvation. Just who can this historical Jesus be, such that we can participate in him?

The first point to make about the historical Jesus is that he is not limited to the individual studied in the quest for the historical Jesus. Rather, the historical Jesus includes the reception of that person by his community after the crucifixion, just as any one else's identity includes how they are interpreted and responded to. The reception is the historical reality of Jesus, just as historical as the events of Jesus' own subjective life. Furthermore, given the care with which Christians have constantly worked at receiving Jesus generation after generation, the real historical Jesus includes all the directions of Christian dispersal around the globe, and in all generations down to now. Jesus is received in the cultural forms of the diverse cultures receiving him, as in Stella's *Creche* (figure 12, p. 170 below). This chapter about the historical Jesus is thus very little about his personal biography, including birth legends and miracle stories, and very much about his objective identity in and for the Church, today as much during the time of his subjective life.

This is not the only meaning of historical identity. Many people, including most of the scholars in the quest for the historical Jesus, would insist on limiting it to a person living with subjective consciousness. But a person's influence and reception is what a historian would include in writing a biography, for instance of Caesar or St. Francis. Jesus' particular self-consciousness is only part of the historical Jesus. So I would say that the identity of the historical Jesus includes Jesus' own personal life as a living subjective consciousness plus his identity as a personal force among those who have known and responded to him. These two aspects of his historical identity overlapped in time during his ministry on Earth, and the documents for the quest for the historical Jesus express how he was received, from which some historians attempt to get at his own inner beliefs as a subjective person. The attempt to isolate the personal Jesus from his relations with his community of disciples is not a helpful abstraction. The concrete reality of his life on Earth included and was much defined by the community of love he attempted to establish among his disciples (John 13–17). This point is especially powerful for Western readers when encountering a Christology arising from an Indian context centering around Jesus as guru.[4]

After his death, Jesus was no longer personally present interacting with his community. Some members believed they encountered him in resur-

---

[4] See M. Thomas Thangaraj's imaginative *The Crucified Guru*.

Figure 11. Michelangelo Merisi da Caravaggio, *The Supper at Emmaus*, National Gallery, London

rected form. But clearly what they encountered was not quite the same Jesus in the sense of his personal life, body, and subjectivity that it was before. The accounts of the resurrection appearances agree on nothing except that it was Jesus in some changed sense, and a different sense in each case. Whereas according to Matthew (28:9) the women who found him at the tomb grabbed his feet and worshipped him, in John (20:14–17) Mary can't recognize him at first and then is forbidden to touch him because, as Jesus put it, he has not yet ascended to his father, the resurrection being a kind of way station. Titian's *Noli me tangeri* (figure 10, p. 144 above) wondrously depicts this strange encounter between Mary Magdalene and Jesus. The most unusual, however, is the account of the disciples on the road to Emmaus. No one, according to Luke (24), had seen Jesus at the tomb, although both Mary and Peter had been there and looked. But two disciples, not of the Twelve, walked and talked much of the day with a man who didn't look like Jesus until he blessed and broke the bread, a Eucharistic gesture; then he did look like Jesus, and vanished from their sight. Caravaggio's picture of the supper (figure 11) at that moment of recognition is striking for the vitality of the man seen to be Jesus, but certainly a person much younger than the over-thirty

Jesus crucified a few days prior, and with no stigmata. My best hypothesis about what "really happened" is that the disciples, in their emotionally charged grief and disappointment, construed people and events to be the resurrected Jesus and responded to those events as if Jesus were still among them directing the community. But he was not steadily with them, and then appeared no more (except once years later to Paul; e.g. Acts 9, 22, 26, or Gal. 1). One function, among many, of the symbol of the ascension is to get the ghostly apparitions of Jesus out of the way. The disciples instead had to imagine what Jesus would want them to be and do, and they used their memory of his personal presence to discern this. This was exactly what they had been doing when he was actively with them, only their imagination got much quicker and more direct feedback then (for instance, "Get behind me, Satan," Matt. 16:23). Knowledge of the Risen Christ, historical though that is, remains more ambiguous as I will point out shortly. The point is that the Risen Christ is present in the imagination of his community even though absent physically. All the gospel accounts of resurrection appearances were recorded years later when the Gentiles were the main audience; so they obviously are interpretive rather than reportorial.

The second thing to say is that the way Jesus has been particularly and historically received is very complicated. It would be easy to simplify things by saying that the Church pure and simple is the body of Christ and that Jesus is present as the spirit animating his own body. Then the full reality of the historical Jesus would be his own personal life plus the history of the Church. Paul's (Rom. 7:4, 12:5, 1 Cor. 12:12–31, Eph. 1:22–23, 4:11–16, 5:25–32, Col. 1:18, 3:15) great image of the Church as the body of Christ has considerable power. Nevertheless, two things stand in the way of this simplification of the historical Jesus.

The Church itself manifestly has been *not* the body of Christ animated by his mind on many occasions. Most of Paul's letters complained about persons or practices within actual congregational life and relations between Jewish and Gentile Christians. The dramatic narrative in Acts has largely to do with conflict within the church. Christianity is splintered into hundreds of denominational branches and slivers, nearly always because one or both parties to a given split believed the other was not the body of Christ. What to think in the face of this? It is tempting to distinguish the historical entities that have claimed to be the Church from the true Church that Christ wholly moves as his body, or where the Holy Spirit really is, as Tillich claimed.[5] This is an idealistic move: the

[5] Tillich's definition of the Church in *Systematic Theology*, volume III.

Church exists only where it is the true church, and all those other congregations and organizations are "mere historical realities," without the mind of Christ and the Holy Spirit. The advantage of this idealistic move is that a given historical organization can be understood as sometimes the Church and sometimes not. But the fatal disadvantage of this move is that it lets the historical communities that think of themselves as Christian off the hook. Instead of judging them as bad in various respects, it excuses those bad elements as not being the true Church. When the Christian movement has done terrible things it is devious sleight of hand to say that it just was not the Church then and that Christianity was not responsible. It is far better to say that Christianity, the Church in its divided fashion, consists of all those social movements and organizations that have thought of themselves as Christian, attempting in their ways, however mistaken or even self-deluded, to function as the body of Christ. In this way Christianity, and every one of its branches, stands under the judgment of history and the historical Jesus as risen Lord for the quality of its faithfulness, a very helpful judgment to have in hand when confessing.

The other main consideration against the simplifying move of considering the Church to be the body of Christ and locating Jesus' historical identity that way is that it flies in the face of the symbols of the risen Christ. At least one system of symbols of the risen Jesus is that he has ascended to Heaven from which he judges his followers, among others. According to this symbol system Jesus is significantly external to the Church, not coincident as spirit in body. This is so even in the Ephesians passage that develops the body of Christ theme:

I pray that the God of our Lord Jesus Christ, the Father of glory, may give you a spirit of wisdom and revelation as you come to know him, so that, with the eyes of your heart enlightened, you may know what is the hope to which he has called you, what are the riches of his glorious inheritance among the saints, and what is the immeasurable greatness of his power for us who believe, according to the working of his great power. God put this power to work in Christ when he raised him from the dead and seated him at his right hand in the heavenly places, far above all rule and authority and power and dominion, and above every name that is named, not only in this age but also in the age to come. And he has put all things under his feet and has made him the head over all things for the church, which is his body, the fullness of him who fills all in all. (Eph. 1:17–23)

From its side the Church in any circumstance has to look to its imagination of the risen Christ to help it determine what to do and be, the "spirit of wisdom and revelation." The very openness of the Church, its recognized need to go beyond the patterns and inertias of the past to new forms and directions, requires it to construe Jesus as a transcendent judge. The agony of its deliberations, with all their risk for losing something good for something bad, is the Holy Spirit working through the travail of historical life for the Church. Another part of that symbol system is that Christ will come again to judge what the Church has done and become.

So the particular historical reality of Jesus through the ages lies in the complicated dialectic in which the Church in its particular places and times responds to its imagination of Jesus as judge, based on memories from the gospel of his personal life and as expanded and developed by imagined applications to the new circumstances and places. The historical Jesus in this dialectic includes the history of the images that the Church ought to have to grasp the truth, and that it sometimes does have. Moreover, the imagination of the Church does not just leap from the recorded biblical situation to its own at any one point, but is complicated, enriched, and usually confused by intervening in Church life with imagined judgments by Jesus and imagined applications to different circumstances. Invariably, there is intervening tradition behind the Church at any one time imagining the demands of the living and risen Christ for itself. That Jesus lives from age to age in the imaginations of people in the Church does not make that identity anything less than historical. The imagination of the Church in its consideration of Jesus relative to its own particular life is historical, and can be studied as such.

The third thing to say about the historical Jesus as historically present to the Church though not coincident with it is that the truth about the risen and still historical Jesus can only be embodied from within the Church. This is to remember that such truth would be the carryover into the Church of what is important about God in the respects in which Jesus represents God to the Church. Someone from the outside might be able to *judge* the truth of an alleged carryover, as any one part of the Church does when it judges another part of the Church. But the *locus* of truth is in the transformation of the interpreting Church accomplished by the interpretation. A simple way to say this is that Jesus represents God in the respect in which the Logos should be normatively embodied in the Church as community and as individuals. In the perilous deliberations of how to live out the life of Christ in its present circumstances, the Church has a true grasp of Jesus as the symbol of God if and only if that symbol leads to an accurate pursuit of justice, piety, faithfulness to existential location, and the religious quest in those circumstances. In the Prologue above I expressed this as finding ways to be kind, both personally and corporately. We now have the Logos-categories to spell out something of what kindness means.

The historical identity of Jesus consists in the difference he has made to himself and others, and this comes from his personal life plus the true images of Jesus that have been involved in the Church's dialectic of growth in its Lord. The actual history of what the Church has imagined Jesus to be is part of the history of the Church. But sometimes that Church has imagined wrongly, with understandings of Jesus and the application of that imagination leading to deep alienation as well as miserable unnecessary failures in justice, piety, faith, and hope. In these occasions, the reality of the historical Jesus is the image that was missed, that was not grasped, or that was distorted. This is no less historical, because it is related to the real circumstances for which the image of Christ was sought. The historical identity of Jesus as the risen Christ is in the *normative* images of him for each circumstance of life, whether or not anyone imagined them. They are what the Church should have imagined. That is, they have the normative status of obligations for Christian imagination, obligations sometimes failed. In hindsight and larger perspective, we often can second-guess the Church regarding who Jesus really was for it in some circumstance, and what it should have done to be faithful.

The concern of this book is with the truth of such symbols of Jesus as the historical risen Christ as it might be grasped and assessed today. To make the historical risen Christ "present" today, truly, requires consideration of our present circumstances. This of course cannot be undertaken with any thoroughness. Nor can I as an author express what the Christ might be to individual readers in the particularity of their personal circumstances. What can be done, however, is to lift up relatively new circumstances in which the Church is defining itself today and ask how Jesus might have historical identity relative to each. The South American nativity scene of figure 12 should not be a surprise. Following the schema of the Logos (though with a different order of elements from my earlier discussions), the next section will discuss contemporary cultural pluralism and its implication for the Church as an instance of problematic existential location. The third section, on Jesus and justice, will discuss the needs for global justice of distributive, retributive, and reparative sorts. The final section will deal with the contemporary situation of deference in reference to ecological concerns. The next chapter, on Jesus

Figure 12. Joseph Stella, *The Creche*, c. 1929–33, The Newark Museum, Newark

as friend, will deal with the contemporary problem of the religious quest itself, the fourth element of the Logos.

EXISTENTIAL LOCATION: JESUS CHRIST AND CULTURAL PLURALISM

The existential situation of Christianity today is multifarious. Consider social contexts. The churches in North America and Western Europe are recoiling from the manifest collapse of Christendom as that had come to be understood in terms starting with Constantine, that is, Christian cultures associated with Christian nations and more or less approbation of Christianity by governments. The recoil of the churches from this collapse takes many forms, including conservative efforts to repristinate some authentic forms from the past, liberal efforts to extend Christianity into collapsed Christendom as to a mission field, and charismatic attempts to find radical Christian novelty while sitting loose with regard to culture.[6] For all these European and American church movements, there is an underlying sense that the problem is themselves in their own past traditions.

By contrast the twentieth was the century of greatest growth in the history of Christianity, mainly in the Third World. The growth in Latin America has been mainly among charismatic Protestants in reaction to a particular Roman Catholic culture. In Africa and Asia Christianity has entered as rather much of a new religion, finding its ways among cultures previously formed by other religions. Begun by European and American missionaries in previous centuries, these Third World Christian movements have become much shaped by issues of inculturation and indigenization, and hence are extremely sensitive to the tensions of openness between received forms of Christian life and belief and new circumstances where those have to require new meanings. The Independent Churches of Africa do not have roots in missionary work, except indirectly; their emphasis on tree planting is not a European ritual.[7] The Third World is by no means monolithic. Christianity worked out against Islam and traditional tribal religion in Africa is not much like Korean Christianity whose context is shamanist, Buddhist, and Confucian.

A third social context for contemporary Christianity is in Eastern

---

[6] H. Richard Niebuhr's *Christ and Culture* is an old but still brilliant analysis of some of these issues.
[7] See the fascinating account in M. L. Daneel's *African Earthkeepers*.

Europe and the Islamic states of the former Soviet Union across Asia. Here the churches face two difficult fronts. One is the legacy of seventy years of virulently anti-religious secular communism that seriously weakened Orthodox church structures. The other is the resurgence of Islam in the states from Albania and Bosnia across the southern borders of Russia to the eastern end of Central Asia, a resurgence fueled in part by resentment against colonialist Christians. What should Christianity become on these two fronts?

The above remarks have addressed differences in current social settings for Christianity. These need to be read also against differences in histories, the "denominational" differences marking the split of the Christian Church into churches. To most readers of English the stories are familiar of the Reformation of the Roman Catholic Church with the quick splits between the classic reformers and the Anabaptists and free churches, and then the split of the Church of England from that of Rome. Thence denominations split on national, ethnic, and social class grounds, as well as through attempts within a tradition to recover its essential spirit, as the Methodists were led away from the Anglicans and then the Nazarenes from the Methodists. In many respects these divisions should be viewed benignly as different indigenizations of Protestant Christianity as it spread into new lands, even the New World; as the cultural differences have fallen away, the denominational differences have ceased to matter much.

Much more serious, and probably intrinsic to any religious movement that insists on cultural adaptation and relevance, is the failure to achieve unity from the very first. Consider the beginning of Acts. Returning from the Ascension (Acts 1:12–14) the group of witnesses gathered in a single upper room in Jerusalem for prayer. The group included the Eleven remaining apostles with some women among whom was Jesus' mother, and also Jesus' brothers (listed in Matt. 13:55–56 as James, Joseph, Simon, and Judas; Matthew also cites a number of Jesus' unnamed sisters who are not cited as such in Acts). The next thing that happened (1:15–26) was that Peter addressed a group of about one hundred and twenty "brothers" (and perhaps an equal number of "sisters") and pointed out that Judas Iscariot had broken the fellowship of the Twelve by betraying Jesus. According to Peter, Judas had then used his blood money to buy some property on which he fell, his body bursting open to spill his bowels on the ground (as earthy an image for dividing the community of Jesus as might be imagined; the alternative version of Judas' death, Matt. 27:5, is that he hanged himself). Peter then arranged the selection of a replacement by lot, setting the condition that the candidates had to have been part of the group since the early encounters with John the Baptist. That condition excluded Jesus' brothers, and we might imagine the dissension that resulted soon when Jesus' brother James became the chief leader of the Jerusalem Church, sufficiently powerful to give Peter a hard time (Gal. 2:11–12). The early Church's initial experiment in communal living followed upon phenomenal growth of the movement at Pentecost and immediately after. Yet when two members of the commune, Ananias and Sapphira, declined to contribute the whole of their estate, they were struck dead and the communal form of Christian life was not mentioned again. The Jewish and Gentile factions of the first-generation Church likely never functioned very harmoniously; the Jewish faction withered fairly soon in Palestine, though it might have survived among Jewish nomads in Arabia encountered centuries later by the first Muslims. Conflicts between "Hebrews and Hellenists" were present in other, non-Christian, forms of Second Temple Judaism. The European Christian churches have not kept track of the first-century Christian mission to India, attributed to Thomas and claimed by the contemporary Thomas churches, or of the effects of Mark and Philip's missions to Ethiopian Africa.

The most disastrous event for Christian unity was the Council of Chalcedon. On the one hand it condemned and excommunicated the Nestorians who represented most of the Christians living outside the Roman Empire, especially those in the Persian Empire. With the Nestorian missions to China and India it is likely that their numbers in the next four centuries surpassed those of European so-called Catholic, or Roman, Christians. The Nestorians went their own way, not worrying that the Catholics thought them heretics. By limiting their vision of true Christianity to those within the Roman Empire, the Roman Catholics allowed their sense of Christianity to become closely associated with the state and its political culture, Christendom. The Nestorians, never a majority religion in their lands, did not make that move. The other result of Chalcedon was that some of the Nestorians' opponents were also dissatisfied with the decisions and left to form the Monophysite churches of Syria and Africa, of which the Coptic Church is the strongest today, that were removed from the Roman Empire with the rise of Islam. Most Christians whose lineage runs through Europe do not recognize the Nestorian or Monophysite churches as legitimately Christian.

So what is the existential situation for Christianity today regarding its

self-identity? It is multifarious both in social contexts, calling for different inculturations of Christian life and belief, and in histories that bring
divergent and often mutually hostile traditions to those contexts. I would
venture the following observations, none very profound or reflective of
much of a particular point of view.[8]

1. Good faith requires each congregation (and individual Christian) to
recognize itself to be the outcome of particular historical developments
and to have a particular social and cultural context in which to find
appropriate forms for the life of Christ. Not to recognize the first clause
would be to fall into some kind of denial of existential particularity, often
the kind that says there is only one legitimate form of Christianity. A
single form of Christianity would be plausible if there were only one situation of life in which to embody the normative Logos of Christ, which
is manifestly false even in the records of the New Testament and in the
histories of those trajectories of Christianity that lead to each congregation's own historical resources.

Not to recognize the second clause would be an existential denial of
the particular obligations to discern, in the Holy Spirit, what Christian
living might be in that congregation's own circumstances, its issues of
justice, piety, faith, hope, and love, and its particular struggles with alienation. The tempting denial here would be to cling to some past form of
Christian life as especially normative; but that would be to affirm a dead
Christ, not one living now to lead each congregation in its special
context.

2. Each congregation needs to see the other congregations with their
different histories and different circumstances, attempting different
forms of Christian life and belief, as *prima facie* members of the body of
Christ, equally creatures loved by God, acknowledging the same Lord
though in different ways, led by the same Spirit, and like itself, struggling
to find ways of being optimally faithful in their circumstances. This does
not mean that upon further discernment other congregations might not
be found seriously wanting; few people now would tolerate the Nazi congregations as anywhere near the mark of Christian faithfulness. Nor
does it mean that certain practices or beliefs within other congregations
might not be judged in serious error even after understanding the meanings they have in those contexts. Probably there are no social contexts in
which Christianity should have tolerated the denigration or abuse of

---

[8] See the boisterous celebration of contemporary religious pluralism in John H. Berthrong's *The
Divine Deli.*

unusual, disfigured, or disabled people, the practice of any kind of racism, disrespect of people of different social class or historical background, pride in nationalism or ethnocentricity, condemnation or disrespect of homosexuals, or the subordination of women. The inclusiveness of Jesus' table fellowship and the universality of saving grace across all creation would condemn those practices even when they have been typical of the larger culture. These negative judgments on other congregations or elements of their beliefs and practice are the same kinds of judgments each congregation would make on the stages in its own ancestral history, with care to discern how things mean different things in different contexts.

3. Given the difficulty of each congregation's discernment of its own true life, its posture toward the others even after deliberate and careful judgment should be one of acceptance, curiosity, sharing of common struggles, offering of encouragement, and the rendering of reproof where that is the careful outcome of discernment. Each congregation should be aware of the ease with which it might misunderstand the circumstances of some other and so should approach others with openness and curiosity so as to be able to understand the others. Only when understanding across differences is deep might it be possible to share spiritual riches and judgment. To invite others' critical judgment before offering that which comes from one's own position probably is also a good policy in order to keep faith with the existential situation of extreme pluralism within Christianity.

4. The attempt to agree upon a universal organizational structure for the Church, which was the dominating metaphor for the Protestant, Orthodox, and Roman Catholic ecumenical discussions of the mid-twentieth century, probably should be abandoned. Rather, the diversity of forms of church organization should be celebrated as indicative of the diversity of circumstances of church life. No form of universal organization could be agreed upon that would not be an imposition of some culture's order on others, and that would be a denial of the existential situation of radical pluralism within Christianity.

5. Rather, each congregation, recognizing that existential situation, should welcome the presence, gifts, and services of Christians from other contexts and traditions, and welcome them especially to the Eucharistic table. Whereas in the past it is conceivable that some groups would legitimately be excommunicated from other groups' table fellowship, that is likely not conceivable in the present radically pluralistic situation.

6. On the other hand, in light of the pluralism, it would probably be

bad faith to insist on participating in the rites of others unless invited, or to insist that they use one's own rites. The reason is that pluralism at this particular moment in the history of Christianity is rife with misunderstanding from context to context, from history to history, and also with an inability to participate emotionally in the forms of alien Christian practices. Therefore, deference in common worship needs to be observed.

7. The sum of this is that each congregation has a somewhat doubled existential situation: on the one hand being true to Christ in its own particular context and on the other hand being the particular neighbor to other congregations in other situations with other histories. In past times it might be enough for a congregation in a new environment to focus exclusively on discerning what forms Christianity should take there. In our time few if any environments are so insulated from others as not to have the development of relations with other forms of Christianity to be part of their particular mission.

Multifariousness within Christianity itself is only part of the impact of the existential situation of pluralism today. Another part is the encounter of Christianity with other religions, including local or new religions and the great world religions, as well as with the secular movements with religious dimensions such as humanism and Marxism. The multifariousness of religious pluralism is not spread evenly across the globe. Some parts of the world already see vital mixes of the world's religions, like the situation in the Roman Empire during the first generations of Christianity. Other parts have a very strong domination by one religious tradition with others enjoying or suffering minority status that might be hardly acknowledged; parts of the Islamic world might be like this. Rural areas often are more religiously homogeneous than urban ones.

Nevertheless, the current existential situation is that cultural boundaries are being crossed at a terrific rate. First there is the relative ease of modern travel, which means a few people can emigrate to other lands, and where they have gone their families can follow. Second, there is the increasing integration of the world into a global market, moving foods globally as seasons change, and moving money and employment in search of profit. Christians might have occasion to question the justice of this global economy. But they cannot question the fact that it brings into contact and partnership people from different religions. Third and most important of all is the power of the internet to ignore cultural boundaries and national identifications. Access is relatively cheap so that the boundaries of economic difference, between oppressing nations and oppressed, for instance, are being crossed with great frequency, and so are boundaries between elite and popular cultures. The cross-cultural communication through the internet is becoming the medium through which people engage the causally significant structures of their world. All these forms of radically increased global interaction create the existential situation in which Christians in nearly every form of Christianity engage people with other religions. How should the churches be true to this?

1. The first thing is to acknowledge the existential situation of religious pluralism as defining our time and take steps to understand the other religions. Various particular forms of Christianity contain historically generated images of other religions, for instance European Christianity of Judaism and Orthodoxy of Islam. To be faithful in the current situation is to learn about the other religions and examine the ways in which previous images of them are true and false. To the extent that those images are false, they are likely to be harmful in treating people in those religions as neighbors (remember Jesus' illustration of neighborliness was a cross-religious encounter, Luke 10:29–37).

2. Although Christians need to focus their own identity on the life of Christ as it might optimally be expressed in their particular circumstances, no principle exists within Christianity to limit what the grace of God might do through other traditions. In fact, the Christian principle is that the grace of God as Creator is unlimited, though always particular. As we have seen, Christianity is itself a very particular cultural development constructing a religious and cultural world out of signs and symbols that have a history. The meaning of Jesus as Messiah, Lord, Savior, and the rest comes out of the history of Israel as reinterpreted in a multitude of different directions. The Christian way of life would be an alternative to those other religious cultures that could not buy into that history as Paul's Gentiles did. The symbols of engaging God by "going to the Father" (John 14:6) are affirmed as true by Christians, but they entail living in the semiotic world defined that way. Radically different religious symbol systems for engaging what Christians engage as God the Father might not understand those terms. The Buddhist goal of release from suffering, the Vedanta goal of actualizing Brahman, and the Confucian goal of being one body with the world, are not easily scaled onto a map where Christians can claim an exclusive truth.

In Jesus' one recorded (John 4:1–45) serious interfaith dialogue, his move was not to defend Jewish worship in Jerusalem over against the

Samaritan woman's worship on the mountain but to deny the significance of those differences. In his encounter with the Canaanite woman
(Matt. 15:12–28) he tended to be dismissive but was turned around (the
only instance where he is recorded to have accepted instruction from
someone else) by her faith that he applauded. Similarly, in his dealings
with Romans, Pilate excepted, he responded positively to their faith (e.g.
John 4:46–55); John said a Roman official's whole family became believers (long before Jesus' family did so). The demoniac possessed by
"Legion" was presumably not Jewish, living among swineherds (Mark
5:1–20). When he was healed he asked to become a disciple but Jesus sent
him off to preach in the Decapolis, mainly non-Jewish cities in eastern
Palestine; this was before he sent his own disciples out on their own
(Mark 6:6–13), and Jesus generally told Jewish people whom he healed
not to talk about him but to seek ritual purification from the priests. So,
taking these texts at face value (but remembering they were written for
a largely Gentile church), Jesus' first missionary or evangelist was a
Gentile sent to Gentiles. Jesus' encounter with Pilate (Matt. 27:11–14,
Mark 15:1–5, Luke 23:1–4, John 18:33–38) was characterized by what we
today would call an unfair power differential. According to the synoptic
gospels Jesus was uncommunicative to the point of rudeness. According
to John's, Jesus carefully distinguished his claim for authority ("not of
this world") from that of Pilate so as not to be competitive; he had earlier
advised rendering to Caesar what was Caesar's. All in all, Jesus' recorded
interactions with Gentiles was marked not by any explicit rejection of
their religion but with respect, and with enthusiasm for the power of
God he felt in himself and shared with the Gentiles in healing ways.

Paul's only recorded interfaith dialogue (Acts 17:16–34), debating with
Stoics and Epicureans in Athens on the Areopagus, shows him using the
altar to an unknown god, not to reject it but to argue that he knew about
that god, and proceeding to tell them about the Creator and the resurrection of Jesus. In rejecting the worship of idols in favor of the living
God, an old Jewish theme, Paul was not contradicting the Stoics or
Epicureans. In his argument for God the Creator he used Greek proof
texts, quoting the Stoic Aratus, "for we too are his offspring," and probably Epimenides for the line "for in him we live and move and have our
being," just as in arguments with Jews he and others would proof-text
the Hebrew Bible. Jesus and Paul were both respectful of the religions of
Gentiles, not hesitant to proclaim or demonstrate their own truth but
neither rejecting the validity of others. Openness to other religions has
powerful biblical warrant.

The question of the validity of other religions is an empirical one, is it not? Allowing that the Creator has infinite, though always particular, power, and that the Christian commitment is to the graciousness of God to all, it would be highly unlikely indeed that other religions would not have their own truth. There is no special likelihood that their truth would be more or less purely expressed than historical Christianity expresses the Christian revelation. In the existential situation of radical religious pluralism, it would be a faithless denial to assert without investigation that only Christianity has interesting religious truth, or defines the only way to live before the ultimate. Rather, faith in this situation is to engage the other religions so as to learn from them, leaving assessments until serious comparisons can be framed in common cultural language.

3. Because the interfaith encounter is happening, and not always intelligently, a special task of Christians in this situation is to develop in some respectful detail what is sometimes called a "theology of religions." This has two sides. One is to understand each of the other religions and express how Christianity relates positively and negatively with it. The other is to understand how Christianity looks from the standpoint of the other religion, also seeking to understand and relate to Christianity. Both sides are essential for Christian identity in an existential situation of radical religious pluralism. This process is obviously a dialectical one, for Christianity itself changes as it comes to learn from and criticize Buddhism, Daoism, New Age religions, and the rest. The interaction of world religions is nothing new and Christianity has been massively shaped by it. In the present existential situation, the deliberate attention to theology of religions is an imperative, failure of which results in a denial of the real character of the situation.

4. Meanwhile, the overall posture of Christianity to other religions, and of different Christian congregations, should be neighborliness, as illustrated in Jesus' tale of the Good Samaritan. Neighborliness is a prior condition for any aggressive Christian inquiry into other religions. Not to acknowledge this is to deny the underlying current of suspicion in inter-religious matters occasioned by the last four centuries of Western colonialism from which Western forms of Christianity did not decisively dissociate themselves until very late, if yet.

Many other dimensions of the contemporary existential location of Christianity than pluralism are important. Moreover, the existential locations of Christian congregations are diverse within the current global context, as noted. But these discussions illustrate the general point that, in order to embody Christ today, special dimensions of faith relative to existential location call for special forms of Christian life and thought, perhaps forms not called upon earlier.

JUSTICE: JESUS CHRIST AND GLOBAL DISTRIBUTIVE, RETRIBUTIVE, AND RESTORATIVE JUSTICE

A similar qualification should be made immediately to the discussion of the presence of Jesus Christ today in the Church's pursuit of right form or justice. The vast diversity of situations of the Christian churches gives them different agendas for living justly among themselves and also for pursuing justice in their communities. The demands and programs of the individual churches for justice in their particular situations might be more important and pressing than any of the more global issues to be discussed here. Nevertheless, because of the world-wide causal connections that are making the globe one society, if still a great diversity of cultures, some relatively new issues of justice have arisen that go to defining what it means to be the body of Christ today.

Another qualification should be made as well. The obligations of right order are not peculiar to Christians. They fall upon anyone who might be able to act so as to affect outcomes for better or worse. The rhetoric of justice that Christians use might have some bias, but the forms that it would take in context are justified by the considerations that would apply to any rhetoric articulating justice. Christians do not have a monopoly on good thinking regarding morality, politics, or political economy. Through the ages, Christian thinking has been as biased by circumstantial interests as that of any other group. What Christians have is a commitment in principle stemming from their faith in the normative reality of the risen Christ and their understanding of the community of the New Covenant to give themselves to the causes of justice. Three such causes stemming from global social causation will be discussed here for illustrative purposes. These are causes for which it is important for Christians in our time to witness as part of their faith in Christ whose mind they struggle to share and whose bodily ministry they give themselves to extend.

The first cause is that of *distributive justice*, distributing the riches of the earth and human endeavor, and also the prices to be paid for all that and civilized life, in due proportion. This anciently recognized kind of obligation has been articulated through many tensions. One is the tension between ideals of equality on the one hand, justified in Christian thinking by the equality of all people as children of God, and on the other hand the ideals of human identity and worth resting in work and its rewards, family solidarity, and history regarding particular land and artifacts, all of which justify "ownership" as important for human life. Another tension, associated obviously with the first, is between the particular values things have for individuals such that they barter them for other things that have value for them, and the translation of all value into money, which is required for most schemes of equality. Yet another tension is between the ideals of distributive justice, however they balance the above tensions, and the realities of power imbalances that often lead the richer and stronger to become more so and the poorer and weaker also to become more so. In modern times, moreover, we have come to see all of the above filtered through social class structure; whereas in premodern times in Europe and in many other cultures today social class location is part of the meaning of life, and distributive justice is modulated accordingly, the modern, more egalitarian, outlook interprets class distinctions as themselves offenses to distributive justice, at least in theory.

The social sciences now are sufficiently advanced to enable us to understand some of the global interactive causal structures that provide the tools for altering large-scale patterns of the distribution of resources. In a sense, the debates about distributive justice are interesting but frivolous when nothing can be done to make a difference anyway. The debates can be positively harmful when they inspire ideologies of change that seriously misunderstand the causal processes; the disastrous seventy-year experiment with communism failed because its applied economic theory led to an actual decrease of wealth that put intolerable strains on increasingly totalitarian distributive structures. Now we understand more, though perhaps not enough.

The Christian concern for justice on a global scale needs systematically to be rethought in terms of the causal patterns that do indeed distribute the world's goods and evils (who gets what and who pays for it). The old tensions need to be rethought in terms of knowledge of the shifting of wealth in a global market economy. Entitlements need to be rethought in terms of the conditions for being able to take advantage of them. The claims of immediate needs versus history need to be rethought in terms of the causal consequences of any pattern of balancing those. Most of all, the Christian ethical imagination needs to investigate where causal interventions can make a difference. What are the possibilities for the United Nations, for blocks of governments of First, Second, and Third World nations respectively, for multinational holding companies involved in many businesses, for international, national, and local labor groups, for professions such as medicine and law, for various *pro bono publico* organizations in different advocacy fields, for organizations involved with ethnic self-consciousness and celebration, for institutions of education at all levels, for the academic world of research and scholarship, for the world of popular and investigative journalism, for institutions that let the voices of people be heard that ordinarily are unnoticed, and especially for Christian churches, both in their denominational offices and their congregations? Christians should remind the world that it is foolish to think that any one of these causal entry points, even government, will be able to solve the whole problem of distributive justice, though each may think its entry point provides the right perspective for the whole. Christians should also remind the world that it is foolish to think that any one total vision can map either the definition of distributive justice relevant to our time or a comprehensive program toward achieving it. The best we can hope for is a little progress here and a little there, not worrying too much about coordination.

I see the general contribution of Christian churches, at all levels from congregations to denominational offices embodying the life and work of Jesus today regarding distributive justice, to include the following five programs: First, to insist that any change effect greater kindness, whatever other ideological considerations might be involved; second, to give voice systematically to people who otherwise might not be heard, and have what they say conveyed to the relevant places; third, to foster ongoing conversation, inquiry, and debate into the complexities of distributive justice, reminding simple perspectives of the complexities involved, and insisting that all perspectives be taken into account where possible (the Church might be the only institution with this mandate); fourth, to require that complexity and ambiguity not inhibit action but insist that something can always be done, even if only in small matters that affect large ones; and fifth, to be prepared to model sacrifice, to be reticent to insist on self-interest, and to be willing to accept changes that work to one's own disadvantage but to the advantage of others to whom justice is due.

Retributive justice is punishing offenders. An eye for an eye, a tooth for a tooth, was its ancient biblical paradigm. As a form of legal justice, retribution aimed to let society through government take over blood vengeance that was socially destructive and might not be balanced in due proportion to the offense. Jesus' claim in the Sermon on the Mount that we should not judge in order that we be not judged, has to do with an individual's arrogation of a kind of divine judging position, and is not inconsistent with the government regulating retributive justice. Like distributive justice, its conception has been riddled with tensions. It does not lend itself easily to a single-order formula. A classic tension exists between viewing the perpetrator as a victim of circumstances and holding the perpetrator personally responsible. The former denies the perpetrator's humanity, at least with regard to the offense, and the latter ignores the possibility of extenuating circumstances; modern law codes attempt to balance these. Another tension exists between retribution for the sake of rebalancing some cosmic good upset by the offense and service to society by reconditioning the perpetrator not to be bad any more and deterring others from committing like offenses. Yet another tension is between the social need to apprehend, try, and punish the perpetrator and the very grave possibility that the wrong person has been identified, a tension particularly acute in capital cases.

Among the many controversies about retributive justice in our own time of global interaction is the significance of the human rights movement, especially as codified in the United Nations Declaration of Human Rights. Instead of letting both the definition of crimes and the measure of their punishment be determined by local communities and their traditions, the human rights movement sets limits to local autonomy. It defines new crimes, namely the abuse of universal human rights, and sets limits on what should count as penalty and punishment. A new tension is thus set up between the local definitions of the very meaning of crimes and their punishments and more universal definitions of those things. Recent examples are the European outrage at Muslim practices regarding sacrilege in the case of Salman Rushdie, at practices of forced clitoridectomy in some African societies, and at the United States's practice of capital punishment.

The special Christian contributions regarding retributive justice in our time seem to me to be three programs: First, to insist that the practices of retributive justice manifest kindness to both the aggrieved party and the perpetrator, however kindness is defined in each case and the two balanced together; second, to remind the public in all appropriate circumstances that the ways in which a society manages retributive justice have grave consequences for the society itself, defining both personal responsibility in perpetrators and what people are owed by society in the case of victims; third, to mediate deliberately between the sensibilities of local perspectives and those of more universal perspectives, taking the Church's communicative structures as a model embracing local inculturations of the life of Christ within the solidarity of Christ's life in the world. Of course, until the Church thoroughly addresses the issues of its own existential identity in a pluralistic world, it cannot make much of a contribution to this last point.

Reparative justice is something of a new notion that builds upon both distributive and retributive justice. It focuses on the victims as much as on the perpetrators of large-scale social injustices, both distributive and retributive, and aims to repair the broken social harmony to end the cycle of resentment and vengeance. Examples arising from distributive justice are where classes of people defined by ethnicity, gender, historical poverty, military defeat, or some other way, are oppressed by others economically, politically, and/or psychologically: for instance, Indians and mixed-blood poor in Latin America, African-Americans and Native Americans in North America, Africans and Colored in apartheid South Africa, women and homosexuals in most societies, and perhaps Third World nations generally. Examples arising from retributive justice are where cycles of revenge and grievance have gone on so long that the original causes of conflict have been forgotten or turned to legend, or where conditions of oppressed and oppressor have switched or been confused, as in conflicts between Jews and Nazis in Germany, between Catholics and Protestants in Northern Ireland, between Catholics, Orthodox, and Muslims in former Yugoslavia, between Hindus and Muslims in parts of Pakistan, India, and Bangladesh, and between Hutus and Tutsis in Africa. Looked at from a long enough perspective, no people on Earth live in a place to which some other people do not also have claim.

Reparative justice is the attempt to stop the resentment and revenge by bringing the sides together to share their experience in the hope that each side will internalize the perspective of the other. The victims get to express their hurt, pain, outrage, and hatred so that the other side sees what it is responsible for and acknowledges that. When both sides are the victims, this requires much learning to accommodate and own up to the other's perspectives. When one side is mainly oppressor and not victim, reparative justice requires the acquisition of uncommon humility, and on the part of the victim side, forgiveness. The cases for reparative justice are rarely those where restitution can be made, the grievances often going back generations and involving long-past social conditions. But where reparative justice succeeds in internalizing the perspectives, histories, sufferings, and ambitions of each side in the other, a new more unified social consciousness is created where the sides do not so much identify themselves against one another as include one another in their sense of common social definition. This means that issues of both distributive and retributive justice can have a more meaningful and comprehensive scope.

Institutions of reparative justice are only beginning to be formulated. They include the "official apologies" that some groups or governments have made to those whom they have oppressed, and also the legal dialogues in South Africa where families of people abused by the apartheid government are able to face their oppressors and make them listen to what was done to them.

Christian churches in our time have a great stake in the promotion of reparative justice, especially in developing institutions for its legal standing and to which automatic appeal can be made in times of trouble. The Christian stake comes first from the deep Christian commitment to peace and reconciliation, which has a striking opportunity in the form of reparative justice in our time. The Christian stake comes also from the fact that Christian factions have themselves been set against one another in paradigm cases, as for instance between African-Americans and Euro-Americans, or the sides in Northern Ireland. Most of all in our time, situations of serious economic and political oppression often exist as the result of Western imperialism associated with Western European and American Christianity: Christians with an imperial heritage have extraordinary opportunities to invite the communications of reparative justice.

These discussions of justice on a global scale should not detract from the responsibilities of Christians in various places to attend to local issues of justice that might be far more focused. As noted earlier, the circumstances of contemporary Christians are so diverse that little can be said that applies with equal strength to all. But every congregation is part of the global network of social connections, as well as the global Church, and therefore part of its efforts in the Holy Spirit to embody living Christ in its practice of justice is to attend to these considerations.

PIETY: JESUS CHRIST AND NATURE

The issues of deference or piety in terms of which to embody a Christian way of life in our time could hardly have a better illustration than in the ecological crises of the environment that have forced themselves on the attention of the late-modern world. Human beings from time immemorial have subordinated nature to their own interests. Most of the time we can imagine that it was not even objectified as "nature," only as the resource for food, the forces from which to find shelter, the very context of life itself.

Modern technology has made a qualitative difference to the capacities of human beings to alter their environment. Industrially produced fluorocarbons threaten the ozone layer; tankers spill oil fouling oceans and beaches; fumes from energy production and heavy industry spread from one country to the next; pollution from industry and waste from huge cities contaminate land and water; nuclear radioactive products cannot be put anywhere safely, reminiscent of the nightmare of the medieval alchemist seeking to invent a universal solvent: what to put it in? Elementary measures of modern sanitation and hygiene, as well as international charity, have enabled huge populations to grow, for instance in India, China, and Africa, with inadequate economic base so that the land is overcultivated, overgrazed, and denuded of firewood. The greed fostered by unregulated market capitalism and cultures of consumerism threatens to deplete forests of their usable lumber and the seas of desirable fish, and to turn wilderness areas into farms and resorts for cash.

All this and more has been brought acutely to the consciousness of the public in both developed and undeveloped countries, with the latter concerned that they might be inhibited from exploiting the environment before they are on a par with the former. No one wants to give up what they have, including their dreams for more. But most now recognize that they are likely to lose even what they have if the environmental conditions for their wealth are destroyed. Modern science is beginning to spell out the causal systems in which the environmental disasters lie, pointing out that both the initiating cause and the places of possible intervention might lie far from the effects, with the victimized people or their governments having no jurisdiction over the areas in which corrective change needs to take place.

Some of the issues here are those of justice, for instance the exploitative powers of the rich and powerful over the resources of the poor and weak, or the practices of some groups to have more children than they can support, placing the burdens on others. But there is another dimension of the environmental problems that is relatively new to our time and of a distinctly religious character. How should human beings relate to the environment as the set of natural components that are integrated with human life? As regards justice, the elements of nature are related as means to the end of the flourishing of human life, defined however that be. But as regards deference, how should people relate to the elements of the natural home that gives them life?

The contemporary Christian answer, I believe, lies in the conception of the Logos. The natural components of the human world, like the social and personal, are parts of creation and should be revered and deferred to as such. Christians, like most people, know to be grateful for what we enjoy. But gratitude is a dangerous and competing attitude for deference. Gratitude suggests that nature is for us, thanks be to God! From the human perspective gratitude is appropriate, of course, because we can and often do appreciate the things that make life possible. Gratitude should be expressed to the Creator for the creation that makes our lives possible. But deference is to attend to the values things in nature have in themselves, from their own perspectives, and explicitly not for us. Part of deference is deep remorse, even to the extent of blood-guilt, for the human use and consumption of nature.

Here lies the importance of the recognition of wilderness. Wilderness is nature without being ordered for human life. It can be observed only delicately without human destructive intervention. But wilderness is necessary to be recognized, protected, and experienced if human beings are to begin to develop proper deference to nature. In the history of many peoples, especially the European, the wilderness was the enemy. The forests were dark and full of threat. One of the great contributions of the medieval Christian religion to Western civilization was to provide strong, directed, monastic workforces to clear human habitations in the great forests of Europe. The biblical injunction to care as stewards for nature as a garden was interpreted as a call to arms to conquer nature. That was only just. But it was not deferential, and it poisoned the roots of deference in the biblical tradition.

The founding myth in Genesis 2 and 3 was that Adam and Eve were created to care for the garden and one another under a commandment of restraint, and they broke that restraint. For that they were expelled from the garden in which they might have had a proper relation with nature into a literal wilderness where they had to eke out a living from uncooperative soil with hostile beasts, pain in childbearing, and a family whose first act was murder and with descendants upon whom civil order needs to be forced. Seen from the perspective of the problematic of deference, the founding biblical myth is that the created ideal human condition is one under a covenantal constraint that people are free to break. When they do, the human condition is turned into a kind of general warfare to win civil justice by swords and spears and to battle against nature with plowshares and pruning hooks, instruments that are not really so different.

The dominant images of God in the biblical tradition have had to do with the governance of the human sphere. Yahweh the mighty Warrior advanced his people over the Egyptians and Canaanites, and as the righteous King enforced the laws of his covenant with Israel, showing both stern judgment and mercy. The martial aspects of kingship were not exclusive. God was also pictured as a Father, a patient Husband with a wayward wife, a Shepherd. The New Testament intensifies some of these more tender and loving images. Even though Jesus depicts the human situation in terms of the kingdom of God, as remarked before the head of the kingdom is a Father, not a King. Nevertheless, Christian reflection quickly understood Jesus himself as King, as we have noted in the previous two chapters. The Bible's concluding images in the Book of Revelation are all about justice overcoming evil with great retribution, establishing absolute divine rule and at the end (Rev. 21, 22) a new city for human beings, a city absolutely square and unnatural, with high walls on all sides, and in which the originating natural distinction between darkness and light is obliterated, all at the cost of great destruction of stars, mountains, rivers and seas. Is cosmic justice for human beings worth all that?

I suggest that the ecological crises of our time constitute a wake-up call for wildness. We need to find, preserve, and learn from the wilderness. Even more, we need to retrieve and cultivate the images of God as wild. God is the creator of the entire cosmos, vast beyond human importance. As the Psalmists knew, we are a bare flash in the cosmic time of God. With the Earth an incomprehensibly tiny speck among the debris of the cosmic Big Bang, how can our salvation-history be of much note in the cosmos? The world God has created is largely a whirl of expanding gases where the elements for human habitation clump briefly between initial fire and the final dissolution (see Beth Neville's *From Caves to Cosmos*, between pp. 158 and 159 above, especially plates 6 and 7). The creation that reveals God's nature is wild, untamed, not domestic at all. The domesticated God of Kingship and War against Evil is but a tiny prismatic ray of that great Wild Light, shining on human affairs just because there is a difference between what we can do and what we should do. Only because we live under obligation does it make sense to think of God relative to justice. We live within that obligated context, to be sure, and so for us those domesticated symbols of the divine have cosmic significance, especially when we ask how *we* can be at home in the universe. But of what large importance is it that we be at home in the universe, except to us?

Late-modern science has created new images of the Wild God of infinite blasts, dances of expanding gases, and a cosmic finish more profound than any king's imagined tortures of final retribution and fulfilling peace. And it is from the perspective of these images that we need to reread the lessons of the environmental disasters that have come upon the entire globe. The real problem is not that human beings are ruining the environment that makes their life possible. The real problem rather is that God's nature has been truly wild east of Eden (Gen. 3:24) all the while. God's nature changes the composition of the sea when chemicals are added to it, regardless of its hospitality to the biosphere. God's nature turns earth to sand and clay when nutrients are leached out, a victory of geochemistry. God's nature dissipates the ozone layer when the atmosphere changes, allowing new cosmic radiation to create a new earth. God's cosmic dance of gases can smash the globe with comets and end us like the dinosaurs or the supernovae. That Wild God has a different holiness from the Heavenly Court holiness of biblical images based on pharaohs and emperors, a much greater, truer, and now inescapable holiness.

The cultivation of a human sensibility of true worship before the wild holiness of God, a worship subtly re-conceiving how human beings ought to defer to the elements of nature that necessarily must be taken up within human life, is a genuinely monumental task for Christian life and thought today. The covenantal obligations that define the human condition, according to the Christian theology expounded here, are no more exclusively those of deference than they are exclusively of justice, or of existential location, or presenting oneself to God. Yet the obligations of justice have been vastly over-weighted in most Christian, indeed monotheistic, history. That imbalance needs redressing. The redress is most likely to come from a re-evaluation of what is worshipful, less the Cosmic King than the Wild Creator of fecund blasts.

The obligations of deference necessarily must be compromised with those of justice, existential location, and the religious quest. Not everything human can be abandoned to wilderness. But we shall not have a proper attitude in deference if we view it merely as the compromise that needs to be made in order to secure the human sphere. We need rather to apprehend nature on its own, as it moves around and through us, destroying as it pulses to create something else. We need to see this as revelatory of God just as much as of the obligations of justice. In fact, what we have been taught so abruptly lately is that the human sphere itself needs to be reconceived as a fragile harmony floating temporarily on the cosmic river of forces. We have an urgent need to achieve our excellences neat and find meaning in our God-given part of the wild world (the main lesson of *From Caves to Cosmos*), which requires worshipping the right God, the Wild One. Psalm 29 stretches the image of God as enthroned king to command creative wildness. Another sea-change is required in human sensibilities that is as profound as those caused by the feminist revolution and the rejection of slavery and oppression. The Wild-God/Wilderness-World sea-change is an extraordinary responsibility for Christianity today, and it needs to take place in and through Christian bodies across the globe. Perhaps the greatest hope is that it has started in the tree-planting rituals of the African Independent Churches before it has in the theological academies.

The arguments of this chapter have taken as their premise the thesis that the meaning of embodying the life of the Risen Christ in contemporary Christian living requires determining what the Logos-obligations of justice, deferential piety, existential location, and the religious quest require for contemporary circumstances. Those requirements are likely to be different from what they were for earlier circumstances, and so the life of the Church needs to be led by the Spirit to re-embody Christ in appropriate new forms in each circumstance. The arguments here have proceeded from the observation that ours is a time of great interacting pluralism, with Christianity meaning different things in different contexts, but united in its intermeshed histories and solidarities, and called to unity in Christ. The dialectic of particular differences requiring different forms of Christianity, and the common task of all this constituting the contemporary unity of the Church, has been worked through three main illustrative topics, pluralism itself, Christian approaches to justice, and proper deference in connection with environmental concerns. The theme of the religious quest is the topic for the next chapter.

Who then is the historical Jesus? First, Jesus was the person we know by that name through the witnesses of the New Testament, knowledge of a determinate quality according to historical science. The same person, Jesus, is also the one who was meaningful for those early witnesses who believed him resurrected from the dead, ascended into heaven, represented in their midst by the Holy Spirit, and the judge of their commitment to live together as he had taught and to continue his ministry. As their own conditions changed, particularly with regard to membership in the community of people who had no connection with the religion of Israel, they had to imagine Jesus' leadership under those circumstances. Thus began their adventure in openness to a future for the continued heavenly-but-present life of Jesus, imagining also that he would judge them in the end.

The question of who the historical Jesus is remains open in the sense that Christians today are trying to discern how the Logos Jesus incarnated in the past might best be embodied today. "Embodied" is just another word for "incarnation," perhaps a less threatening one to modern ears. The difficulties of finding out who Jesus was before the crucifixion by means of historical science are different from but probably less difficult than finding out who the historical Jesus is today.

CHAPTER SIX

Jesus as friend

THE RELIGIOUS QUEST

The religious quest is undertaken alone. Facing death is part of it, and that is alone. Whether one undertakes a religious quest, and how, is probably the single most important character of one's soul over time and in eternity, and that is the essence of one's singularity. William James defined religion for the sake of his discussion in *The Varieties of Religious Experience* as "the feelings, acts, and experiences of individual men in their solitude, so far as they apprehend themselves to stand in relation to whatever they may consider the divine."[1] Alfred North Whitehead had a similar notion when he wrote, in *Religion in the Making*:

Religion is what the individual does with his own solitariness. It runs through three stages, if it evolves to its final satisfaction. It is the transition from God the void to God the enemy, and from God the enemy to God the companion. Thus religion is solitariness; and if you are never solitary, you are never religious. Collective enthusiasms, revivals, institutions, churches, rituals, bibles, codes of behavior, are the trappings of religion, its passing forms. They may be useful or harmful; they may be authoritatively ordained, or merely temporary expedients. But the end of religion is beyond all this.[2]

James and Whitehead, as well as those who agree with them, have been subjected to thorough criticism for the overweening individualism of this approach to defining religion, and I have been part of that attack.[3] Many reasons make it an inadequate approach to understanding religion. First, it seems to fly in the face of the obvious truth that nearly everything we do or think is a conjoint action with others. This is so even in the most remote negative sense: to take time out to attend to one's soul has the social meaning of taking time away from other things. Second, even to think about religious matters in one's solitude is to employ the

---

[1] Chapter 2, p. 31, in the Penguin edition.   [2] *Religion in the Making*, pp. 16–17.
[3] See my discussion of the texts quoted here in *The Truth of Broken Symbols*, chapter 1.

semiotic structures of one's culture in which lie embodied all the culture-making work of others. And, third, religion itself is a social way of life with myths, metaphysics, and cosmologies, with ritual and communal practices, and with spiritual practices for individuals that are culturally created and communally overseen. These are the kinds of things the critics have in mind who object to the solitariness approach for understanding religion. As the quotation from Whitehead illustrates, those social aspects of religion are easily dismissed as ephemera, indeed distracting substitutes for the real thing. I hope by now that in this book the steady march from symbols of God as Creator of people in covenant, to the stark intimacy of substitutionary atonement, to the cosmos as a kingdom, to the community of God with people in covenant, to the continuing life of the historical Jesus in living communities, convinces the reader that religion, at least the Christian one, is ineluctably social. The Christian religion is a way to live before God as a people.

And yet: There is something ineluctable about the solitariness of the religious quest, and I think part of it lies here, that the religious quest walks precisely along those boundaries where the religious symbols, ideas, language, senses of authority, social structures, communal habits, projects, and hopes are called into question. All those things that religion, including Christianity, employs to shape its Way are social constructions, symbols worked out through time and practical implications and habits developed from those symbols. They constitute what Peter Berger calls a "sacred canopy," like a tent, but vast, like the canopy of heaven.[4] The sacred canopy through its myths, cosmologies, theologies, narratives, and other symbols defines what the human world is, its beginning and ending, its placements of things, its values and very meaning. The terms of the canopy are learned with culture, or invented to deal with crises, discoveries, and advents; they are internalized, and then projected out onto the world, whence they are modified and internalized again and on around in a constant dialectic. The sacred canopy shifts bit by bit in its terms and meaning as individuals mature, and a culture's sacred canopy itself changes with changing conditions. Previous chapters have given accounts of how basic, world-defining symbols can be true or false, depending on interpretive positions, and how in experience they grow and people learn new elements of the sacred canopy. The previous two chapters dealt with the evolution of the Christian sacred canopy from the mixture of Second Temple Jewish ones to a tent that encompasses Gentiles.

---

[4] See Berger's *The Sacred Canopy*.

Part of the very meaning of a sacred canopy is that it marks the boundaries of the human meaning-world. It gives definite shape to a world in a context in which everything really might be different. Or if one wonders about why there is a world at all, a question of the monotheistic sacred canopies, there is a necessary hint at the possibility that there need not be, indeed that the infinity behind the finite is more real than this contingent world. In every sphere of the sacred canopy the very finiteness of the defining founding element of the human world points beyond itself to the infinity, the non-finiteness that would obtain if the finite element were not there, or were wrong. Perhaps the cosmic geography is not a stack of heavens on top of Earth which itself rests on the waters over Hell. Perhaps there is no afterlife as everyone thinks; or perhaps the afterlife at which one has scoffed does indeed exist, with punishments for scoffers!

Some religious people are so secure within their sacred canopy, including some Christian ones, that they let their whole lives be interpreted according to it. For them birth is a destiny and death a transition according to a formula; the major events in life are passages with proper ceremonies and the great calamities have a justifying reason. Or if their sacred canopy is secular, birth is just being thrown into existence without meaning and death the absurd end; major events in life have no proper ritual form and thus no significant shape, with childhood lasting a lifetime; great calamities are as meaningless as the other chances of life. Neither of these sorts of people has a significant religious quest because the sacred canopy covers everything without question. Some other people do not have much of a sacred canopy at all, with inconsistent bits of world-founding shaping pockets of order within life, but not with much reflection and no integration with the rest. Peter Berger fears that modernity itself with its dissolution of meaning structures might make the very existence of sacred canopies next to impossible.

But for some people, those with a religious quest, the sacred canopies are significant precisely in their gesturing beyond themselves while they provide a social construction for interpreting ordinary affairs. Wesley Wildman has pointed out that every major Christian theologian has admitted that even the best theological categories (namely one's own) fail to articulate the depth and mystery of the divine reality. Every one of them is a social construction that at some level is false, too limiting.[5] There is mystery in the sacred canopy that opens itself to those who attend to it.

---

[5] See Wildman's "Theological Literacy."

Moreover, for many people the events of life are not always taken care of by the sacred canopy. Theodicy problems are devastating in this regard in late-modern culture. What Jewish or Christian sacred canopy including a providential God and a Chosen People could survive unquestioned after the Holocaust? For Christian sacred canopies that take God to be a well-intentioned, all-powerful, all-knowing personal being directing history, the ravages of war in the twentieth century were far too devastating to be justified by desert, and the suffering of innocents is irreconcilable without a concomitant belief in an afterlife where no suffering matters for long. The depths of evil and the blind brutality of suffering have caused many not to rest unthinkingly with their sacred canopy but to quest about its validity and what lies beyond its boundaries.

Theology gets interesting precisely at the points where crucial elements in the sacred canopy crack and where their consolations and interpretations of meaning do not work. Wildman distinguishes between that ordinary kind of theology that teaches the sacred canopy of a group and keeps it up and running, adjusting it to new circumstances, and the extraordinary but genuine kind of theology that operates on the boundaries of the canopy itself.[6] Most of what I have argued in previous chapters is an attempt to pitch the Christological tent on new ground, albeit calling attention to its apophatic tent-like character. Genuine theology, Wildman argues, always balances positive and negative moments, the kataphatic and the apophatic; it is genuine also when it loses its balance between those two. People sensitive to that questioning of the sacred canopy have a religious quest, and it is solitary because the community and solidarity constituted by the sacred canopy is itself in question, set in abeyance at some deep level.

Rents in the sacred canopy are not the only reasons the religious quest is solitary, however. I have used several metaphors for the religious quest in previous chapters, deliberately keeping the symbolic field fluid. The "quest" metaphor suggests a journey. "Presenting oneself before God" spatializes that. Relating one's finite life to the infinite, the ultimate, the unconditioned, is another metaphor. "One's identity as creature before the Creator" is yet another. The Logos theory schematizes the problematic by means of the notion of value: a creature with such and such form harmonizing such and such components, in such and such existential location, achieves such and such value. This concrete value is its reality, its identity. One cannot come to terms with one's own most

---

[6] Ibid.

important identity without determining what that is in ultimate perspective, in relation to the Creator and the rest of creation. The religious quest is that singular quest for that which registers one's own identity. It is the quest for meaning in the most profound sense, and that meaning is singular and unique to oneself, however contextual.

If there is any truth to the "relational metaphysics developed here, every person's identity involves all the components of life, the person's background, metabolism, educational resources, and most particularly the personal relations in family, jobs, friendships and public life that are individuated through maturation. A person's identity includes all those other people and contexts that are part of that person's life. No one has an identity apart from those connections.

But in another sense one's true identity is not just the things that happen to make up one's life but rather the cumulative responsible character that grows from all one's decisions large and small. There are many degrees of responsibility, moving from immaturity to maturity, and from the constraints of conjoint actions to actions with a wide degree of freedom and control.[7] One's unique and singular value in the cosmic scheme of things includes all those things that are components of one's life, particularly insofar as one takes responsibility for them. If the scheme developed here has merit, responsibility has many modes, including the orders one affects, the deference one pays, the ways one owns existential situations, and even one's attendance to the meaning of life.

The value or achievement of one's life is not just a sum of all these things. It includes as well how one relates to the obligations as such, that is, to the meaning of life, or standing before God. Augustine knew that the whole state of his soul was put in jeopardy by the incident of his thoughtlessly joining some adolescent friends in stealing pears, not an issue of moral gravity or even of centered deliberative responsibility; his barely conscious motive was to steal for the sake of being bad. It was a turning from God who had created the world in which people live under obligation.[8] That we live under obligation is one of those world-founding boundaries, the rejection of which amounts to a rejection of the founding of the world.

The religious quest is to find that world-founding element that makes our accumulated responsible identities meaningful, that establishes the

---

[7] On identity and conjoint action, with differential senses of responsibility, see my *Normative Cultures*, chapter 6.   [8] See Carl G. Vaught's "Theft and Conversion."

obligations responsibility to which defines moral identity. Christians say this is God the Creator. The deepest question of life is not just how to fulfill the obligations of our time, including all those specific to Christianity as continuing the historical identity of Jesus discussed in the previous chapter. The question is also how to relate the fact of being who we are in a world defined by being under obligation, to the fact of obligatedness as such, to the question whether the obligations are real, to the relation between the world that would give us meaning if it were well-founded and the founding of it. How does the world of finite valuable human meaning relate to the infinite? Can we trust the Christian sacred canopy that says it is created and that this creation has meaning? In theistic terms, the religious quest is the quest for God who answers these questions. The flip side of the religious quest is coming to terms with who we are in light of God, or before God, or in presenting ourselves to God. This is a solitary, lonely journey.

Not everyone undertakes it. I noted in chapter 3 that not everyone has an ultimate concern, as Tillich had hoped. Relating to God or the ultimate does not make a difference to the lives of everyone. I have now drawn out at greater length the argument that it is possible to relate differentially to the finite world, including to its obligations and to one's responsible self-identity as itself related to its transcendent ground. One way of relating is to turn from the relation itself. Even if it means presenting ourselves for condemnation, to relate to the created world with obligation relative to its Creator is better than turning from the Creator in neglect or rejection and from the responsible identity we have only relative to that creative ground. It is better because it engages a reality, whereas turning from it is to disengage: the question is of faith and existential engagement. Because we have some control over whether we turn to the quest or away from it, and the quest is better, we are obligated to it.

Perhaps one's residence under a rich and true sacred canopy is sufficiently secure that one slides without issue into the religious quest. William James called this the "once born" religious type. For others, the sacred canopy does not provide automatic entry, and turning to the religious quest is a matter of many turns. But for both, the quest requires confronting the sacred canopy with regard to its validity, confronting one's own singular identity as that which one brings to the ultimate, and confronting the ultimate itself in one's finite form.

One of the chief systems of symbols within Christianity is that Jesus is the friend who can accompany us on the religious quest. Not that Jesus makes it less lonely, though perhaps there is a sense of companionship that makes solitariness bearable. Rather, Jesus draws us onto the quest, guides it, allows us to be our true selves, and brings us into the divine presence. These are the symbol systems that will be examined here.

JESUS THE PERSONIFICATION OF DIVINE LOVE

No one can doubt the incongruity of the symbols for Jesus as friend with the symbols of the bloody atonement, the Cosmic Christ Pantokrator, King and Judge of Heaven, and the historical Jesus leavening Christian communities all over the globe. No one could be friends with those figures of cosmic significance and legendary status. Even the ghostly Christ of the resurrection appearances, who walks through walls, who is unrecognizable for long periods of time (figure 11, p. 165 above), who won't let you touch him (figure 10, p. 144 above), and then asks you to put your fingers in gaping spear thrusts in his side – that person could not be your friend. Perhaps only the risen Jesus of John 21 who cooks breakfast for his friends and then talks to Peter (who had recently betrayed him three times) about love, assuring him that he has accepted Peter's love, might be a friend.

The Christian tradition has not given high liturgical significance to the symbols of Jesus as friend. The others discussed in this book are all found frequently in stained glass in the churches of the European traditions of Christianity. That was not often true of symbols of Jesus as friend until perhaps the nineteenth century when it was fashionable to think about the historical Jesus. William Holman Hunt's *The Light of the World* (figure 13) might depict Jesus in a form that could be imagined as one's friend, but only in an eerie way; the same might be said of Warner Sallman's famous "portrait" of Jesus (figure 14, p. 211 below) that was replicated by artistic evangelists in countless "chalk talks" across America in the mid-twentieth century. But the theme of Jesus as friend has not generally been an organizing principle for public worship or community life, and probably for that very reason: friendship is not a mainly public or communal matter. It is personal and private. Being with one's friends in public is always a little delicate because one cannot display an intimacy that is not felt with the larger community without slight general embarrassment or even jealousy. For the lonely journey of the religious quest, you need a friend, not a leader.

Nevertheless, private friendship with Jesus was not a sentimental

Figure 13. William Holman Hunt, *The Light of the World*, Keble College, Oxford

nineteenth-century invention. It has solid biblical foundation, most pro-
nounced in John's gospel. Although the Pantokrator image in figure 1,
is easy to contrast with the sentimental Sallman painting as I did at the
beginning of chapter 3, it has long been recognized as double-seeing:
one eye looks to God and the other looks intimately at the viewer. John's
gospel and the letters attributed to him thematize love to a great degree.
Love, of course, has many dimensions, and often the topic emphasized
is how the community should be loving, and how individuals ought to
love in a public way within the community. Jesus' injunction in the
Farewell Discourses (John 15:12) to "love one another as I have loved
you" can be interpreted as a kind of public love within the community.
The issues for the formation of the community itself discussed in the
previous chapter can be summed up as finding loving modes of
Christian life in the world. But Jesus also meant love and friendship in
a personal, private, and individuated sense, and John went out of his
way to highlight this.

So, for instance, all the gospels (Matt. 26:69–75, Mark 14:66–72, Luke
22:55–62, John 18:15–18, 25–27) tell of Peter's denial of Jesus at the time
of his arrest. Luke reports Jesus turning to look at Peter as the cock crew.
But only John depicts the risen Christ doing anything in particular to
heal Peter's broken heart and repair their personal friendship. That was
part of the point of Jesus asking Peter three times whether he loved him
(John 21:15–17). Peter answered each time, "You know that I love you,"
which of course was the very thing in doubt after the denial. The ritual
questioning was in part to help Peter understand that he really did love
Jesus, despite what he must have secretly doubted about himself, and that
Jesus heard him and entrusted him with his own life – continuing to feed
his sheep.

John depicts Jesus' relation with many of his disciples as more personal, particular, and intimate than the other gospels suggest. Matthew
(4:18–22) and Mark (1:16–20) relate that Jesus walked by the Sea of
Galilee and called Simon and his brother Andrew, and the brothers
James and John, to follow him, and they did. Soon after (right away after
synagogue for Mark 1:29–31, and after the Sermon on the Mount for
Matthew 8:14–15) they went to dinner at Simon's house where Simon's
mother-in-law was sick; Jesus healed her and she served them. Luke
placed that dinner party at Simon's house (4:38–39) before Jesus called
Simon, James, and John (Luke 5:1–11; no mention of Andrew) to
become his official disciples. All this suggests that Jesus, Simon, Andrew,
James, and John had been longtime friends and that the master–disciple

relation developed slowly out of that.[9] The common synoptic reference to the dinner party might reflect an early Church memory of that occasion as being the first meeting of the gathered community as such, for which Simon's mother-in-law was especially honored.

John's account of the calling of the disciples, nevertheless, is far more individualized. It begins (1:35–51) on the day after Jesus' baptism by John the Baptist; Jesus comes back to the Baptist who tells two of his own disciples that Jesus is the Lamb of God. They follow after Jesus who turns and sees them, and asks them to come home with him to where he has been staying in Judea; the evangelist clocks that at four in the afternoon. One of those erstwhile disciples of John the Baptist, now of Jesus, is Andrew who brings his brother Simon to meet Jesus whom he claimed to be the Messiah; Jesus greets Simon and names him Cephas (Peter). Either Simon had already been in Judea, likely also among the Baptist's disciples, or Andrew had made a very quick trip to Galilee to get him, the former being more likely. At any rate, the next day (John is very detailed about chronologies) Jesus decides to go to Galilee himself and finds Philip who is introduced as a fellow townsman of Andrew and Peter (Andrew and Peter is the order in John's gospel at this point in the narrative, not Peter and Andrew). Jesus asks Philip to follow him who is convinced by Andrew and Peter's belief that they have found the Messiah. Philip then goes to his friend Nathanael who, however, is skeptical. So Jesus goes to Nathanael himself and convinces him by means of a vision. That is the end of the account of calling the disciples in John's gospel and, excepting the wedding party at Cana, they are not mentioned again seriously until the end of the sixth chapter where the Twelve have been gathered and Judas Iscariot is named as the one who will betray Jesus. The second disciple of John the Baptist who followed Jesus was not mentioned by name; was that John the brother of James, or the Beloved Disciple, the inspiration of this gospel tradition? Were these the same?

The disciples return to the center of John's narrative accompanying Jesus on the delayed visit to help Lazarus, and from here to the end Jesus is conspicuous with his particular friends, beginning with Mary, Martha, and Lazarus. Some Greeks who want to meet Jesus approach Philip, and he takes them to Andrew (Philip and Andrew are Greek names, of course) and both of them go to Jesus. Personal introductions were important for the fourth gospel. The last evening together is the famous

---

[9] See Thangaraj's *The Crucified Guru*.

portrait of fellowship among friends. Jesus begins by washing the others' feet. Peter attempts to refuse the courtesy on the grounds that Jesus is Teacher and Lord, and Jesus explaines that this is the proper way to behave even where there are such distinctions. Throughout, the discussion returns repeatedly to the theme of who would betray him and John says that Jesus was visibly upset, prompting Peter to ask the disciple "whom Jesus loved" to ask Jesus about this. Matthew and Mark record that the disciples were upset at Jesus' remarks about betrayal, but they do not show Jesus being disturbed as one about to be betrayed by a friend he had chosen (John 13:18). In the subsequent discussion, the so-called Farewell Discourses, Jesus goes on at length. John shows the disciples as discussing among themselves what Jesus says (John 16:19) and Thomas, Philip, and the other Judas are remembered for asking specific questions. John does not record Jesus' prayers in the garden of Gethsemane, but the other gospels (Matt. 26:36–46, Mark 14:32–42, Luke 22:39–46) center that around the interactions of Jesus, Peter, James, and John.

At the crucifixion, Matthew and Mark do not record that Jesus addressed words to anyone save God. Luke records Jesus welcoming one of the thieves into paradise, and the synoptics (Matt. 27:55–56, Mark 15:40–41, Luke 23:49) agree that the disciples, especially the women, "looked on from a distance." John, however, says the group was standing near the cross, and Jesus personally addressed his mother and John the Beloved Disciple about becoming a new family.

For resurrection appearances, Matthew records that Jesus spoke to the two Marys at the tomb and the Eleven together on a mountain in Galilee. Mark reports no resurrection appearances. Luke says Jesus appeared to two disciples (not of the Eleven) on the road to Emmaus, one of whom, Cleopas, is named, who subsequently reported this to the Eleven plus companions, none named, who in turn reported to Peter that Jesus had appeared, a tale of tales. Then Jesus suddenly appeared in the room, according to Luke, invited examination of his wounds, ate some fish, taught about scripture, and then led them out for the ascension, with no one named.

In John's account the resurrection appearances are more detailed, filled with personal names, beginning with an extended meeting with Mary Magdalene at the tomb. John records the same Easter evening meeting that Luke does but says that Jesus gave the assembly his peace, breathed on them (John's version of the Pentecostal Holy Spirit), and commissioned them to forgive sins (not to preach and baptize disciples across the world, Matthew 28:20, or wait for Pentecost, Luke 24:49).

John records that one of the Eleven was missing from that assembly, Thomas, and that when he was with them the following week Jesus returned, offered his body to Thomas to quell his doubts, and received his confession of faith. The twenty-first chapter of John is a kind of epilogue, itself in character with John's emphasis on the individuality of friendship. In addition to Jesus that chapter names Peter, Thomas, Nathanael, and the Sons of Zebedee, and says two others were present who were unnamed (possibly because of controversies over the memory, or because they were not among the Eleven). Jesus gave prophetic fishing advice (a symbolic act surely, not to instruct the professional fishermen), cooked breakfast for the group, and had that long private discussion with Peter about love and death. The Beloved Disciple (presumably John the Son of Zebedee) was the first to recognize Jesus, and the closing point of Jesus' discussion of death with Peter was his assertion of his right to have a more private friendship with the Beloved Disciple than with Peter.

Jesus' special friendship with John the Beloved Disciple is controversial, both for the possibility of its having sexual overtones and also for the fact it is reported most directly in the Gospel that comes from John's tradition. Whereas the synoptic gospels portray John and his brother James as major players along with Peter from the beginning (for instance Mark 5:37, 9:2–8, 38, and parallels), John's own gospel does not name him except indirectly as the one whom Jesus loved or as one of the sons of Zebedee. Unless John was one of the original two disciples coming over from John the Baptist, he is not mentioned specifically at all until the last supper (John 13:23–26) where he is described as sharing a couch with Jesus and as the one most fit to ask a private question of Jesus (who is the betrayer?). Nothing in John's gospel prepares the reader for the extraordinary act from the cross in which Jesus made John the son of his mother, in effect the executor of his estate (despite the fact that Jesus had vigorous brothers and John's own mother was one of the close followers of Jesus). John's gospel's very reticence to speak about John suggests a friendship too private to occupy a large place in the public narrative.

Matthew (20:20–28) and Mark (10:35–45) relate an incident that shows how Jesus treated John and his brother James differently from the others. Full of apocalyptic warnings, when the entire extended company of disciples is marching to Jerusalem for the Last End, John and James ask Jesus to sit at his right and left hand in glory. What an adolescent thing to say! According to Matthew, they have their mother ask Jesus for them, so they probably were very young. Jesus gently tells them that they do not know what they are asking for, but that they will drink his cup; arrangements in glory are not for him to make. But the other disciples took offense at the presumption of the boys, possibly also at the special friendship of John with Jesus. To them, Jesus was blunt, saying that whereas Gentile kings lord it over their subjects in his community each should be the servant of all the others. That might have been a reproof to the boys' desire for high place (or maybe to their mother's attempt to advance her children). Yet by saying it to the jealous disciples rather than the boys Jesus turned the point into a subtle criticism of their jealousy, which of course comes from a coveting of "place."[10] Jesus' treatment of all parties was appropriate, friendly, tolerant, and indeed loving; but it was different for the two parties.

This long textual discussion all goes to show that personal friendship as well as more public kinds of love were recognized as part of the Christian Way in the early Church, especially in John's tradition. To conclude this discussion about private love or friendship, think about Paul's famous disquisition on love in 1 Corinthians 13. Its context in the letter treats love as a community virtue more important than all the offices of the congregation discussed in the preceding and succeeding chapters, superior in fact to faith and hope which are dominant Pauline motifs for general Christian virtues. That chapter has become an emblem of married love and is frequently recited in weddings, although it addresses none of the special problems of married love such as material support, housework, and raising children. Considered in the context of private love between friends, however, substituting "friendship" for "love," it makes perfect sense, even to the effects of friendship being clearer sight, not as in a glass darkly, and knowing one's companion fully even as one is known.

Friendship, of course, even at its most private, has elements of social construction. On the one hand it has to have signs with which to express itself, and these are social; on the other it must fit itself into more public life. Friendship therefore has a history in its various cultures and has been analyzed in many wonderful ways. One of the most powerful recent analyses is by Andrew Sullivan who uses the classic Western literature on friendship but focuses it on the situation of American gay people in the AIDS crisis. So many gay people have been abandoned by their families and predeceased by their lovers that only friends are left for company on that last journey home. Because there have been so many such journeys

---

[10] I owe this point to a sermon by Wesley J. Wildman, "God Is Friend."

for gay people, many have learned the nature and offices of friendship quickly.[11]

Paul, of course, did not intend that 1 Corinthians passage to refer only to friendship, and he had a cosmic extension for it. If we are to understand how Jesus might be a friend to us, we need to swerve briefly from this discussion of friendship's intimacies to divine love on the cosmic scale again.

Recall the account of creation in chapter 1. The eternal creative act produces determinate things that have form, components formed, existential location, and value. Creativity within time does the same thing, moving from one swarm of determinate harmonies to the next, making the earlier components in the later, or dissolving them, but always moving on to new harmonies that themselves are part of larger swirling processes. Each determinate harmony is something real and good and made by the Creator. The Christian tradition has identified this creative activity with divine love, and that is just and true. On the human scale, we love when we make good things. Love is especially directed to people, and we are loving when we help people become themselves and to become better. Parental love is a literal making. Human love does not create *ex nihilo*, always beginning instead with given components such as genes and neighborhoods. The analysis of the Logos developed here throughout gives more content to love within the human sphere, for it suggests that to love someone is to help them with their justice, piety, faithful engagement with their place, and their religious quest. Put together, this means to help them become better lovers themselves. So part of the formal argument for the special divinity of Jesus is that in his historical person he initiated a movement to make people into decisively better lovers.

Another dimension to divine love needs to be lifted up here, the kenotic. Unlike a potter or architect who creates out of antecedent materials, or a God who dips into the infinite divine substance to ladle out some finite world-stuff, the Christian God creating *ex nihilo* holds nothing back but is completely expressed in the creation. God is not something reserved after creation but the creative act with its product itself, and within time the creativity moves inexorably from moment to moment, not lingering. That too is registered as love, giving oneself over to what is loved with no reserve or judgment.

---

[11] See Sullivan's *Love Undetectable*.

What are the best paradigms for creative love? The Chinese are clear that it is parental love, and Jesus' intimate address for God, "Abba" (Daddy), might agree with this. But the Christian image of families is that they are broken, often as not. Rather, the Christian paradigm is the love of a friend (John 15:13). So it is with this paradigm that we ask how Jesus can be our friend.

IMAGINATIVE FRIENDSHIP

In the relevant sense of intimate friendship, of course, Jesus is our friend only in our imagination. The historical Jesus prior to his death knew no one like us, at least not like in culture. The continuing historical Jesus does not have subjective consciousness in the relevant sense for friendship with us. Jesus as friend is one whom we imagine, constrained by what we know of the historical Jesus down to now, and by what we learn of ourselves in the friendship.

The imagination of a friend, and the comportment of ourselves to that imagined person, is not at all strange to our experience. We know many people with whom we interact regularly, with whom we imagine conversations. We imagine what they would think about something, how we might respond, how they might respond to us, and so forth. Even in a face-to-face encounter we imagine what is going on in the other person's mind, we imagine what the meaning might be of posture and body language, and we imagine how they might respond if we did this or that. Interpersonal relations are impossible without internalizing imagined persona of the others and interacting with them imaginatively as we interpret the meanings of what is going on and compose our own intentionality in direct engagements. This is the very meaning of having a semiotic system as a means of communication between people. Contemporary computers can signal intelligent information back and forth to one another, but they do not imagine the intentions of the other, think about alternative meanings and strategies, and ask how their own signs might be interpreted or misinterpreted when they are internalized in the other computer. Or if they do interact with virtual images of one another as well as with the real signals, they have an interpersonal relation, at least in rudiment.

Face-to-face encounters usually provide pretty quick feedback correcting our imagination. In some circumstances, however, we legitimately doubt whether the responses that in fact are given reveal the true intentions of the other: our imagined intentions might be the real ones, we suspect, covered over by deception, or a failure on the other's part to understand his or her own true deeper intentions. Moreover, under even the most felicitous of communicative conditions, the actual responses give only the barest and most abstracted expressions of the intentionality we imagine the person to have. In imagining another person's intentionality, we take it to have not only a cultural perspective and a feeling for being in that person's body, but also a background of personal history, of that person's psycho-social development, relations with parents, deep sexual and spiritual tensions, and configurations of forces. We take the person to be specifically placed in society with family, job, roles of various sorts, to all of which the person's intentionality is related. We construe the person's intentionality to include relations with ourselves and often with people, places, and events shared in common, relations that we imagine to be different from our own. These and a thousand other factors figure in to what we imagine about another person as we attempt to interpret the bare signals of words and gestures, and acts that might be given a merely physical description. For some personal interactions most of the imagined interpretive background for the other person is trivial. If we have reason to think the person can determine the postage for the package we want to send because she is the postmistress, we pay her what she asks without wondering much about her ethnic background or whether her early childhood made her liable to obsessive behavior when under pressure from her children. Most ordinary interactions with familiars and colleagues are more complicated than that, with genuine wonder, sometimes, about whether we have been understood and understand. We wonder about whether what seems to have transpired just now connects beyond its appearance with what we know are ongoing issue for the other: Is Sonny angry now because I wouldn't let him go out, or because it reinforces his belief I am a controlling parent, or do both motives feed the other? There is a sense in which the people we know best are the deepest mysteries, because we have come to imagine so diverse and rich a set of background variables in their intentionality, based on ongoing experience, that any actual situation of communication is vastly overdetermined by imagination and undetermined by confirming signals.

If the above is true for people with whom we interact regularly, how much greater is the importance of imagination in our relations with people who are very significant for us but who are away. Mature people imagine interactions with the parents long after leaving home, often after the parents are dead, and they imagine how the parents would react to their present issues. Most of us have good friends with whom we have imaginary conversations from which we get our bearings. Most authors have struggled to find a "voice" that would communicate with their desired audience, and imagine how someone famous in that audience would react: could Mother Teresa understand this? Paul Tillich? What would Camille Paglia say?

These imaginings are not pure fiction. Even the purest fiction is the composite of images picked up from somewhere and transformed according to imaginably possible transformations. But there are two fundamental constraints on the imagination of the intentionality of others. One obviously is what we know about the other person. Mother Teresa is an ideal imagined audience figure because we know something at least alleged about the charity of her heart, her practical hands-on devotion to people most of us loathe to touch, the simplicity of her faith, and her lack of sophistication regarding social causation. Tillich is a different ideal imagined figure because he was so much at the heart of a long and culturally rich theological tradition, with sharp insights and prejudices, an agenda that might be addressed. Camille Paglia is a brilliant debunker of political correctness and pious verities. Imagining the responses of each would give definite shape to one's argument. Similarly with imagined conversations with absent friends, parents, and significant figures: we can imagine interactions with them and their responses to our present concerns precisely because of what we know about who they are or were from other contexts. That the postmistress is behind the postal counter wearing the postal uniform allows us to imagine her intentionality enough to satisfy the transaction.

So in imagining Jesus to be our friend, we already know a lot about him, or at least have much information. The gospels are full of depictions of Jesus, showing him in many situations. The rest of the New Testament is filled with interpretations of who he was, what he did, and often what he stood for regarding how to live. The great symbols of Christ, including those discussed earlier, are part of our imaginative background for Jesus. Then there are the teachings about Jesus that many people received as children, youths, and as adults living in church communities, including representations of what our elders and the rest of the church have thought he would say and do in situations different from the biblical ones. The post-resurrection living Christ is not without witnesses.

Significant controversy exists about who Jesus really was and whether the Church's interpretation of what he would be, do, or say was right in a given circumstance. It could make a real difference if Jesus were not inclusive in his friendships as it so often seemed but instead was solidly identified with the poor and hostile to the rich. It could make a real difference if he were concerned almost exclusively with the children of Israel and did not care much for others unless they had staggeringly exemplary faith. It could make a real difference if Jesus would have approved excommunicating Nestorians over their Christology, or would have approved the crusades, or would think denominational loyalty is ultimately important.

Nevertheless, the gospels are to be read not as direct communicative signals from Jesus but through the intentionalities we can imaginatively construct of their own authors; they are perspectives of the evangelists on Jesus that we can come to understand. We can come to understand Jesus through the eyes of those interpreting communities just as we come to understand our contemporaries, not only by making inferences from their words, gestures, and deeds, but also by seeing how their intentionalities are construed through the perceptions of other people with their own intentionalities.

Although it might seem that the involvement of imagination to such a great degree as I have claimed here makes the interpretation of others precarious, just the opposite is the case. The interpretation of others needs always to read their words, gestures and deeds against the background of their deep intentional structure that can only be imagined. The deeper our experience with the person, the more clues we have. Some of the most profound clues are how people with different intentionalities from our own interpret the clues of the other. In fact, we count on social interactions with many others to form our imaginative constructions with each. In the case of our special friends, we might see some things few others do; but even so, we use the perspective of those others to help understand the intentionalities of our friends. Therefore it is an advantage to have not just one gospel, no matter how authoritative, but four, plus the memories and interpretations of Jesus in the rest of the New Testament, and the traditions of the Church where Jesus has lived ever since. In fact, if Jesus had written his own autobiography that had come down to us with perfect textual integrity, it would still help to have the other gospels to know what he meant. The plurality of intentionalities imaginatively interacting with Jesus' intentionality can only strengthen our own imagination regarding Jesus and what he would say or do as our friend.

The other constraint on imaginative construction in these matters is ourselves and our situation. We imagine the others responding to us, and of course we have interpretations of ourselves. In the case of the post-mistress we imagine that she takes us as an ordinary customer the weight of whose package is the relevant variable; but if we point a gun at her and also ask for the cash from her drawer, we would be on the lookout for a special response from her. Similarly, with our colleagues and famil-iars: they are interacting in the same situation as we are, responding to the same things we are, as well as to ourselves. Our knowledge of that situation, and of what we ourselves are saying and doing, is a powerful constraint on our imaginative constructions interpreting others. "Constraint" is not quite the right word: the situation adds content to the imagination, focusing what we imagine the others might imagine about what is going on. Although we know what we intend to do and say, the others might misinterpret that; this possibility is itself part of our imaginative construction and leads us sometimes to take extra steps not to be misunderstood. Or the imagined possibility of being misunder-stood gives us the possibility of deceiving. Or, as our friends sometimes point out, what we think we know we are saying and doing is not the real truth, and we are the ones deceived. Personal interactions are greatly shaped by these considerations.

When we imagine what our parents or deep friends would say to us now when they are long absent, part of our imagination is shaped by what we think they knew of us, of our own intentionality. Another part is shaped by our own circumstances, which we know or think we do, and to which we can imagine our parents and friends reacting. Our own understanding of our circumstances is the focal orientation of imagin-ing their responses.

In the case of the imagined friendship with Jesus, the Jesus we know from the scripture of course did not know us or our situation. The his-torical Jesus who is articulated in our community, should we live in a good Christian one, might come a bit closer. But even there that Jesus would be more abstract and public, not concretely related to us and private.

Imagining a friendship with Jesus is deeply constrained by who we are, most particularly who we are in the depths to which our essential iden-tity is related. We have to be able to imagine Jesus as someone who can relate to us and to whom we can relate as friend. Although I know many biblical scholars, I cannot imagine any one of them imagining a friend-ship with Jesus in which the conversation was conducted in ancient Aramaic. We all imagine Jesus speaking our own language. And for those

Figure 14. Warner Sallman, *Head of Christ*

of us who might be seriously bi-lingual and bi-cultural, perhaps Jesus has to be imagined addressing those different parts of us each in its own language. It was no accident that the European representations of Jesus made him look European, or the African representations black, or the Korean like a Korean. Joseph Stella's nativity (figure 12, p. 170 below) seems to be set in South America. Jesus as friend needs to be imagined as relating to us, and our kind, in our situation. The pious twentieth-century representations of Jesus wandering through a modern Western city dressed in a long choir-robe are silly. Yet they have a point. Some people today cannot imagine Jesus as anything other than dressed in a robe with long brown hippy hair. Sallman's blue-eyed Jesus is definitely of the House of Plantagenet, despite the choir-robe (figure 14). For those people, that image is the place to start. And the goal for the sophisticates is not to require Jesus to be imagined as like us, but as radically different, different as the people we ourselves are supposed to be able to befriend.

But to begin with, it is important to imagine Jesus addressing us on our own terms.

Who are we when we engage Jesus imaginatively? That question needs to be answered if we are to bring to bear this kind of constraint on imagining Jesus himself. Ordinary good friendships usually develop with three kinds of experiences. Usually the occasion for a friendship starts with some shared experience such as common schooling, being neighbors, working together, a common trip. This develops into a mutual appreciation of the ordinary life of each person, where they live, how they relate to family and neighborhood, what their jobs and interests might be, and so on. Very good friends discover and cultivate a kind of synergy between some aspects of their lives, even when those lives are different in content. Another kind of experience is the peak ones, those shared moments of intense joy, thrill, deep communion, the moments whose intensification of life helps define what is important in one's life afterward. Children have those moments playing together; schoolmates have those moments, travelers at some great marvel, friends in conversations that change one's life or that bring to articulation feelings struggling for expression. The third kind of experience, to be sure, is the shared moments of suffering, grief, sorrow, and despair. Someone who companions us at those very low times when death would make an insignificant difference is a deep friend; when we can be with someone in their own despair, that marks us as friends.

A serious friendship requires time to grow with all three of those modes of experience, the ordinary living, the peak experiences, and the visits to the abyss. Each of those rests on vast and deep backgrounds of intentionality, different in both parties. To share the experiences in friendship requires working through to imaginative access to what the other is thinking and feeling as lodged within those intentional structures. Perhaps more surprising is that we discover our own hearts, our own intentionality structure in this process of deep sharing in serious friendship. What we thought was most important in our life turns out not to be that at all but something else instead, some unacknowledged ambition, or a fear. What we thought was so thrilling about the shared peak experience was not what was going on at all. The despair we thought we understood came not from the causes we knew but from something else entirely, and our friend helped us to understand. Friendship is an ongoing process of self-discovery and self-revelation, on both sides, with different effects and mutual reinforcements.

Furthermore, the content of our lives, the things that count as peak experiences, and the things that count as dark nights of the soul, all change through life. From childhood to youth to responsible maturity to accomplishment and finally to old age and the contemplation of a world without us, the deep structures of our intentionalities and the ways they register experience change. And so friendships that last also move through these changes. It is rare that a childhood playmate remains a confidant for life, but it happens. Perhaps it is less rare for school and college friends with whom we shared great adventures or all-night soul-searching conversations to grow with us through life. Still, long friendships that endure and grow through changes are always rare. But they are life-forming. A person without good friends is likely not to know himself or herself. Marriage in late-modern Western societies is associated with friendship as well as sex, family, and home; but that association is not made in many other cultures, most of which separate domestic life from friendship, and it does not happen with great frequency in late-modern Western cultures.

To imagine Jesus as our friend is to imagine him relating to our own real selves, which in turn we must imagine. This means finding ourselves as we function in all the rounds of daily life including our dealings with other people, ourselves as brought to focus in peak experiences, and ourselves as laid low in fear, sorrow, despair, and apathy about life itself. In ordinary good friendships we want our friends to know us, and are wonderfully trusting in our own faithfulness to accept our friends as we come to know them; yet we ordinarily hold at least some of our faults in hiding, embarrassed or ashamed to bring them into the friendship. There is a virtue in being embarrassed or ashamed at some things. Yet in a very good ordinary friendship, the acceptance of mutual love allows us to expose and confess more and more. In a friendship with Jesus we imagine our exposure, and imagine our hiding, and imagine Jesus responding to what we expose, and also, like a perceptive friend, to our attempts at hiding.

Imagining Jesus as friend then is a moving dialectic of imagining how he would share our ordinary life, our peak experiences in the flush of life, and our drowning moments in the Slough of Despond. We imagine how he would react to what we reveal of ourselves, and we imagine this by reflecting on his character as we know from other witnesses, ancient and subsequent. With the imagination of how he would respond to us, in our language, like a friend of our time, but out of his own agenda, his own justice, his own mercy, forgiveness, and love, we build a picture of who he is in relation to us. And then, of course, we can look again at ourselves, perhaps understanding things about ourselves we never thought before, or could bring ourselves to think.

How would Jesus, our imagined friend, relate to how we affect the orders of things around us? To how we defer to the things of our world? To how we engage the realities of our life? To how we compose ourselves with respect to what is ultimately important? To how we integrate these things? The more concretely we imagine this, the more we come to understand who we are in these regards, and the more concrete our image is of Jesus our friend. Moreover, what is at stake in each of these regards is not just the surface action or attitude, but the whole intentionality behind it, our way of forming our history, environment, psychic past and deepest passions into the vast and deep but highly personal intentional frames within which our actions, words, and attitudes have meaning. Just as we need to know these things about our close friends in order to interpret and respond to what they really mean and are, so we need our friend Jesus to understand these things about ourselves. For us to imagine Jesus understanding, we need to imagine them about ourselves, as truly as possible for our friendship with Jesus to be true.

So it is that meditation on Jesus as friend takes on the aura of the confessional. This is not just in imagining him with us in our dark hurt moments, but in all of our moments, the ordinary ones and peak experiences as well. For our inmost hearts are brought to the friendship as they form and express themselves in what we do, say, and feel.

I said earlier that our essential identity has to do with the cumulative character we build in making all the little, and sometimes large, decisions that shape our ongoing lives. That remark should be supplemented to include the shaping of the intentional structures through which our choices themselves appear from deep in our hearts. The choices about which we speak easily are but the most outward expressions of deep personal structures that give them meaning, that relate them to the rest of who we are, and that constitute our deepest grasp of the world, how we feel about possible outcomes of actions, how we take in and process the components of our lives, how we construct our engagement of life itself, and how we already have arranged a posture toward the ultimate. Our essential identity is all of this, and this is what we bring to the friendship with Jesus and in terms of which we imagine him responding to us as friend. Friendship with Jesus, imagined over time with a passion for friendship that overcomes our dishonesty, is a way to come to know ourselves, and know whom it is we present to God.

The confessional aspect of friendship with Jesus might seem to be better imagined as a friendship with Omniscient Freud. For we can use the techniques of psychoanalysis associated with him, and newer improved techniques and conceptualities that can be imagined into his omniscience. Although there is truth to this, the other constraint on imagining a friendship of this sort is the known character of the friend. Omniscient Freud is a professional analyst paid to accept us and our dirty secrets without judgment (if we can imagine Omniscient Freud we can imagine ourselves rich enough to afford his fees). But Jesus is no professional who accepts us because of a role. We know Jesus' take on justice, deference, existential engagement, and the love of God, and it is not Freud's. We can imagine how Jesus would respond to our character in those respects, both as a ruthless judge who makes us naked with his imagined glance and as a merciful, forgiving, faithful lover who would cover our sins with his body.

The sexual imagery of friendship with Jesus is never possible to avoid completely. St. Theresa made it explicit: her enjoyment of Jesus was orgasmic. Not only the Church has been represented as the bride of Christ, but individuals too. Heterosexual men and lesbian women might have some understandable difficulty with this and can displace sexual imagery with other images of being penetrated to the core with Jesus' knowing judgment and being enveloped all round with the warm safety of his love. This sounds sexual too, does it not? Perhaps sado-masochism arises from the imagined, longed for, experience of being fully known and loved. With ordinary friends there are decent boundaries to this. What a great kindness not to require our friends to know us fully or participate in the deepest recesses of our hearts! When those boundaries are not respected and regularly renegotiated fairly, an ordinary friendship, even the best, is likely to crash. But an imagined friendship with Jesus, long term, has no need for such boundaries.

There is another root of the sexual imagery below the surface (if not up front) of meditation on Jesus as friend, namely, our own libidinal impulses (Omniscient Freud is right about that). Perhaps sexuality with its paradigmatic meaning of copulation is not the right word for libido, for surely we have libidinal impulses toward people to whom we are not at all sexually attracted, something Freudians sometimes attempt to explain as displaced sexual attraction for someone else. However that goes, we know that the heart of our intentionalities is formed by the impulses of our bowels (to use the biblical expression, Col. 3:12, KJV), the same stirrings that are set in motion by real ordinary sexual excitement. Though our libidinal impulses are given in our genes and shaped by environments beyond our control, they are among the most important means by which we take up the world in our intentional stances. We take possession of them when we use them to take possession of the world. The impulses are expressed for better or worse in our justice, deference, engagements, and hope for heaven. They are part of our essential identity, and our self-revelations seem to turn more and more to those stirrings. Sexuality itself is a metaphor for them. St. Paul might have had his own problems with sex, but his repeated references to it were on the mark in identifying where to find the heart that comes up for judgment or that expresses the redemptive love of Christ.

I have spoken so far as if friendship with Jesus were a one-way affair, a matter of him loving us and us revealing ourselves, opening ourselves, to be loved. I have spoken of this almost as a therapeutic matter, as something to teach us about ourselves and reveal our deepest intentions. All this is a legitimate but selfish use of friendship. Of course there is the other side as well. Friendship with Jesus involves us coming to love him. The same is true in ordinary friendships. No friend would bother with us unless we were attracted to perform analogous offices of understanding, sharing, judging, and appreciating as well. Moreover, accepting the helping offices of friends is difficult unless to some degree we give ourselves over the friends in strongly felt affection. Only because we love them and are committed to them can we accept their knowing judgment of us and their bad taste in loving us. Friendship with Jesus is the same way.

With respect to the Lamb of God who nails my sins to the cross, I can be grateful beyond words. With respect to the Cosmic Christ, the Alpha and the Omega, the King of the Universe, I can be overwhelmed with glory and thankful in passing for my own place in the universe. With respect to Jesus Christ the Son of God, Second Person of the Trinity, I can find my place as a creature fundamentally related to God. With respect to the historical Jesus, I can rejoice in finding a way to live with divine glory in my community, participating in the ministry of Jesus, functioning as a member of his body, struggling with the Holy Spirit to give glory to God in my place. But through none of those symbols do I find occasion to love Jesus as I do my friends only better. Only when I imaginatively construct a long friendship with Jesus, imagined as the lover of my own soul, imagining Jesus himself transformed as he comes to know and love me, do I have a symbol of Jesus through which I can love heart and soul.

Narcissism haunts the loving of someone imagined to love us.

Perverse displacement, perhaps masochism, arises in loving someone imagined to judge us, a heaping up of self-hate. But these are precisely the kinds of things that are worked through in a friendship, and worked through thoroughly in friendship with Jesus. Though the friendship is a construct of the imagination, it has two realistic constraints that become more real and vivid as the friendship proceeds. One is who we are ourselves, and the other is who Jesus can be imagined to be relative to us given what we know of him. From what we know, Jesus cannot be imagined to be anything less than a knowing judge and forgiving, desiring lover.

In friendship with Jesus we can learn two fundamental things down in our muscles, bones, and bowels: First that we are lovable because we are loved, and second that we too can love with our whole heart, mind, strength, and soul because that is what we feel for Jesus. How does this bring us to God?

LONELINESS, THE CROSS, AND THE ABYSS

Jesus is the Christian symbol of God, and we engage God by means of that symbol.[12] Jesus to be sure is many symbols, and it is through Jesus as our friend that we engage God as fully lovely with our own full love. To understand this, however, we need to confront the paradox at which our argument has arrived: the coincidence of loneliness and love.

I began this chapter by reflecting on the loneliness of the religious quest, the sense in which, despite all the relational inter-definitions with other things and personal individuation through concrete relationships, we face God alone. The search for what our lives ultimately mean, however socially intertwined and nested in nature, is ultimately solitary.

We have now explored something of that solitariness. It rests first in the directionality and intentional density of our subjectivity. Our actions toward others, especially communicative actions in speech and gesture, themselves have no reality in us except as coming through our intentional structures of background, life-history, early childhood learning, environment, psycho-sexual passions, and purposes large and small, known and hidden. Although most of the elements of our intentionality are given in genes and the resources of the particular natural and social environment, our intentionality structure is composed of what we

---

[12] This point is beautifully expressed in the title of Roger Haight, SJ's new book, *Jesus: Symbol of God.*

do with all these. Little babies turn from genetically human metabolic organisms into personal human beings by organizing their responses with intentionality into more intentionality. What starts as a laconic or especially sensitive nervous system turns into a laconic or excitable little person. Within a few years the child has a sufficiently well-formed intentionality structure that we say he or she acts from purposes, not merely instincts. By the age of eligibility to drive a car, vote, or join the military, we say that the person has such a well-developed intentionality structure that it is his or her own responsibility to see that it is a good one.

As Jesus pointed out in the Sermon on the Mount, a person is responsible in some deep religious, if not moral, sense not only for external acts but also for the promptings of the heart behind them. So when I said earlier that the essence of a person is his or her cumulative character resulting from choices, I did not mean only the overt actions and such conscious choices. I meant all the little choices that transform mechanical responses to primitive intentional responses, primitive intentions to more complicated coded ones, developing eventually a complex intentionality by means of which the person participates in the meaningful, semiotic, exchanges of society. Many of those choices are made so early in life, or so deep in the bio-psychic structure of the human organism, that the person cannot possibly be held personally responsible for them. But they are *parts* of the lasting intentionality structure and its life of relation to the world that the person presents to God. The person is responsible also for how other elements in the intentionality structure relate to, take up, and give more meaning to those primal pre-responsible elements. Some of the given matters in intentional life are those of blood-guilt; but how those are taken up is more a matter of responsibility.

The issues of how one is a sexual person illustrate this point at its heart. Everyone has a base-level sexuality given in some combination of genetic readiness and early learning that seems to be deeply fixed long before the child can be held accountable for sexual decisions. If we believe in the goodness of creation then that base-level sexuality is good, so far as it goes. The question of the "goodness" of homosexuality is settled positively by this consideration, a matter hotly debated among Christians now. But no person ever acts or lives sexually on that base-level sexuality alone. Sexuality is taken up into other intentionality structures so that it is intertwined and expressed through affection, intentionally shaped instincts for care and domesticity, and the management of emotion and energy. Sexuality (of any orientation) is easily expressed as selfish egoism, anger and violence, and can take brutally anti-social and disrespectful forms toward others. It also can be expressed through the most sublime intentionality structures of friendship, love, and care. Perhaps Jesus had this character of soul in mind in both his examples, condemning the intentionality of anger behind murder and of lust behind adultery. So the "how" of a person's sexual expressions throughout intentional life is far more than the base-level given, and involves considerable personal responsibility. All of this is presented to God.

The directionality in intentionality is from the heart outward. What is the soul? It is the vitality of responsiveness to the world shaped by the intentionality structures through which it moves and in part are its own creation. The essence of a person is how that person moves through intentionality structures uniquely his or her own and in significant measure the person's own responsible creation. Moreover, the person's essence is not merely intentional life at a moment, but the cumulative history of intentionality through the person's lifetime, a topic to be explored in the next chapter.

The religious quest is to come to terms with who one is essentially in relation to the ultimate. Given all one's worldly connections and inter-definitions, one's soul still has a meaning to be found as such, irrespective of those connections that are among its most important constituents. In that respect, the soul is absolutely alone because it is absolutely itself. It presents itself to the ultimate ground of meaning, or to God, as the absolute other. One stands before God as only oneself, not as anyone else.

What our argument has also shown, however, is that we discover who we are through friendship. In serious friendship we go beyond social roles to relate to people and discern their intentionalities at some deep level. To do so requires coming to terms with our own intentionalities that are brought to light by the friend, and this process is dialectical, going deeper and deeper as the friendship deepens. Both parties are brought to terms with deeper structures of their own intentionalities that they find accepted by the other, indeed interpreted, and also with the deeper structures of their friend. I said above that serious friendship operates through time in relation to the ordinary details of living, and also through peak experiences of shared friendship and the pits of despair where the friends support each other. The ordinary times are where the full range of intentional structures come into play in the assorted contexts, and the peak and pit times are when they come under pressure. In the pressure times, intentionality structures become a little ecstatic, leaping ahead to new levels of meaning and intensity, or collapsing to more primitive forms. Friendship helps bring this out. I can never understand myself fully, or even accept what I do understand, only by myself. For of course I am not by myself: I am in part who I am intentionally for and with others and, to understand and accept that, I need to read it in them. So in friendship we learn to love and be loved, a paradox to juxtapose to the solitariness of the self we bring to friendship.

An imaginatively constructed friendship with Jesus has many obvious disadvantages compared with a real friendship, the most particular being that we can always lie and cheat in our imagination whereas real friends sometimes catch us up on that. But the advantage to an imaginatively constructed friendship with Jesus, the reason it has been a part of Christian piety for ages, is that we cannot but imagine Jesus as the symbol of God the Creator. Jesus is the one who not only insists on the proper human orientation to the Creator in justice, deference, faith and the hope of the religious question, but does that in our imagination as it applies directly to our circumstances. Indeed, "circumstances" puts it too externally. Jesus as friend relates to every nook and cranny of our hearts, interpreting, letting us understand, judging, and loving. This friendship is creative because it allows us to love in return. Jesus as visible image of the invisible Creator is the personification of God as judge and lover, the divine creative agent who makes us into lovers, and the one loved when we love the Creator.

Even when we imagine Jesus penetrating to the depths of our hearts in knowing judgment that strips us naked and covering our sins with his body, Jesus is other. Jesus has an intentionality with a different direction from ours, one to whom we are objects of interpretation, judgment, and love. We cannot imagine Jesus as friend without that otherness; without that there is no interest in Jesus' intentional framework, or in the possibility of his having a perspective on ours. Even in imaginative friendship, there are boundaries that mark the differences in intentional direction, boundaries that let us imagine Jesus as partly opaque to us, and rightly so, and ourselves as different from Jesus, not what he would be or do in our circumtances. In real ordinary friendships we need such boundaries for letting the other "be," and letting ourselves be as well. Jesus must be imagined as having a different essence from ourselves, as being a different soul, albeit one that expresses the Creator creating in our circumstances and very soul.

All of this discussion has been very psychological. Good, so far as it goes. But there is another sense of loneliness that expresses the human condition in ways that go far beyond psychology. Once our very ancient forebears thought their trees and streams, mountains and seas, were populated by deities so that the mysteries of transcendence spoke out quite close to home. With the development of Axial Age religions, including Exilic and post-Exilic Judaism and Christianity, our ancient parents thought of the world as a whole with a steady sphere for human life, perhaps other realms for angels and heavenly beings, but with the Creator God as transcendent of the entire creation and ruling things in ways defined by human meaning. The general principle of this human meaning was that human beings are the center and purpose of the universe and God arranges things so that human goodness is rewarded and evil punished, appearances to the contrary notwithstanding. There were early tears in the fabric of that anthropocentric and divine monarchical sacred canopy in the ancient world, for instance as expressed in Job. Now that canopy has shredded and blown away. We know, as I have rehearsed several times, that the large causal processes of the cosmos pay little regard to human life, that the hospitality of Earth to human habitation is a serendipitous and temporary fluke, that the Earth is on the edge of one small galaxy out of billions, and that one's fortunes in life have little to do with one's goodness or evil and everything to do with inertial natural and social forces, luck, and prudence. God does not manage affairs within history to reward good and punish evil.

And so we are desperately alone in the cosmos, relative to the dreams of our ancestors. We want God to take care of our needs like a Father. We want our people to be great but discover that their achievements float on blood. We want our jobs and projects to be successful but discover them often to be trivial and fragmentary. We don't want our parents and friends and children to die but they do. We don't want to grow old but we do, or, worse, don't get to. We are like Job accusing God of a bad job. Instead, the Preacher (Eccl. 1:2–9) was right about God's created nature and us:

Vanity of vanities! All is vanity. What do people gain from all the toil at which they toil under the sun? A generation goes, and a generation comes, but the earth remains forever. The sun rises and the sun goes down, and hurries to the place where it rises. The wind blows to the south, and goes around to the north; round and round goes the wind, and on its circuits the wind returns . . . all things are wearisome; more than one can express; the eye is not satisfied with seeing, or the ear filled with hearing. What has been is what will be, and what has been done is what will be done; there is nothing new under the sun.

Though lacking a sense of the evolution of the cosmos, the Preacher surely caught its indifference to human meaning. The senses described in previous chapters of Christ as King of the Universe were careful not to contravene this picture of the cosmos and lack of domestic divine management. When we imagine ourselves approaching God for our reward, what we find is the Abyss.

So not only are we in solitary companionship with friends who are more other to us the deeper they penetrate our souls, we are together in a cosmos indifferent to human desire save by the accidents of Earth.

Who knew that better than Jesus? He was a teacher with poor students, a healer who could never do enough, the leader of a band that abandoned him. He was betrayed by one of his chosen friends, convicted of a crime that had little to do with his life or ministry, and executed naked and bloody in front of his mother at an early age. And as he twisted against the nails he gave up any hope he might have had for last-minute angels and cried the accusation of devastating cosmic loneliness: "My God! My God! Why have you forsaken me?" Then he commended his spirit to God.

That is our friend. What is our loneliness next to his? As we come to share his devastation, our own desire to be understood, judged, and loved comes home and we give our hearts to him. This is the friend who understands us in love, calling us to responsibility, and whom we have come to know in the intimacy of imagination. This is the friend who can take us to God, not the domestic God but the Wild one, the Abyss from which spring the Preacher's circling winds.

For the divine creativity is merely love, making lovely things and then making more. In its very singularity it is wholly alone. God creates in no medium, and there is no alternative or complement to creation. The created world itself is not other than God but is the terminus of the creative Act. The act of love is totally lonely, solitary, and singular. Like Jesus totally giving himself with nothing left over, not his life, or even his dignity.

God is the glorious source of all creation, the most lovely, beautiful, awesome act of being something imaginable. But considered under the aspect of friendship God is utterly alone, like Jesus. And like us in the Last End.

How should we think about this God, Creator of all things good, but utterly alone, who abandons the Lover of Lovers? Perhaps the right posture needs more than to present ourselves as ready for judgment and thankful for the love shown in our living. Perhaps it needs also to offer friendship. Is that not the point of Jesus' Farewell Discourses, to bring the disciples to God as friends? Is that not the true way of glorifying God, to be God's friends? Friendship with Jesus is the symbol that allows us to relate to God in friendship. Jesus as Logos in the garden when the dew is still on the roses is the visible intentionality structure of the invisible Creator whom we can befriend through Jesus. Because we can have such a friend in Jesus, God can become our Beloved, our Lily of the Valley (Song of Solomon 2:1–2), and we can glorify God by being lovers.[13]

[13] Such sentiments as these are better sung than spoken. Sing the transformation from pleas to God for love and succor to loving God as our beloved Lily of the Valley in Charles Albert Tindley's hymn "Stand By Me," number 512 in the United Methodist Hymnal. As for the Logos in the garden, sing C. Austin Miles' "I Come to the Garden Alone while the Dew is Still on the Roses," number 314 in the same hymnal, a hymn usually criticized as selfish and individualistic by critics who do not understand the logic of the symbol of Jesus as friend.

CHAPTER SEVEN

Jesus as Savior: the Eschaton

No symbol of Jesus has captured the Christian imagination through the years more powerfully than that of his return in judgment and glory. Though an ancient theme elaborated in the biblical Book of Revelation, Graham Sutherland's *Christ in Glory* tapestry (figure 9, p. 139 above) was completed as late as 1962.[1] The Lamb of God, the symbolic sacrifice that covers sins, appeals to depths of soul *in extremis* and also symbolizes the end (figure 5, p. 66 above). The Alpha and Omega of the Cosmic Christ is stately, and it is part of the Apocalypse (Rev. 1:8 and 21:6). The symbols of the divinity of Jesus, crossing back and forth the infinite distance between God and human creation, have great metaphysical significance. The symbols of the historical Jesus and his continuing incarnation resonate through a dialectic of presence and absence and define human responsibility to God. The symbols of Jesus as friend (figures 13 and 14, pp. 199, 211 above) connect the general claim that Jesus is the Savior of the World with the specific blessing that Jesus is my personal savior, personalized in imagination so that through this friendship I become the person I should be, for whatever that is worth. But none of these symbols has the decisive force of the ultimate summing up of things, the Eschaton, the Apocalypse, the Second Coming of Jesus Christ. The eschatological symbols are strange in their force. Jesus is the Good Shepherd, carrying us home when we are lost, weak, and clueless (figure 16, p. 237 below). Jesus is the triumphant Lamb of the Apocalypse from whose mouth the words turn to a sword (figure 5; Rev. 19). The eschatological imagery of the New Testament is extraordinarily rich, not at all consistent, but deeply resonating, symbol with symbol.

---

[1] Sutherland's tapestry was commissioned for the rebuilt Coventry Cathedral whose predecessor had been bombed in November 1940. The text for the tapestry was Revelation 4:2–7 and Sutherland was determined to depict this glorified Christ as the one who could have created the world in the beginning. See Susanna Avery-Quash's discussion in Finaldi's *The Image of Christ*, p. 202.

Today the eschatological symbols are almost wholly rejected as pro-phetic or predictive of the end of the world, while at the same time late-modern culture is obsessed with Apocalypse Now, Doomsday, and Armageddon.[2] The first century might have imagined that only God could bring the Earth and history to an end. Our time threatens the world with nuclear holocaust, environmental catastrophe, lethal viruses, and colliding comets. European late-medieval anxiety over Heaven and Hell was in no way fiercer than late-modern anxiety over The End, The Last Thing, which is what "Eschaton" means.

Whereas eschatology considers The End of things in general, apoca-lyptic specifically imagines the end as a bang, not a whimper. Apocalyptic is a kind of thinking that intensifies what looks on the surface to be historical claims about the triumph of good over evil into cosmic, trans-historical claims. Just as images of Heaven are ways of schematizing going to a God who is not in time or space, so apocalyptic is a way of representing the eternal judgment of the Infinite or Ultimate God in finite historical ways. Apocalyptic turns up the intensity so that something more than historical is meant. A vivid example of this is in Isaiah 23–24. Chapter 23 continues earlier prophetic criticism of tribes, places and cultures, in this instance Tarshish, Sidon, and Tyre, claiming that the destruction of cities and their economic life, especially their ships, was caused by God, not just by the other nations who defeated them. Suddenly with chapter 24, continuing through chapter 27, not just cities but the whole Earth will be desolated, withered, and laid waste, the Heavens opened for a flood more thorough than Noah's, and the planet itself will be broken apart by earthquakes. This passage is a late interpo-lation and distinct from the thoroughly historical and political prophecy that surrounds it. The panorama of Memling's *The Last Judgment* (figure 15) is replete with apocalyptic markers. Beth Neville's *From Caves to Cosmos* (between pp. 158 and 159) is intense entropic apocalyptic of a thoroughly modern genre, especially plates 6 and 7. Thomas J. J. Altizer, the most radical Christian theologian of the twentieth century, is notorious for proclaiming the death of God; but this is a comparatively trivial point to be properly understood only in the context of his larger apocalyptic thinking.[3]

The Gospels attribute apocalyptic thinking to Jesus, say, in Mark 13

---

[2] Popular movie titles of the late twentieth century.
[3] See his *The New Apocalypse*, and *History as Apocalypse*; see in particular his *Genesis and Apocalypse*, which, like Sutherland (figure 9) and Beth Neville (plates 1–7), links creation and ending, the Alpha and the Omega, or, as he would put it, the coincidence of opposites.

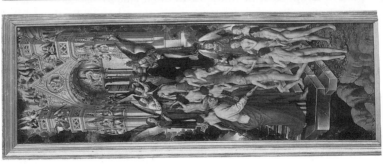

Figure 15. Hans Memling, *The Last Judgment*, the National Museum, Gdansk, Poland

(see Matthew 24–25, Luke 12, 21, John 8). Jesus predicts the end of the world in climactic judgment that will come unexpectedly like a thief in the night, and that very soon: the disciples themselves should watch for signs of it. Of course these gospel accounts were written some years after Jesus' crucifixion, probably after the destruction of the temple. But the conclusion of the nineteenth-century quest for the historical Jesus is that Jesus himself did very likely hold views such as these. In them, Jesus was careful to distinguish God from himself, only God knowing the time of judgment. The Book of Revelation also distinguishes Jesus from God, but makes Jesus the chief instrument of the cataclysmic judgment in the form of the Son of Man, the Son of God, the Lamb of God, and the avenging White Rider.

Christian imagination has been extraordinarily intense with apocalyptic. Memling's *The Last Judgment* has a central panel of judgment, with saved souls ascending the stairs into Heaven in the left-hand panel. They pass the lily of resurrection as they reach the staircase where they are greeted by St. Peter and welcomed by angels. As they approach the gates they are clothed in recognition of the modesty they display before being admitted. In the towers of Heaven are angelic musicians playing a lute, a harp, a shawm, and a trumpet. The right-hand panel shows damned souls falling into Hell, blasted down by an angelic trumpeter and welcomed by devils with fire and torture. The limbs of the damned are splayed as with a loss of personal integrity in contrast to the modesty of the saved who cover themselves. The central panel of judgment is split horizontally between the lower resurrection of the dead from the Earth for judgment, superintended by the military Archangel Michael who weighs souls, and the upper heavenly court where Jesus Christ sits on a rainbow uniting Heaven and Earth (see also plate 3). The globe of earth is Jesus' footstool and he is surrounded by the twelve apostles, Mary, and John the Baptist. From his head extend the lily of resurrection and the bloody sword of judgment. Celebratory angels hold the cross, the crown of thorns, and other symbols of his life. Several trumpeting angels aim their blasts from Heaven to Earth. Only after the trumpet's last sounding in judgment do the sounds of creation blend in Heavenly harmony, for Memling.

Roger Wagner's *The Harvest is the End of the World, and the Reapers are Angels* is a different vision of the apocalypse, one without the ancient and medieval geography. Figure 17 (p. 260 below) in black and white does not show the painting's stark contrast of the hues of ripe wheat with hues of purple, blue, and magenta sky. Shading of the angels on the ground is in the sky colors, and the arboreal silhouettes against the sky are the autumnal shades, a dualism of color and horizontal composition that marks uncompromising judgment. As in Neville's apocalypse, no people are here, though the reaping angels are "like the son of man." Wagner's apocalypse celebrates the lushness of the finite world, its flourishing, and its finish. For the soteriological imagination of ancient world (figure 16, p. 237 below) human beings are comfortably represented as sheep. For Memling's Renaissance apocalypse (figure 15), the central subject is human beings. For the late moderns Wagner (figure 17) and Neville (plates 1–7), the subject of judgment is the vast cosmos in which human beings will have played out their part long before the end. No wonder, for the late-modern imagination, the human place is a problem of homelessness and the Last End cannot be represented geographically.

Whereas Jesus, and also Paul, might well have believed that the Apocalypse would come within history soon, perhaps within their lifetime, they nevertheless did not imagine it as a mere historical event such as the defeat of the Roman occupation forces. Liberation theology today has an eschatological hope for change within history, but not an apocalyptic hope for the abolition of history. Apocalypse abolishes the Earth and Heavens and ushers in a perpetual, static, non-historical New Heaven and New Earth, with the New Jerusalem.[4]

Eschatology is not the same as apocalypse. It affirms a union with God in which the truth of everything is revealed and judged. Sometimes this is imagined as at the end of time and in a new non-historical and non-earthly place, Heaven. Other times, as in the Colossians passages and John's Farewell Discourses already discussed, the eschatological union is imagined as not abolishing history but running alongside it, as it were, so that those already at the throne of God also have to keep their attention on negotiating their way through persecutions and ordinary life. In "realized eschatologies" such as that of John and the author of Colossians, the imagery of end-time is retained but transformed. The connotations of immortality, as living temporally in quasi-history after death, are subordinated to those of eternal life, defined by its presence to God rather than continuities within history. Both kinds of eschatology are clear that the whole person is brought into proper union with God, the bodily as well as the "spiritual" parts.

Despite the penchant for apocalypticism in the contemporary

---

[4] For a devastating review of contemporary academic approaches to Jesus, from the standpoint of contemporary apocalypse, see Altizer's *The Contemporary Jesus*.

imagination, not all "end of the world" scenarios are Christian. This chapter will deal with four main symbol systems for Christian eschatology: Jesus as the Redeemer who brings his own home to God, as the Way, as the Truth, and as the Life.

JESUS THE REDEEMER

There's a place I know where the train goes slow,
Where the sinner can be washed in the blood of the Lamb.
There's a river by the trestle down by Sinners' Grove
Where the Willow and the Dogwood grow.
Down there by the train

Down there by the train
Down there by the train
Down there by the train
Down there where the train goes slow

You can hear the whistle, you can hear the bell,
From the halls of Heaven to the gates of Hell,
And there's room for the forsaken, if you're there on time.
You can be washed of all your sins and all of your crimes,
If you're down there by the train

Down there by the train . . .

There's a golden moon that shines up through the mist,
And I know that your name can be on that list.
There's no eye for an eye, there's no tooth for a tooth.
I saw Judas Iscariot carrying John Wilkes Booth.

Down there by the train . . .
So if you live in darkness and if you live in shame
All of the passengers will be treated the same
And old Humpty Jackson and Gyp the Blood will sing
And Charlie Witman is holding on to Dillinger's wings
They're both down there by the train

Down there by the train . . .

If you've lost all your hope, if you've lost all your faith,
I know you can be cared for, and I know you can be safe.
And all of the shamefulls, and all of the whores,
And even the soldier who pierced the side of the Lord,
Is down there by the train

Down there by the train . . .

Well I've never asked forgiveness, never said a prayer,
Never given of myself, never truly cared.
I've left the ones who loved me, and I'm still raising Cain.
I've taken the low road, and if you've done the same,
Meet me down there by the train
Down there by the train . . . [5]

The first job of Jesus as Savior is to save us from our sins. The other jobs are to lead us in a way of life appropriate for redeemed sinners, to enable us to live the truth about God, and to bring us to God so that the full vitality of our life is God's life. In classical theological terms, the first job is justification and the next three together comprise sanctification or holiness.

Many people, especially those influenced by Reformation piety, identify salvation almost exclusively with the first. For them, the chief question is *whether* they are saved and is often cast imaginatively as whether they are destined for Heaven or Hell. This prime question decided, the other jobs seem like works of supererogation. Other Christians suppose that the first job has least human interest because it is mainly a work of God to which the human response is only praise and thanks. The three parts of sanctification are the primary loci of human responsibility and thus of greater practical interest for them.

The sacrificial imagery of the atonement, explored in chapter 2, was founded in the Levitical conception that atonement can be made only for sins that are unintentionally committed (Lev. 4:2; Num. 15:27–31). When Moses sought atonement for Israel after it had intentionally turned from Yahweh in the Golden Calf episode, God said No (Ex. 32:30–34). When the Christian author of Hebrews replayed the sacrificial role of the high priest, he limited the sacrificially redeemable sinners to the "ignorant and wayward" (Heb. 5:2). The Book of Revelation, admittedly about vengeance more than mercy and the triumph of righteousness by means of destruction of the wicked, describes the saved in the white robes thus: "they who have come out of the great ordeal; they have washed their robes and made them white in the blood of the Lamb" (Rev. 7:14; see figure 5). Later in Revelation, God (or Jesus, it is not clear) says from the throne:

It is done! I am the Alpha and the Omega, the beginning and the end. To the thirsty I will give water as a gift from the spring of the water of life. Those who

[5] Song written by Tom Waits under the title "Down There By The Train," published by Jaima Music (ASCAP). A popular recording was made by John R. Cash, ("American Recordings, 1994") and it is this recording that is discussed in the text.

conquer will inherit these things, and I will be their God and they will be my children. But as for the cowardly, the faithless, the polluted, the murderers, the fornicators, the sorcerers, the idolaters, and all liars, their place will be in the lake that burns with fire and sulfur, which is the second death. (Rev. 21:6–8)

There seems to be no mercy for the great deliberate sinners, only atonement for unintentional sins and perhaps for a little waywardness. Those who thirst for righteousness and God shall be satisfied, but not the rest.

My exposition of the atonement symbols of the Lamb of God followed the Levitical root. Blood-guilt, as I developed the notion, is the guilt one has just by being human. It is not exactly the guilt of inadvertent ritual uncleanness or impurity, although I did introduce a Confucian sense of ritual into the constitution of the human, a ritual spoiled by blood-guilt. The line between the inherited and unintentional on the one hand, and the deliberate and intentional on the other, is not clear. Chapter 2 acknowledged that inherited blood-guilt itself gives rise easily to anger and resentment about the human condition. A person can turn away from the creator, whose inheriting child one is, and indulge in quite deliberate sins as a protest, falling into bondage to those sins as to an addiction. Identifying with the blood-punishment and death of the crucified Jesus is a means of release from that bondage, I argued, applying to inherited blood-guilt and its extension in rebellious blood-guilt.

But what about all those sinners who do not enjoy the dignity of metaphysical rebellion, the exquisite pride of Milton's Satan or Augustine's delight in evil as a way of turning from God? Most of us hear ourselves addressed in Johnny Cash's bass rumble about the place where the train goes slow. The causes of our sinning are not important in the long run, whether they are the human condition as such, being born into a broken family, living in a community that defines status by crime and addiction, suffering plain bad luck, or making original fully conscious life-choices for wickedness. Once we are on the low road, it is hard to move to higher ground and only heroes do it. Like an addict, we might protest and make some effort at reform. Surely we know the sinful life is wrong. Sometimes we are to be pitied. Other times we choose to remain in our own misery. In honest moments we know we belong with "all of the shamefulls, and all of the whores." Cash sings his confession: never asked forgiveness, never prayed, never gave of himself, never cared for others, left those who loved him, and still leads the lawless life. Most of us would not quite say "never," but surely we would say "too rarely." And given the deceptive subtleties of hypocrisy, perhaps "never" is right after all: contrition, prayer, self-giving, love, faithfulness, and righteousness can all be faked, fooling even the faker. Is there no hope for those of us who just do wrong and live wrongly?

The Waits/Cash song is explicitly anti-Levitical. It denies the eye-for-an-eye, tooth-for-a-tooth principle. It allows salvation to Judas Iscariot who is shown bringing Lincoln's murderer to the heavenly train and to the soldier who pierced Jesus' side. No reformation is asked of these people, only the effort to get to the place where the train slows enough to hop on. The only ticket is a desire for Heaven. Is this the Christian gospel of salvation?

Nowhere is the move from Second Temple Judaism to a decidedly different religion more evident than in the claim, indeed proclamation, that Christ died for every sinner no matter how bad. The only sin that blocks redemption is the rejection of the Holy Spirit itself (Mark 3:28–29), which is merely the rejection of redemption. Paul's early understanding of justification by faith, not works, is the most direct expression of this. Anyone who has faith is redeemed, all the shamefulls and whores, all those on the low road; whatever follows from this later is sanctification, not justification or redemption. With this understanding, of course the Gentiles are welcome. The Levitical system of distinguishing intentional from unintentional sins, and of atoning sacrifices as defined within the covenant with the nation of Israel, can easily become one metaphor among others for God's saving power. People who have no serious identification with the history of Israel and can adopt it only second hand at best are as welcome to the mercy seat as the Levitically righteous. The train to Heaven is for bums and hoboes who catch it when it slows by Sinners' Grove. All you need is to want the ride, and you can bring your worst friend. The blood of Christ avails for all, not only for the qualified.

Perhaps Paul's language (say, in Rom. 4–8) was unfortunate in that it allows faith to be interpreted as a subtle kind of work. The logic of justification has seemed to some to be the following: first repent of your sins, second have faith that Jesus Christ can save you, and third receive justification in faith. On this logic the question of the source of faith assumes enormous proportions. Does it come as a matter of human choice? Then it is a work attempting to earn justification. Or does it come from God? Then God is responsible for giving it to those who have it and withholding it from those who do not, and the sterile problematic of predestination (single versus double) ensues.

But this logic is wrong. The right logic is this: first want salvation, second go to Jesus for it, who receives you, and third learn to repent which is in fact part of sanctification. The desire for salvation does not have to be of a specific kind; it does not have to be strong enough to override sinful behavior, or steady enough to provide consistency. The desire for salvation can be fickle. Perhaps only the words of a revivalist can provoke it, or the intensity of a religious service, and the return to ordinary life can damp it. Perhaps salvation is desired only when everything else goes wrong and fades when the world turns hopeful: vows made in desperation turn to embarrassment later. The desire for salvation does not have to be well understood. Nor does salvation itself have to be well conceived. A train to Heaven is as good a symbol as any.

Salvation vaguely means the surmounting of the present state of felt pain and sin to reach a state of happiness and purity that is not ruined by pain and one's own sin. One's own sin might be the reason salvation is thought to be unobtainable. But because salvation is obtainable by merely the wanting, one's own sins do not really count for much. Pain and suffering are just as much part of what salvation delivers people from as their own sins.

Christianity has been criticized for concentrating on saving sinners rather than relieving suffering, a Buddhist perspective.[6] This accusation is another kind of works righteousness, however, a kind of liberationist achievement of salvation by social justice. Relief from suffering and pain comes into salvation rather as characteristics of the life left in order to be with God. In the popular imagination Heaven is pictured not only as the place where you give up your wicked thoughts and destructive behavior but also, and more importantly, where you don't hurt, where you are healthy, not crippled by age, where you get along with your difficult relatives, are reconciled to enemies, and where the joys of sense, heart, and mind are readily available. Cigars in Heaven do not cause cancer, do not smell bad to others, do not exclude women from the smoky rooms of power, and do put phallic symbols in a positive light.[7] The desire for salvation does not have to be right about Heaven any more than it has to be analytically right about what salvation is from.

In the true logic of salvation for Christians, you go to Jesus for it. What "going to Jesus" means does not have to be very precise. Accuracy about the historical Jesus is not required. Understanding subtle symbols can

---

[6] See Andrew Sung Park's *The Wounded Heart of God*. See also Altizer's *The Contemporary Jesus*, chapter 9.

[7] For an extensive defense of this theory of cigars in Heaven, see my *The Truth of Broken Symbols*, pp. ix, 270f., *et passim*.

come later, but is not necessary. A person can come to Jesus on hearing about him for the first time, when virtually nothing of Christian thought and culture is known. All that is required is the belief that Jesus can accomplish your salvation, however that is conceived. The minimal belief is that by taking your desire for salvation to Jesus, by looking to him rather than to yourself or others, God's power in him saves you. For Jesus is the one who loves you with no strings attached, and can free you from sin and pain and take you to God. Whether other religions might also have paths of salvation is not a relevant issue: the issue is that Jesus does have the power of salvation and that you are saved by wanting it from him. Countless symbols express "going to Jesus," from psychological "surrender" to the cosmic "journey to Heaven" by train or by the Christian version of Noah's ark, to joining Jesus' band of disciples, the Church. All these symbols, however, lead off from simply looking to Jesus for salvation to sanctifying consequences.

The third step in the logic of salvation, learning to repent, is itself part of sanctification, however paradoxical this seems. I made this point earlier by quoting from the prayer of absolution in the 1662 Anglican *Book of Common Prayer*: "He pardoneth and absolveth all them that truly repent and unfeignedly believe his holy Gospel. Wherefore let us beseech him to grant us true repentance and his Holy Spirit . . ." Once one has accepted Jesus as one's savior, accepting Jesus' saving love however symbolized, one can then proceed to analyze one's sins and repent. Spiritual life is characterized by increasing honesty and self-revelation as one comes to trust God's love enough to accept oneself, as analyzed in chapter 4. Salvation becomes more determinate, the more one learns to repent and live in the Holy Spirit. Salvation is free, but has subsequent costs in commitment to holiness.

Does any of this make sense to the late-modern world? Can Jesus really symbolize such all-embracing redeeming love? The metaphysics in this is plain. God's creative powers are constant and ever available, perfectly exemplified in Jesus imagined as friend to one's own condition. The love of God in creation does not somehow metaphysically turn off for sinners. It is present in suffering too because suffering is part of creation. The sinner's standing before God in the worst of times is as fresh as the morning of birth. All of the problem lies with the sinner who has turned from the Creator or strangled the creativity; by giving up that problem to Jesus, a fresh start is available. The fresh start, of course, is to live with God, to live before God.

How can late moderns relate to symbols of salvation? We obviously do, given the great popularity of imagistic religion and books and television programs about angels. Perhaps much of this is a resentment of the indifferent, impersonal universe in which our science shows us to live, and a nostalgic longing for supernatural saving powers and places. But I believe that even today the symbols of heaven for presence with God negotiate the dialectical relation between time and eternity just as they did in the ancient and medieval worlds, and as they do for all religions. Within time we know that salvation does not mean the quick end of suffering or pain, that our projects necessarily prosper, that we easily climb up from the low road, or that we escape illness and death. For life within time, salvation means engaging those things with God, which is the topic of sanctification to be explored in the next three sections. With respect to eternity, the boundaries between our own lives and the life of God are erased. The features of our lives remain what they are, with no mystical blurring of determinate identity. But they are set within the larger life of the Creator which itself becomes our life and value. Though our lives are painful, the tears are wiped away; though in time we shall die, death means nothing in eternity, is trivial and not mourned (Rev. 21:3–4). Because the content of eternity is what happens in time, not abstractly considered through the flow of time but concretely considered in all time's dimensions together, the understanding of eternity is a dialectical symbolization through time. This too is the topic of sanctification, to be addressed shortly.

How shall we understand Jesus as redeemer? As lover, of course, the lover who will accept anyone, regardless. One symbol for Jesus as lover is the one who allowed himself to be sacrificed for our atonement, not just suffering and dying as a substitute for our punishment but doing that out of love for us. Another symbol is Jesus as the Cosmic King who judges us righteously but extends mercy to the condemned. Yet another is the deified Jesus who perfects the human so as to contain divinity, and shows us how. The historical Jesus of ministry and nurture in the Church is also a symbol of love. Most of all, the symbol of Jesus as lover is the friend whom I imagine in all concreteness to know me better than I know myself and love me despite all. These symbols are all fancy and difficult, however, no matter how necessary they are to elaborate a complete notion of Jesus as lover. They all require work and self-transformation in order to be appropriated in any significant way. To engage God with them requires more work than can be required for turning to Jesus when you desire salvation.

Not excluding these symbols, but superseding them, are the immediate symbols of Jesus as lover, the symbols somewhat embarrassing to theologians but beloved in popular piety. Jesus gathers the children around him, not so much to teach about the kingdom of heaven, but because he loves children. The loving Jesus is the shepherd who leaves the ninety-nine sheep to find the one lost lamb (oneself) and carry it home on his back (figure 16). The loving Jesus stands at the door and knocks (Rev. 3:20, but not v. 21; figure 13, p. 199 above). The loving Jesus calls us to a meal as he did with his friends of old (figure 11, p. 165 above). The loving Jesus is hard to describe in words because they lead into complicated explications. But he is easy to depict in visual arts doing loving things, holding his bleeding heart, staring at us with the face of compassion and desire for our love. These depictions have a bearing not on historical likeness, but on whatever might mean for us a loving friend whose love can accept us and make us whole.

All the images of Jesus as lover, however immediate in their force, are mediated in their presentation. Artists draw them, evangelists write them, and institutions and media bring them to our attention. The most powerful images of Jesus as lover are those that are expressed personally by individuals whom we encounter. Not that any of them would be candidates for the other symbols of Jesus analyzed here, but quite broken individuals can themselves possess and communicate the love of God. The love we see in a glance or gesture, that we encounter in someone's kindness or timely word, can be the love that sets us free to give ourselves to God. Christians attempt to do this by associating that love with Jesus. Others might do it with no connection with Jesus whatsoever save that God's love in them actually redeems and therefore is subject to interpretation in Christian terms. In Christian living, Jesus is most powerfully symbolized as the lover whose love can take the worst of the shamefulls home to God.

JESUS THE WAY

Paul characterized the Christian life as living "in Christ" (for instance, Rom. 12:5, 1 Cor. 15:18–22, 2 Cor. 15:17, Gal. 3:26–29). We might say that "justification" is getting into Christ and "sanctification" is what we do when there. In John's Farewell Discourses, Jesus characterized himself as the Way, the Truth, and the Life (John 14:6). He also said that Christians abide in him as branches on a vine (15:1–8). The symbols of the Way, the Truth, and the Life are signs for engaging life with or before God, or holiness.

Figure 16. *The Good Shepherd*, Musei Vaticani, Rome

To say that Jesus is the Way is to look to him, and symbols of him, for how to live in this life in proper relation to God. Neat as it might be to articulate a single version of this Way, that is likely not the truth. Nevertheless, we should begin with the version to which the name "Way" was first attached, namely, the Church.

The Church is the self-conscious community of Jesus' followers constituted very shortly after his death by the remaining Eleven (with a twelfth, Matthias – Acts 1:26 – soon added), the leading women who had traveled with Jesus, some of Jesus' own family, and others who were also close such as the travelers on the road to Emmaus. We should not think of the twelve disciples alone as constituting Jesus' community. A significant number of people had accompanied him from the time of his own baptism, according to Acts 1:21–26, and many more had joined later in his ministry, including some of his own family who had scoffed at first. We have no accurate numbers for this group, and surely some people must have been more committed than others. Yet their commitment to sustain something of the community Jesus had founded was sufficient to keep them together despite his ignominious crucifixion, confused resurrection appearances, the tarnished credibility of Peter as leader, and the obvious competition from at least some in Jesus' family for leadership. Pentecost is the Jewish feast celebrating the harvesting of wheat and, by the first century, the giving of the Law (Lev. 23:15–21, Ex. 23:16, 34:22, Deut. 16:9–12). Jesus' community, however ragtag, gathered to celebrate this festival that came fifty days ("pentecost" means fifty days) after the Passover festival at which he died (Acts 2). Then and there they were so enthused by the Holy Spirit that they found definite identity, purpose and, direction as articulated in Peter's sermon. Others caught the Spirit and their numbers grew.

I stress the historical beginning of the Church in order to emphasize its historical particularity (even if the history told about it is not always accurate) down to our own time. By the first Pentecost, the peculiar dialectical interaction of gathered people, the Holy Spirit, and the Christ Jesus who lived in memory and contemporary imagination as founder, animator, and judge, was operative. Chapter 5 drew out the character of this community as related to God in Christ, a character that can be understood as well in the terms of our own pluralistic time as in the terms of the first century. That chapter focused on the transformation of the Church as it admitted Gentiles. The Church was founded, indeed, as a community in transition.

This use of the word "church" emphasizes the particular historicity of the institution and its members. Shortly I shall characterize other Ways of being Christians, Ways of Jesus; these might but need not overlap participation in the Church, and can involve marginal, even critical antagonistic relation to the institutional Church. In some sense, all can be called "church" because they are all ways of being "in Christ," hence in his body. But to preserve a strong sense of historical institutions I shall refer to all as Christian Ways and only the institution as the Church Way.

What does it mean to participate in the Church as the Way of Jesus? Not everyone has the leadership roles that are important for the discussions of transition and relevance to the living Christ. What everyone in the Church does have is the order of communal worship around which to organize the rest of life. The liturgical order is a kind of scheduling that gives shape to life, and the orders have differed in intensity and form in various places and periods of the historical Church. The weekly order of Sunday worship is the most universal. In some places and times there is a denser weekly order of prayer meetings, choir practice, fellowship groups, Evensong, and Morning Prayer, and such like. In some times and places there is a daily order of offices. The yearly liturgical calendars celebrate now some or all of the following seasons or festivals: Advent, Christmas, Epiphany, the Transfiguration, Lent, Passion Week, Easter, Ascension, Pentecost, and Trinity, called by these or other names. In some communions saints' days are also celebrated on a yearly calendar.

In a sense the liturgical ceremonies of the daily, weekly, and yearly Christian calendar are only the outward organizing points. Each service has institutions and a culture built around it with many gatherings of parts of the community to perform them. Moreover, what goes on in the services has many consequences for the rest of life, such as the readings from scripture and sermons that are reflected upon later, the organization of the community into roles and offices, the material elements of the community (such as worship and teaching places, art, music, architecture), and the ethics for the internal behavior of members of the community and the ministry of the community to the larger neighborhood and world.[8] To function as a member of a Christian community is to be much affected by its images for engaging the world, to have one's time and energies ordered around the life of the community, and to have one's identity shaped in some measure by one's communal roles.

[8] This "way" of living before God is religion as Ninian Smart analyzes it in seven dimensions, not all of which are discussed here: the ritual and practical, the doctrinal and philosophical, the mythic and narrative, the experiential and emotional, the ethical and legal, the organizational and social, and the material and artistic. See his *Dimensions of the Sacred*, pp. 10–11.

Membership and participation in a congregation of the Church need not be very reflective. It can be undertaken for no special reason other than participation in a larger culture shaped by Church life. People can participate richly in such a Christian Way without any dramatic salvation experience and with simplistic and deeply mistaken theological ideas that embarrass their sophisticated children. Whether the ordered Way of their specific community is authentically Christian depends mainly on its leaders who struggle with the issues of making Christ live in the communal context, as discussed in chapter 5. The importance of critical leadership cannot be overestimated for the guidance of the community in its ongoing dedication to the living Christ in a changing set of circumstances. A form of the Way that is authentic in one situation might be stultifying and Christ-denying in another. People who participate in the ordered community depend on its leaders to order the community so that through it the living Christ responds to its context.

The variety of different contemporary patterns of Christian Church life reflects different contexts in which the Christian Way needs to be embodied. Every pattern is a compromise of dialectical tensions between faithfulness to its authorizing past and openness to new needs and conditions. Each might have its virtues and also its weaknesses, virtues that are sustained by the very patterns that entail the weaknesses. Each of them offers a Way to be "in Christ" in the historical Church. So, the first meaning of Jesus as the Way is that he defines, by first authorizing and by continuing to live in and above, a special communal life in which a person can participate; this is the Church Way.

Another form of the Way is what might be called the Cultural Way. By this is meant the serious devotion of life to ascertaining and living out the meaning and implications of Christianity for one's cultural and social context. Persons devoted to the Cultural Way of Jesus rather than the Church Way might also belong to a congregation, participation in which might affect their Cultural Way. But persons in Christ on the Cultural Way might not be affiliated with a congregation and indeed might find the work of congregational maintenance a distraction from the center of gravity of the Cultural Way. Whether or not they participate in Church congregations, people who live in Christ on the Cultural Way take their focus to be the meaning and implications of Christianity for their culture or society, perhaps even the global society.

Christians on the Cultural Way sometimes offend Church Christians because they do not take congregational Church life as their center of gravity, and even might reject it. One of the great Cultural Christians of the last century, himself a sometime devout churchman, was the poet T. S. Eliot. Nearly all his poetry is devoted to saying a Christian word to his culture. That word was rarely celebratory or prophetic in the social gospel sense, the styles of word most often found in church. Rather it brought to speech the deep inarticulate longings, pathos, and mysteries of his culture and time, things too ambiguous to find much play in church communities that demand definiteness on which to base decisions and behavior, a definiteness that is more fictitious the closer it comes to ultimate matters. The same devotion to saying a Christian word was true of Emily Dickinson, W. H. Auden, and now of Geoffrey Hill. In political life, Martin Luther King, Jr., and Jesse Jackson were and are respectively active Church Christians. But the center of their Christian life was bringing Christ to American culture, not to convert it to the Christian Church but to transform it to be more just, pious, engaged, spiritually deep, and loving. Many writers and artists, musicians and builders, environmentalists and social activists, academics in all fields, especially religious studies and academic theology, are Christians devoted to the Cultural Way, whether or not they also participate in congregational life.

The marks of being in Christ on the Cultural Way, of course, have to do with devotion to the elements of the Logos as incarnate in Jesus. To put it in a formula, it is to be devoted to discerning and following out the implications of the needs of justice, deference, engagement, and the religious quest, as well as the cultural balancing of these in what might be better called charity than love. Secular people and non-Christians of other faiths can be devoted to these Logos elements as well. But they do not relate them to their incarnation in Jesus or take their devotion to them to be a Way of being in Christ. Insofar as the devotions of the Cultural Way are articulate, they employ and perhaps advance the imagery of Christianity, especially the symbols of Jesus. Insofar as those devotions involve action and commitment, the Christian's motive is not only the merit of the cause but the fact that this is a Way of giving oneself to Jesus.

As argued in chapter 5, the life of Christ in the Church requires the Church also to walk the Cultural Way. The same devotion to the elements of the Logos as incarnate in Jesus and as relevant to the larger cultural situation is a requirement for Church life as well as for the Cultural Way. Yet the Church is necessarily preoccupied with the critical development and maintenance of its own culture, in but not of the larger world. People who live in Christ within the Church Way have their lives ordered by the patterns of the congregational community, and this is where their center of gravity is, however much they or their leaders also attend to the Cultural Way. People whose center of gravity lies in the Cultural Way pattern their lives differently, perhaps observing Church order, but not as the most important way in which they work out their life in Christ. They are usually careful to prevent themselves from being compromised by the "church-speak" that forms congregations as insider groups and so often covers over the deep ambiguities that are truer than the community-constituting certainties. Some people attempt devotion to both Ways of being in Christ, a project requiring great energy, a sense of humor, and tolerance of much cognitive dissonance.

I have spoken of the Church Way and the Cultural Way in terms that suppose an intensity of following the Way of Jesus. Both patterns of the Way of Jesus allow of elite and popular forms. The Churchly elite are the leaders and common Church practice is popular Christianity. Both can be intense. The elite in the Cultural way are also the thinkers and the leaders, but we should not forget the cultural followers, the expositors and foot soldiers, whose lives can be just as intense in their devotion to the Way of Jesus. Both Ways present patterns of life in which it is possible to be "in Christ" before God.

JESUS THE TRUTH

A person can be said to be "the truth" of something when he or she embodies that thing in a superlative way. Often that thing is an ideal, as when we say that Lily Pons was a "true coloratura" soprano, embodying the ideals we associate with that voice type and style. Other uses of the expression refer to carrying on something in accurate continuity, as when we say that a certain man is a "true son" of his father. More generally we say that a person is true when he or she goes beyond merely knowing something truly to embodying it fully in life, taking it to heart, working out all its ramifications, conforming to what is important in the thing to as great a degree possible in human terms.

Many religions speak of spiritual virtuosos as being "fully realized" or "fully actualized." What this means is that they have so internalized what they know of fundamental religious power, usually associated with power of creation and transcendence of space-time limitations, that they possess something of those powers themselves. Jesus, for instance, was reported to have worked miracles of healing and of food and wine production, to have had visions of things when he was not present, to have walked on water, and to have been transfigured into unearthly company with Moses and Elijah. These things were taken in Jesus' time to have proved that he was an adept, like other adepts, not that he was superhuman.[9]

What Jesus likely meant in John 14:6 when he said he was "the truth" is that he was a true son of his heavenly Father, that is, that he completely and accurately actualized what God could be in human form, at least the human form of his historical circumstance. Jesus made this claim in response to Thomas' question as to how they were to know where Jesus was going when he said he was going to his Father's house. He went on to elaborate that if the disciples knew him, Jesus, then they knew the Father. This was because, first, the words he spoke expressed the Father, and second, his work did as well (which they could see even if they did not believe his words). When he said "no one comes to the Father except through me," he did not mean "No Jews or Buddhists Allowed" but that what he embodied in his teaching and work was God, and that this was being passed on to the disciples (John 14:12). He elaborated this in terms of the community of love, from the Father to Jesus, Jesus to the Father, Jesus to the disciples, the disciples to one another, and the disciples to Jesus, with the result that Jesus can bring the disciples to the Father.

Jesus' emphasis in the Farewell Discourses was on the transformation of the disciples from an uncomprehending and fairly selfish lot to fully realized people who were bonded with God and one another in mature love, and capable of carrying on Jesus' own teaching and work, that is, carrying on his divine nature. The Orthodox tradition calls this transformation *theosis* or divinization: making people divine as Jesus was divine. Western Christianity has generally called it sanctification, making people holy as God is holy, insofar as that can be embodied in human form.[10]

How does the transformation take place? In simplest terms, it takes place through living life as shaped by the teachings and symbols of Jesus, set in the context of the larger understanding of the religion. The disciples accompanied Jesus on his ministry of teaching and healing, listening to his teachings, watching what he did, and learning to help out, even to the extent of going on mission themselves under Jesus' supervision (Matt. 10). The synoptic gospels detail many activities of ministry and many teachings about God, the Kingdom, and about how to

[9] See, for instance, Sanders' *The Historical Figure of Jesus*, chapter 10.
[10] For the Jewish background to the Christian ideas about holiness, see Fredriksen's *Jesus of Nazareth King of the Jews*, pp. 65–73.

live. John's gospel focuses more on Jesus' teachings about himself and his relation to God, and develops many of the great symbols of Jesus in the "I am" sayings. In the Farewell Discourses Jesus promised that after his death and ascension the Holy Spirit would come to continue the process of transformation with the disciples who would then be functioning otherwise on their own. The accounts given above of the historical Jesus as the living Christ and also as intimate friend continue this line of reasoning.

What happens in transformation? The practice of life, as shaped by the teachings and the symbols, changes the way by which people can engage God. At the beginning, people need milk, as Paul said (1 Cor. 3:1–2), and slowly through growing maturity they come to solid food. Paul had in mind that some things are easy to understand and beginners should be taught those things. He also might have had in mind that things are understood one way by beginners and in another way by those who have come to see through the glass less darkly. We know that stories and symbols are understood by children one way, and by adults another. What makes the difference? In the case of simple maturation, the older and more experienced a person is, the more symbols or teachings can be set in broader contexts of meaning and inference, given more resonance with other symbols, and taken as having many layers of meaning. The loss of childhood innocence in adolescence means that symbols are taken to indicate much more than the child thought and sometimes the extra meaning is unwelcome: that loving parents are revealed also to have clay feet does not mean they love less but that the adolescent needs to engage them in more complicated ways.

The theory of symbols operative throughout this book allows for a fairly precise description of spiritual transformation of the sort at stake here. Recall that symbols function within interpretations to engage us with their object, namely God and related matters in the case of religious symbols. Three things are involved in the interpretation: meaning, reference, and context with interpretive purpose.

A symbol's meaning is given in the semiotic code of which it is a part. The semiotic code provides a grammar and also the other symbols and systems of symbols in terms of which it is defined. Its definition is not just the limiting ideas that distinguish it from other symbols, as a dictionary tries to provide. Its definition is the whole of the associations and resonances the semiotic code allows. To learn all these things requires time and experience. A small child can hear God called Father and bring to mind an image of his or her own father, and maybe the fathers of playmates. Growing up, the child might learn to associate divine paternity with creation because fathers play important roles in procreation, turning the simple paternal image of God into a simile. Further reflecting on the gospels, the person might realize that Jesus used the notion of God to create an idea of a perfect Father, rejecting his own family in favor of a pan-human family based on the universal paternity of the Creator. So God provides an ideal for human fathers who should not give their children stones instead of bread or snakes instead of fish. Then again, ideal human fathers, such as the one in the parable of the Prodigal Son, give a sense of the all-accepting love in the divine Father. All of these new associations enrich the person's meaning for the Fatherhood of God. No self-respecting fourteen-year-old would admit to friends to believing anymore that God looks like his or her father, however much that childish image might remain locked and blocked in the heart. Then suppose the person studies Christology more seriously and asks how Jesus might be the son of God, learning what goes on in Luke's genealogy for Jesus that traces him back to "son of Seth, son of Adam, son of God" (Luke 3:38). "Son of" in the Hebrew Bible is the one who carries on the father's work, as we have seen, and now the person can interpret Jesus' claim in the Farewell Discourses that he and the Father are one because he speaks the Father's words and does his work. Moreover, the person might realize that every other person, including him or herself, is also descended from Seth, Adam, and God and therefore has the same heritage and capacity as Jesus. Then suppose the person steps back to reflect on the creation by virtue of which God is called Father and sees it to encompass a universe of vast age and extent, violent beyond imagination, indifferent to human needs save in the fragile environment of the third planet out from Sol on the edge of a minor galaxy. Our life-world is an engine of consumption, microorganisms eating smaller ones and in turn being eaten by larger ones. Species live on other species and are prey in turn, finally vanishing to extinction when their habitat no longer tolerates them. The blood of human beings has about the same saline proportion as the seas from which our slime-mold ancestors emerged, and we bear the genes of the crabs, frogs, reptiles and tigers, as well as the sensitivities and stresses of the founders of civilization and human morality. So when the person prays the Lord's Prayer, the meaning of "Our Father who art in heaven" is that God is the Father of *all that*, a wild, fierce and destroying Father as well as the Father of justice and human order, and moreover *we* are part of all that down to the saltiness of our blood, the snake in our genes, and the life of others in our diet. "Hallowed be thy name" hallows all that awesome majesty, not merely an honored father like one's own, and the Father's will approved for earth as well as heaven includes the will for cosmic blasts and a universe of expanding gasses. The juxtaposition of all that to "give us this day our daily bread, and forgive us our trespasses" puts our daily life in a wholly different perspective from what it would be if the Father were conceived only as a domestic God managing the earthly kingdom. The first element of transformation is the growing enrichment of symbols so that their meaning for the transformed person is vastly different from that for the beginner.

The second part of interpretation is reference. In addition to conventional reference determined by the semiotic code, our theory of symbols distinguishes two kinds of primary reference, iconic and indexical. The iconic dimension of reference, it will be remembered, refers to the object as being like the symbol. It takes the symbol to be descriptive in some sense, a sense that might include metaphor, simile, analogy, allegory, and other tropes. The iconic dimension of reference has no transformative power, however, except insofar as it adds to meaning, that is, gives additional symbols with which to enrich the meanings of symbols: the transformation is the enrichment. The indexical dimension establishes a kind of causal relation between the object and the interpreter, like pointing, so that the interpreter is reoriented. If the indexical reference is true, then the person is reoriented so that something symbolized in the object can be carried over into the interpreter's experience. Indexical reference is necessary for real engagement with objects.

Religious symbols are referred so as to engage us with God and related matters. Transformations here are of two sorts. In the first place, a symbol at the beginning might engage a person very simply, one-dimensionally, as it were, and with a vagueness in the respect in which a symbol is interpreted to represent its object. Living with that symbol, however, the person becomes more ready to grasp its object, partly through greater familiarity, partly through the experience of drawing out associations and implications of meaning, but also partly through having the intentionality structure reformed around that symbol. All of the great symbols of Jesus discussed in this book are of the sort that living with them reshapes the intentionality structure of fundamental orientation: to blood-guilt in the instance of Jesus as atoning sacrifice, to the universe as a home for human beings in the instance of the Cosmic Christ, to the identity of human beings relative to God in the case of Jesus as divine Person of the

Trinity, to the human community as the residence of the divine in the instance of the historical Jesus, and to our individual selves relative to God in the instance of Jesus as friend. All of those orientations have to do with the human condition relative to God, and as the orientations are reshaped by these Christological symbols, the relations to God in those conditions are transformed. Or to put it another way, the soul is transformed so as to be better oriented to God in these dimensions of human existence.

All the major symbols systems discussed here are bizarre, outlandish, and somewhat embarrassing to the late-modern imagination. The first thing we want to say about them is that of course we don't believe them in any literal sense, that they are ancient metaphors that are somewhat offensive to us who do not like blood, kings, divine beings, ruling spirits, or imaginary friends. So, when we let ourselves be shaped by these symbols, they have to be given new meanings for the late-modern imagination. That has been the plot of this book, reconciling the symbols to our imagination.

But then as we live with these symbols, letting them shape us, do we not see that the issues of late-modern life are such that nothing will do for our guilt but blood, that nothing will make the universe our home but justice and mercy on a cosmic scale, that our glory and shame both together stem from the divine heritage of creativity, that the twists of history require an open, continuously creative, living spirit of authority, judgment, and hope, and that any serious actual friendship or love is based on an imaginative capacity to relate one's intentionality structure to another's? As the person of Jesus is present to us in these and other symbolic ways, we come to see our own time and its imagination in new ways, and through them our relation with God. Having lost the first naiveté of these symbols, we recover a second naiveté by living with them.

The second sort of transformation in reference has to do with secondary reference. Whereas primary reference is to the object referred to, secondary reference is to the kind of person who can engage the object by means of the symbol at hand. To use the previous examples, a small child is not a good secondary referent for a complicated theological symbol; a person with an abusive father is not likely to engage God with the symbol of Father, no matter how well and benignly the meaning system of divine paternity is understood. But sometimes living with the symbol, assuming that other symbols effect an engagement with God, can transform someone who is not a good secondary referent into one who is. A small child can use sophisticated symbols as nonsense pieces until they become meaningful with maturity; an abused person can be healed of resentment and come to understand God as Father. Perhaps a better example is the symbol of eternity, so common in the ancient world, including Christian scriptures, but so degraded today. For most modern people, eternity can mean little more than static form (as it meant for the philosopher Whitehead) or an expanded temporal consciousness that is present but with very long memory and anticipation seeing all things "at once," or a fixed plan for the unrolling of world affairs as in deterministic physics of predestinationism. For the ancients, however, eternity was the fullness of life, not a one-point perspective on life. Living with the biblical and other Christian symbols of eternity can change the modern imagination to encompass the ancient.[11] That change is difficult, and requires much metaphysics to bridge the gap, but it is possible.

The third part of interpretation is the interpretive context that provides a culture with its problems, needs, values, and purposes, as well as the specific situation of the interpreting people, including their own purposes. This complex contextualized set of purposes determines the shape of interpretation: which objects will be interpreted by which symbols in which respects. Persons are transformed by living in contexts shaped by the Christological symbols, adopting the culture, problematic, needs, values, and purposes of those contexts. In the Church Way discussed in the previous section, this obviously means living in a Christian community whose worship and community life transform their members so as to adopt the culture and purposes more closely. This means that God is engaged more and more with the Christological symbols shaped by Christian purposes. In the Cultural Way the larger society is queried ever more intensely by the Christian symbols: its cultural problematic and needs are questioned, its values and purposes. Moreover, persons on this Way are transformed by their engagement of their culture with the Christological symbols, becoming more Christ-like as they do so.

The three elements of interpretation – meaning, reference, and interpretive context – are transformative together. I have attempted to separate the senses in which they transform in order to show how interpretation works transformatively, not just to provide information or

---

[11] These points are developed in my *Eternity and Time's Flow*, which discusses the process theologians as those who make God temporal.

redirect behavior. But in fact a transformation of soul through enriched meaning also transforms modes of reference which in turn engage people so that their interpretive culture and purposes are transformed, and on around.

As indicated these transformations can take place while on the Church Way or the Cultural Way, and obviously on both together. But an additional Way needs to be mentioned, the Devotional Way. The Devotional Way is an intensification of the process of transformation through spiritual disciplines. The disciplines might be prayer and meditation, or travel, or exposure to the wilderness, or total immersion in some cause (not mainly for the sake of the cause but for the spiritual discipline). The disciplines are shaped in relevant ways by the Christological symbols and their aim is to make the devotees more Christ-like, as relevant to their circumstances. In Christian devotion, Jesus becomes more real to the devotees as they become more like him, more identified with him, more connected to him in love, and to God through him, and to one another through the love that Jesus embodied.

The Devotional Way is not exactly a Way, a pattern of life, for it becomes most intense when the patterns and their symbols break. When the rents in the sacred canopy show the abysmal sky above, transformational devotion has to find a way to live without as well as with its symbols. Such apophatic divestment of religion is another profound meaning of the crucifixion, opposite in its semiotic sensibility to the thickly invested Levitical symbolism of the atonement.

Transformation to become the Truth as Jesus is the Truth has two sides, as discussed here. One is the symbols by means of which transformation takes place. We cannot engage something for which we are totally lacking symbols. Christian life in our time is impotent to engage God if we do not have the symbols for the engagement. The argument of this book has been that at least some of the classical Christological symbols are indeed right for our time, properly understood.

The other side is that symbols transform when they are actually used in engagement. The practice with the symbols is as important as the symbols themselves. Only on some Christian Ways are the symbols practiced with much intensity. Of course examples exist of people who just stumble upon a Christian symbol and in a moment encounter God in life-transforming ways, a kind of accidental engagement. But if one comes to Jesus for redemption, and gives oneself to him, then one is on some Way to sanctification.

It is possible to be on one of the Christian Ways – and I do not presume that the Church Way, the Cultural Way, and the Devotional Way exhaust them – without paying much attention to transformation. Transformation to become the Truth of Christ requires something of an intentionality to do so. Jesus described that intentionality in some detail as the learning of love and the connections with God, himself, and other disciples constituted by that love. Loving one another because Jesus loved them lets the disciples love the God in Jesus, the ways in which he and his Father are one. The intentionality of transformation toward being the Truth of Christ can start off feeble and ill-focused, as it is in new Christians. But it gains intensity and focus with practice. One of the few comforts of advanced age is that the intentionality of spiritual discipline and formation often reaches a fevered pitch of intensity and efficiency. The reason Grandma prays so much and quotes the Bible all the time might be not the enfeeblement of age but ancient power burning white-hot.

JESUS THE LIFE

Life cannot be understood in temporal terms alone but is fully real only within the eternity of the divine life. In chapter 5 I interpreted the very long historical life of Jesus in terms of his presence to the Church, keeping the variously contextualized congregations open to the future and to future realities of the living Christ. In this section the orientation is reversed, reading temporal life in terms of eternal life.

Christianity promises fullness of life, which is the same as the fullness of creation as creature and heir to, or extension of, the Creator. In light of this, redemption from sin is but the removal of an obstacle to fullness of life. For those who believe in something like literal hellfire, redemption might have more immediacy than the instrumental removal of an impediment to life. Yet what is Hell but the absence of God, or distance from him (Luke 16:19–31)? In light of the promise of abundant life, the Christian Way of being in Christ is the context or medium for full life, and in that sense also instrumental. Following Jesus as the Truth, seeing the Truth of God in him, becoming transformed to be like him in the Truth – that is something like the content of life abundant as shaped through specifically Christological symbols. Life itself is where all this comes together, the Last Thing.

Life itself is not a single symbol in the Bible but an intense vague symbol with many systems of meaning feeding into it. Three from the Hebrew Bible indicate something of its complexity. In Genesis 2:7, God "formed man from the dust of the ground, and breathed into his nostrils the breath of life; and the man became a living being." Though modern science has softened the distinction between the inanimate and the animate, it has not eliminated it. God made the man as a clay doll that he then brought to life by breathing in his nostrils. God's breath, or spirit, makes the difference of life. In the Hebrew tradition, the difference between life and death is made by the functioning of cardio-pulmonary system, as when Jesus "breathed his last" (Matt. 27:50). This contrasted with the ancient Greek tradition that relied on the functioning of the nervous system: soldiers in the Iliad died when "the light in the eyes went out." Michaelangelo followed the Greek tradition in his Sistine Chapel representation of the quickening of Adam by God's electrifying touch (figure 3, p. 271 above). Divine energy as well as divine breath can serve as an appropriate symbol for God making the difference between the animate and the inanimate.

A second symbol system about life is in Deuteronomy 30:15–16, 19–20, in the speech Moses gives to the Israelites about to invade the Promised Land:

See, I have set before you today life and prosperity, death and adversity. If you obey the commandments of the Lord your God that I am commanding you today, by loving the Lord your God, walking in his ways, and observing his commandments, decrees, and ordinances, then you shall live and become numerous, and the Lord your God will bless you in the land that you are entering to possess . . . Choose life so that you and your descendants may live, loving the Lord your God, obeying him, and holding fast to him; for that means life to you and length of days, so that you may live in the land that the Lord swore to give to your ancestors, to Abraham, to Isaac, and to Jacob.

Here life means human flourishing, prosperity in the land, length of tenure for the people and their descendants down through history, the enjoyment of a country flowing with milk and honey (Deut. 31:20). The condition for such life is obedience to God; disobedience entails death. In this context death means not only physical death but also hardship in the land, trouble holding it against enemy attack, social disorder, and the degradation of the land itself and the herds and flocks to conditions of drought and famine.

Although the agricultural context for the Deuteronomist's depictions of life and death might seem limiting today, we still appreciate the sense of life as human flourishing, and of death as human suffering and degradation. To be fully alive, to have life abundant, means at least to enjoy health and prosperity for oneself and one's family and friends in a society with just and economically rich conditions and with a vital culture of sophistication, zest, beauty, peace, and a sense of creative adventure.[12] Something like this sense of life as abundant human flourishing is normative across all cultures. A good society makes a very great difference to life and death in this sense of abundance. The norms of the covenant, as discussed earlier, are relevant to making this sense of life possible. Moses was clear that this sense of life depends on choice and human effort, and that the corresponding sense of death comes from wrong choices and wrong or failed efforts.

A third text from the Hebrew Bible is from Ezekiel 37, the famous vision of the dry bones. Ezekiel prophesies as God tells him, and the dry human bones scattered across a valley clack together and are covered with flesh and skin. Then Ezekiel commands the four winds, or spirits, to breathe into the bodies, and they come alive. Like the Genesis passage in adding breath to inanimate bodies, this text is an addition of life to the dead. In context, it refers to the Israelites who have died in foreign lands who will be brought back to Israel. But it is easily generalized to mean the resuscitation of any dead. The stories of Jesus' resuscitation miracles in the New Testament, such as that of Lazarus, are continuous with it in the sense of life involved. Some constructions of the resurrection of the dead in the Last Things involve this sense of recovering life that has departed, including the reconstitution of a livable body. In Ezekiel's case, the resuscitation of the dead of Israel was coupled with the Deuteronomist's sense of life abundant: the return to Israel would bring back what Moses had warned them to choose and the abundant way of life that involved. But in other cases, for instance the healing of Jairus' daughter (Mark 5:21–43), the widow's son at Nain (Luke 7:11–17), and Lazarus (John 11), there is no indication that restored life meant any restored fortunes of abundant life, although Lazarus and his sisters did give a subsequent dinner party for Jesus and his companions (John 12:1–8) at which Mary's pound jar of expensive perfume was the recorded topic of conversation.

The resuscitation of dead bodies itself is a metaphor for coming to spiritual life after being spiritually dead, a metaphor especially beloved of Paul and his school. For instance, Ephesians 2:4 says, "But God, who is rich in mercy, out of the great love with which he loved us even when we were dead through our trespasses, made us alive together with Christ

[12] I take this list in part from Whitehead's discussion of a good civilization in *Adventures of Ideas*, part 4.

– by grace you have been saved – and raised us up with him and seated us with him in the heavenly places in Christ Jesus." People who are alive in the physical sense and in no need of that kind of resuscitation can still be dead spiritually. For Paul this is so even when they are following the law. The most famous Christian passage on spiritual life and death is John 3:1–10 in which Jesus is quoted as saying that one must be born again from the spirit, which Nicodemus notoriously misinterprets as requiring a physical rebirth from one's mother's womb. The grace of Christ brings a spiritual life and vitality that allows one to live richly before God.

This metaphoric extension of new life is related to the one discussed earlier from Colossians 2–3 in which Christian baptism is a dying to sin with Jesus in his crucifixion, and also a rising with him to glory in Heaven, a state enjoyed now while also living on Earth. In the concurrent earthly life all the old problems remain, including bad habits of character for which sanctifying amendment should be sought, and yet earthly life lived in the spirit is free from bondage to the flesh and its bad habits.

Scholars seem agreed that Jesus believed he was heralding a Kingdom of God soon to come (though he could not predict when) which involved all of these senses of life, combining the flourishing of God's people in the sense of abundance and the recalling to life of the faithful departed, along with judgment, all fulfilling the original creation.[13] Paul also agreed with this, as illustrated in his discussion in 1 Thessalonians, at least early in his ministry. The Kingdom did not come when Jesus and his followers expected it. The author of 2 Peter 3:8–10 (in the late first or early second century) cites the divine time-scale from Psalm 90:4 to the effect that one of God's days is like a thousand of our years in order to explain the delay, though he still expected the day of the Lord.

The gospel of John was clearly focused on the dialectical relation between life in time and life in eternity, as illustrated in passages from the Farewell Discourses already quoted and discussed. There is nothing in that gospel to suggest that Jesus did not believe in a coming kingdom. Indeed, in 5:25–29 he says that even the dead will have the word preached to them (see figure 8, p. 100 above) and rise to the resurrection of life or to condemnation (spiritual death), depending on their merits (figure 15, p. 226 above). But the point is that, for John, the kingdom is already present in the person, teachings, and works of Jesus, which is

---

[13] See the discussion in Sanders, *The Historical Figure of Jesus*, chapter 11.

why Jesus talks so much about himself in this gospel. Jesus does not in this gospel predict that things will be made right in history. If there is an end, it is an end of history in eternal judgment. The disciples should expect history to go on as before, which is why they need the Spirit as a guide through life's ambiguities. Meanwhile, the religiously important point is that Jesus has already overcome the world and that by being in him, through love, the disciples can be in God through love, which is proper eternal life. When Jesus says he is the Life, he means something like this complex of historical and eternal living according to which he is the connection between God and the disciples, indwelling each and allowing them to dwell in each other.

What can twenty-first-century people make of this? If Paul and the author of 2 Peter got discouraged about the delay in the kingdom, the day of the Lord, most of us have given up hope. Or, most accurately, most of us no longer think in terms of a historical day of reckoning with a transformation of human society into a perfect kingdom of God. We know the world can end for any number of reasons but rarely imagine the Last Things as the coming of the kingdom in any historical sense, only as the destruction of Earth and its inhabitants. Part of the reason for this change in sensibility is that the expanded scale of the cosmos in our imagination does not lend itself to the root metaphors of distant-but-not-too-distant kings who might come conquering Earth, or re-establishing a reign. Another part is modernity's grim realization that the course of history is a matter of human responsibility to a very large extent, not a matter of battles between cosmic forces such as Satan and God, and not a matter that can be left to God. The passivity of the New Testament about social change and human responsibility for historical conditions stands in sharp contrast to our own sensibility about responsibility. As to historical eschatology, most of us warm less to the images of the coming of a historical kingdom than to those of the parables, say in Matthew 24–25, which warn each of us to be awake because any day might be our last.

Eternity rather than a future kingdom is another matter. For eternity is a notion that can very well find expression in contemporary life. The metaphysics for it has already been sketched in chapter 1 and elaborated since. To recapitulate, eternity is the togetherness of the modes of time and as such is the divine life. It includes the dynamisms of the growing history of actuality, of the spontaneity of present existence within the limits of the past and future possibilities, and of the structure of the future itself that shifts with each new situation for which it is relevant.

For us it means that within God's eternity we live with all our moments future, all present, and all actualized as past, all together. This is our eternal identity of which our temporal identity is but an abstraction.

Modern philosophers commonly think that consciousness is limited to thinking only of temporal things and static formal abstractions. I doubt this, however. The theory of eternity as the non-temporal togetherness of the temporal modes of historical creation can be understood notionally by people with the patience for metaphysics. Perhaps not all of those can dwell upon this theory meditatively so that it becomes a complex symbol for actually engaging reality in its ultimate and elementary parts, a symbol of vital prayer and practice. Some can, however: I know from personal experience. Many people can engage the eternal aspects of reality by means of temporalistic, indeed apocalyptic, symbols so long as the logic of the metaphysics bounds the extension of the symbols. Eternal life can indeed be imagined as a future heavenly home (with benign cigars!) and any symbols less sensuous, intense, vivifying than that are likely to fail to be true to what is important in eternal life, the divine glory. Another of the glories of old age, along with its spiritual intensity, is both the leisure and the memory to reflect back on past moments in a long life, contemplating them as future possibilities, enjoying or suffering through them as present experience, and assessing them as done deeds. Reminiscence of maturity is meditation not only on the past as past, but on the past as a future spread before a youth and as the days of decision, all together a good simulacrum of eternal togetherness.

The argument I have developed throughout for eternity and the eternal life of individuals and communities has affirmed that everyone has it. Eternity is the locus for ultimate judgment where every decision and every consequence are together as matters of freedom and responsibility. Everyone falls under judgment as argued in chapter 3. So what difference does Jesus make?

All the difference in the world lies between living with a proper orientation to eternity, that is, to God and the creation as contained within the divine life, and living with no proper orientation. Without it we are likely to be alienated by the guilt we bear by just existing. Without it we are homeless, caught in an indifferent cosmos in a no-win situation with regard to our obligations. Without it we are alienated from our Creator whose creativity we share. Without it our historical position has no point of reference or purpose. Without it we do not learn to love or to be alone fully.

With a proper orientation to God we are joined with God, our fellows and the whole creation as integral and interrelated parts of the consummately glorious eternal act of divine creation. Though we do not cease to be who we are with all our finite limitations, we identify also and truly with the larger life of God. What does this identification look like?

When Jesus said he was the Life, it was in the context of intensifying and articulating the bonds of love in conjunction with the Holy Spirit and relating the Spirit to Jesus with the Father. Jesus was the true Son of God, he could claim, because God's loving creativity was perfectly incarnate in his words and deeds. The Logos hypothesis I have proposed here articulates this as the creation of lovely things with form, components, formed, existential location, and value; human beings are such lovely things upon whom the issues of *right* form, components, location, and value are laid as obligations. The harmony of those four elements of the Logos is love. In creating a community of loving persons, Jesus was doing the work of his Father, which he did by word and deed. That was a community of people who could love one another despite their failures to perfect the Logos, accepting that as part of the human condition. By doing likewise, the disciples also did the work of the Father, functioning like proper sons (and daughters as the case may be). By continuing that through history, Christians participate in the life of God normatively, not in alienation, but in harmony. Sanctification in this life is coming to live in greater harmony with the Creator in whom we live and move and have our being.

The symbols discussed here allow us to engage Jesus more comprehensively and deeply. Most of these symbols were not of Jesus' own personal origin but were worked out subsequently by Christians attempting to understand him and know God through him. I argued in chapter 5 that the historical Jesus is still alive in and above the various congregations of the Church and in the larger sense of Church that goes beyond congregations. Insofar as contemporary Christians continue to discern the developing mind of Jesus for the situations arising, Jesus has not said his last word. As our own friends change, so does Jesus. We should not be overly past-oriented, therefore, not overly biblical, in looking to Jesus for our redemption and sanctification. Although we live in the Last Things now eternally, in our time we live in the living Christ through the Holy Spirit, life abundant.

CHAPTER EIGHT

Epilogue: "And the Holy Spirit"

The prologue of this book concluded with the claim that the kind of theology undertaken here is Pneumatology, theology of the Holy Spirit. The Holy Spirit, of course, is another large Christian symbol, officially as large as Jesus Christ and God the Father. Historically, however, the Holy Spirit has been the least developed theologically of the great Trinitarian symbols, the last to be elaborated in the Patristic debates, and even then discussed more in terms of its origin than in terms of its nature and work. Yet the fundamental arguments made in this book, intrinsic to a Christology of symbolic engagement, have centered around locating the issues in the tests of the Spirit.

This strategy is a recurrence to that of Josiah Royce in his master-piece, *The Problem of Christianity*. In that book he developed a theory of interpretation from the same ideas of Charles Peirce that have inspired the present work.[1] He then claimed that Christianity is to be understood as a community of interpretation that he explained in ways that bear many similarities to the arguments here. The principal difference between his approach and mine is his confidence in the coherence of the community. He believed that differences within the community can be overcome by unifying interpretation, a belief that reflects the residual absolute idealist character of his thought even after he had given up that metaphysics. With a different sensibility I allow that at any time the differences need to be respected on their own and that the urge to unify should sometimes be suppressed so that they can work out their own ways without a heavy hand dictating order. Whereas Royce might agree that genuinely unified coherence can only come in the infinite long run, never at any finite time, I would celebrate the differences as such. Christians everywhere supposedly confess One God, One Lord and

---

[1] On Royce and Peirce, see John E. Smith's *Royce's Social Infinite*. My own debt to Peirce on religious symbols is spelled out in the introduction to *The Truth of Broken Symbols*.

257

Savior Jesus Christ, and One Spirit: but the very meaning of that confession differs from context to context according to the arguments given here in several places. This difference aside, the theology of symbolic engagement is very much a Roycean project: The symbols from the past are made to save the current situation by interpretation which is the act of the Holy Spirit, as Royce would put it.

So my argument in the case of each of the major Christological symbols has been that the symbol has power to engage us truly with regard to certain profound religious issues of our time subject to the conditions of right meaning, reference, and interpretive context. Whether it in fact does so depends on the Holy Spirit, as the Christian symbols put it, and the assessment of the truth of the symbols in specific contexts is a matter of "testing the spirits" (1 John 4:1, Gal. 5:16–6:10).

To make these claims about the Holy Spirit precise would require a direct Pneumatology, not an indirect one such as this that elaborates the symbols of the Spirit in discussing those of Jesus Christ. Nevertheless, it is possible briefly to indicate something of a direct Pneumatology, though here in the form of summary doctrines rather than in a living analysis of Pneumatological symbols.

In the metaphysics of creation, the Holy Spirit was identified with the creative act itself, eternal within the divine life and manifest within time as the energy of harmony-making. The characteristics of harmony manifest themselves as form, components formed, existential location, and value, together producing harmonies that are both intrinsically good and intrinsically connected with other things. The characteristics of harmony, according to this metaphysics, are identified with the Logos of which Jesus is an incarnation. With the Creator as Father, the Logos as Son, and the Holy Spirit as the creative act, the ancient Trinitarian principle is affirmed that the act of any one person of the Trinity is the act of the others also, and in relative respects that can be understood.

As a more homely principle, the human creative behavior that advances important harmonies is kindness. To be kind is to make things harmonious. Kindness is the baseline ideal trait the prologue attributed to Christianity. A fancier name for kindness is love, which can now be affirmed on the basis of the discussion of these symbols to be the creative act of God, the Holy Spirit, giving rise to things defined by the Logos. When human beings play out that creativity in their finite sphere, they are loving and, by that, children of God, filled to that extent with the Holy Spirit.

Perhaps the most central appeal here to the Holy Spirit has been in the discussion of the resurrection of Jesus that was treated in chapter 5 in terms of the historical Jesus. The argument was made there that the real, particular, singular, historical Jesus is the person who after dying continues to lead the communities of the Church through the medium of the Holy Spirit working in imagination. That Spirit is the creative and open interpretation of the present needs and imperatives of those diverse communities and individuals in terms of the previous life of Jesus, starting off with his Galilean ministry and continuing in diverse places through the ages ever since. The Spirit, with proper discernment of spirits, is the creative interpretation of that long historical life of Jesus as well as of the religious significance of the present situation. As the community recognizes the Risen Christ as its Lord, moving forward in the Spirit, it extends that historical life. Thus the Risen Christ is both within the community but also above it as judge, and the Jesus of the past alone is not the full judge. An individual can embrace the Risen Christ as friend through the Spirit's imagination. With this approach to the res-urrected living Christ, Jesus lives because of the ongoing activity of the Holy Spirit (Rom. 8:11).

This book is written for those who are self-identified with the institu-tional Christian Church as well as for those who are not so identified but who are Christians in some other senses. Beyond this, however, the book is also written for the larger public of those who are interested in the issues. That I write as a Christian is not a necessary requirement for writing on Christology. But I do in fact write as a Christian, and there-fore part of my motive is ecclesial outreach beyond the Church in its largest sense. The intent is to aid the understanding of Christianity as a religion (and perhaps other religions insofar as they have analogous sym-bolic usages) and to be understood by non-Christians as a Christian articulating at least one stream of Christianity.

Christians of all sorts, new and from established traditions, indeed religious people of all sorts, have an ultimate commitment to the truth because "being religious" is "being in the truth" about ultimate matters. How is error possible? There are five ways to error. First and most obvious is that we have the wrong symbols for God and the bearing of the divine on things. Second is that we misinterpret how the symbols refer to their objects, construing indexical reference as iconic or vice-versa. Third is that we mistake whether a given interpreter is a proper secondary referent for the symbol, with the result that the person cannot actually engage the divine reality with symbols that would work just fine for other people. Fourth is that we misconstrue the interpretive context

Figure 17. Roger Wagner, *The Harvest is the End of the World, and the Reapers are Angels,* 1989

so that we interpret the religious object as if it bore on some context other than the interpretation's. Fifth is that we do not put these components of symbolic engagement together properly. In this book I have attempted to call attention to the importance of avoiding all five ways to error by exercising a theory of the truth of symbols in the analysis of Jesus Christ.

Classical Greece was an age of skepticism as well as belief. Plato deconstructed popular paganism to establish a reconstructed, far more sophisticated, "religion" or "way of life" which was called a "philosophy." (Early Christianity was also called a "philosophy" through the time of Augustine.) More or less contemporary with Plato in West Asia, the great Confucians and Daoists in China were deconstructing their ancestral religious practices and ideas and rebuilding what we know as Confucianism and Daoism. Buddhism did the same in India, with parallel responses from the schools that came to be called Hinduism. In all these cases, popular religion was subjected to skeptical analysis and replaced with elite ways of life and new normative theologies.

We face a similar situation today. I have attempted in this book to be faithful to the deepest roots of skepticism in our time, acknowledging not only the foolishness of religious symbols when employed with the wrong meanings, in mistaken reference, and in the wrong context for the wrong people, but also the social and intellectual evils that have been done in the name of these very Christological symbols. At the same time I have tried to show how these symbols, so ancient and pervasive, so appropriately embodied in popular Christian religious culture, also serve to engage us late moderns with the darkest and most vexing issues hardly addressed by other symbols. Without claiming that Christianity is exclusively true, or even superior to other religious traditions, I have essayed to show that it is at least true at some of the deepest levels obscured by most secular imaginative powers in our culture. Without such symbols for engagement, we do not have a chance. With them we have eternity.

Bibliography

Altizer, Thomas J. J. *The New Apocalypse: The Radical Christian Vision of William Blake*. Ann Arbor: Michigan State University Press, 1967.
> *History as Apocalypse*. Albany: State University of New York Press, 1985.
> *Genesis and Apocalypse: A Theological Voyage toward Authentic Christianity*. Louisville: Westminster/John Knox Press, 1990.
> *The Contemporary Jesus*. Albany: State University of New York Press, 1997.
Armstrong, A. H. Editor. *Classical Mediterranean Spirituality: Egyptian, Greek, Roman*. Volume xv of *World Spirituality*. New York: Crossroad, 1986.
Berdyaev, Nicolas. *The Beginning and the End*. Translated by R. M. French. New York: Harper Torchbook, 1957.
Berger, Peter. *The Social Construction of Reality: A Treatise in the Sociology of Knowledge*. With Thomas Luckmann. Garden City, NY: Doubleday, 1966.
> *The Sacred Canopy: Elements of a Sociological Theory of Religion*. Garden City, NY: Doubleday, 1967.
Berthrong, John H. *Concerning Creativity: A Comparison of Chu Hsi, Whitehead, and Neville*. Albany: State University of New York Press, 1998.
> *The Divine Deli: Religious Identity in the North American Cultural Mosaic*. Maryknoll, NY: Orbis, 1999.
De Borchgrave, Helen. *A Journey into Christian Art*. Oxford Lion, 1999.
Borg, Marcus J. *Jesus: A New Vision: Spirit, Culture, and the Life of Discipleship*. San Francisco: Harper & Row, 1989.
> *Meeting Jesus Again for the First Time: The Historical Jesus and the Heart of Contemporary Faith*. San Francisco: HarperCollins, 1994.
Bornkamm, Guenther. *Jesus of Nazareth*. New York: Harper and Brothers, 1960.
Brown, Frank Burch. *Religious Aesthetics: a Theological Study of Making and Meaning*. Princeton: Princeton University Press, 1989.
> *Good Taste, Bad Taste, and Christian Taste: Aesthetics in Religious Life*. Oxford: Oxford University Press, 2000.
Brown, Raymond. *The Death of the Messiah: From Gethsemane to the Grave*. New York: Doubleday, 1994.
Brumbaugh, Robert S. *Plato on the One*. New Haven: Yale University Press, 1961.
Bultmann, Rudolf. *Jesus and the Word*. New York: Charles Scribner's Sons, 1934.

Theology of the New Testament. Volume I. Translated by Kendrick Grobel. New York: Charles Scribner's Sons, 1951.

Theology of the New Testament. Volume II. Translated by Kendrick Grobel. New York: Charles Scribner's Sons, 1955.

Existence and Faith: Shorter Writings. Selected and translated by Schubert Ogden. Cleveland: World Publishing, 1960.

Cady, Susan, Marian Ronan, and Hall Taussig. *Sophia: The Future of Feminist Spirituality.* San Francisco: Harper and Row, 1986.

Cahoone, Lawrence E. *The Dilemma of Modernity: Philosophy, Culture, and Anti-Culture.* Albany: State University of New York Press, 1988.

Campbell, Ted A. *Christian Confessions: A Historical Introduction.* Louisville: Westminster/John Knox, 1996.

Carse, James P. *The Silence of God: Meditations on Prayer.* New York: Macmillan 1985. Reprint, San Francisco: HarperCollins, 1995.

Chan, Wing-tsit. *A Source Book in Chinese Philosophy.* Princeton: Princeton University Press, 1963.

Chapman, J. Harley, and Nancy K. Frankenberry. Editors. *Interpreting Neville.* Albany: State University of New York Press, 1999.

Close, Frank. *Lucifer's Legacy: The Meaning of Asymmetry.* Oxford: Oxford University Press, 2000.

Cook, Michael L. *Christology as Narrative Quest.* Collegeville, MN: Liturgical Press, 1997.

Cone, James H. *A Black Theology of Liberation: Twentieth Anniversary Edition.* Maryknoll, NY: Orbis Books, 1990.

Cove, Sidney. *The Christian Estimate of Man.* London: Duckworth, 1957.

Crossan, John Dominic. *The Historical Jesus: The Life of a Mediterranean Jewish Peasant.* San Francisco: Harper, 1991.

Cunliffe-Johnes, Hubert. Edited with assistance from Benjamin Drewery. *A History of Christian Doctrine.* In succession to the earlier work of G. P. Fisher published in the International Theological Library Series. Philadelphia, PA: Fortress, 1980. Original edition, London: T. and T. Clark, 1978.

Daneel, M. L. *African Earthkeepers.* Volume 1 of *Interfaith Mission in Earth-Care.* Pretoria: Unisa Press of the University of South Africa, 1998.

Deacon, Terrence W. *The Symbolic Species: The Co-evolution of Language and the Brain.* New York: W. W. Norton, 1997.

Deuser, Hermann. "Neville's Theology of Creation, Covenant, and Trinity," in Chapman and Frankenberry, eds., *Interpreting Neville.*

Dewey, John. *Experience and Nature* (1925). Revised edition, 1929, edited by Jo Ann Boydston as volume 1 of *John Dewey: The Later Works.* Carbondale: Southern Illinois University Press, 1981.

Diamond, Jared. *Guns, Germs, and Steel: The Fates of Human Societies.* New York: W. W. Norton, 1997.

Donahue, John R. *The Gospel in Parable: Metaphor, Narrative, and Theology in the Synoptic Gospels.* Philadelphia: Fortress Press, 1988.

Dutton, Kenneth R. *The Perfectible Body: The Western Ideal of Male Physical Development.* New York: Continuum, 1995.

Eckhart, Johannes. *Meister Eckhart: Selected Writings.* Selected and translated by Oliver Davies. London: Penguin Books, 1994.

Falk, Harvey. *Jesus the Pharisee: A New Look at the Jewishness of Jesus.* New York: Paulist Press, 1985.

Farrar, Austin. *Finite and Infinite.* Second edition, London: Dacre Press, 1959. First edition, 1943.

Finaldi, Gabriele. *The Image of Christ.* New Haven: Yale University Press, 2000.

Fiorenza, Elisabeth Schuessler. *In Memory of Her: A Feminist Theological Reconstruction of Christian Origins.* New York: Crossroad, 1985.

Jesus, Miriam's Child, Sophia's Prophet. New York: Continuum, 1995.

Ford, Lewis S. *Transforming Process Theism.* Albany: State University of New York Press, 2000.

Fox, Matthew. *The Coming of the Cosmic Christ: The Healing of Mother Earth and the Birth of a Global Renaissance.* New York: Harper & Row, 1988.

Fox, Robin Lane. *Pagans and Christians.* New York: Knopf, 1987.

Frankenberry, Nancy K.: see Chapman, J. Harley.

Fredriksen, Paula. *From Jesus to Christ: The Origins of the New Testament Images of Jesus.* New Haven: Yale University Press, 1988.

Jesus of Nazareth, King of the Jews: A Jewish Life and the Emergence of Christianity. New York: Alfred A. Knopf, 1999.

"Ultimate Reality in Ancient Christianity: Christ and Redemption," in Neville, *Ultimate Realities.*

Frymer-Kensky, Tikva. *In the Wake of the Goddesses: Women, Culture, and the Biblical Transformation of Pagan Myth.* New York: Free Press, 1992.

Fuller, Reginald H. *The Foundations of New Testament Christology.* London: Lutterworth Press, 1965.

Gadamer, Hans-Georg. *Truth and Method.* Edited by Garrett Barden and John Cumming. New York: The Seabury Press, 1975.

Girard, René. *Violence and the Sacred.* Translated by Patrick Gregory. Baltimore: Johns Hopkins University Press, 1977.

Goldman, Laurence R. Editor. *The Anthropology of Cannibalism.* Westport, CT: Bergin & Garvey, 1999.

Grant, Jacquelyn. *White Women's Christ and Black Women's Jesus.* Atlanta: Scholar's Press, 1990.

Haight, Roger, SJ. *Jesus: Symbol of God.* Maryknoll, NY: Orbis Books, 1999.

Hammill, Graham L. *Sexuality and Form: Caravaggio, Marlowe, and Bacon.* Chicago: University of Chicago Press, 2000.

Hart, Ray L. *Unfinished Man and the Imagination.* New York: Herder and Herder, 1968.

Herrin, Judith. *The Formation of Christendom.* Princeton: Princeton University Press, 1987.

Hinson, E. Glenn. *The Early Church: Origins to the Dawn of the Middle Ages.* Nashville: Abingdon, 1996.

Horsley, Richard A. *Jesus and the Spiral of Violence: Popular Jewish Resistance in Roman Palestine.* Minneapolis: Fortress Press, 1993.

Husserl, Edmund. *Ideas: General Introduction to Pure Phenomenology.* Translated by W. R. Boyce Gibson. New York: Collier Books, 1962. Original edition, 1913.

James, William. *The Varieties of Religious Experience: A Study of Human Nature.* New York: Longmans, Green, 1902. Penguin edition, with an introduction by Martin E. Marty, New York: Penguin, 1982.

Jaspers, Karl. *Way to Wisdom: An Introduction to Philosophy.* Translated by Ralph Manheim. New Haven: Yale University Press, 1954.

Johnson, Luke Timothy. *The Real Jesus: The Misguided Quest for the Historical Jesus and the Truth of the Traditional Gospels.* San Francisco: Harper, 1996.

Jones, L. Gregory. *Embodying Forgiveness: A Theological Analysis.* Grand Rapids: Eerdmans, 1995.

Kasulis, Thomas P., and Robert Cummings Neville. Editors. *The Recovery of Philosophy in America: Essays in Honor of John Edwin Smith.* Albany: State University of New York Press, 1997.

Kee, Howard Clark. *Christian Origins in Social Perspective.* Philadelphia: Westminster, 1980.

Kee, Howard Clark. Emily Albu Hanawalt, Carter Lindberg, Jean-Loup Seban, and Mark A. Noll. Editors. *Christianity: A Social and Cultural History.* With an Epilogue by Dana L. Robert. New York: Macmillan, 1991.

Kirk, Kenneth E. *The Vision of God: The Christian Doctrine of the* Summum Bonum. London: Longmans, Green and Co, 1931.

Lang, Bernhard: see McDannell, Colleen.

Latourette, Kenneth Scott. *A History of Christianity.* New York: Harper and Brothers, 1953.

Leith, John H. Editor. *Creeds of the Churches.* Garden City, NY: Doubleday, 1963.

Lohse, Bernhard. *A Short History of Christian Doctrine: From the First Century to the Present.* Translated from the German by F. Ernest Stoeffler. Revised American Edition, Philadelphia: Fortress, 1985.

Mack, Burton L. *The Lost Gospel: The Book of Q and Christian Origins.* San Francisco: Harper, 1993.

McDannell, Colleen, and Bernhard Lang. *Heaven: A History.* New Haven: Yale University Press, 1988

McGinn, Bernard. *The Foundations of Mysticism* (1991). Volume I of *The Presence of God: A History of Western Christian Mysticism.* New York: Crossroad, 1995. *The Growth of Mysticism* (1994). Volume II of *The Presence of God: A History of Western Christian Mysticism.* New York: Crossroad, 1995.

McGrath, Alister E. *Christian Theology: An Introduction.* Second edition, Cambridge, MA: Blackwell, 1997.

MacGregor, Neil, with Erika Langmuir. *Seeing Salvation: Images of Christ in Art.* London: BBC Worldwide Limited, 2000.

Manchester, Peter B. "The Religious Experience of Time and Eternity," in Armstrong, *Classical Mediterranean Spirituality.*

Marcus, Joel. *Mark 1–8: A New Translation with Introduction and Commentary.* The Anchor Bible, volume XXVII. New York: Doubleday, 2000.

Mathews, Shailer. *The Social Teachings of Jesus: An Essay in Christian Sociology.* New York: Macmillan, 1897.

Mathews, Thomas F. *The Clash of Gods: A Reinterpretation of Early Christian Art.* Princeton: Princeton University Press, 1993.

Meadows, Philip R. *Sadhana and Salvation: Soteriology in Ramanuja and John Wesley.* Ph.D. dissertation, University of Cambridge, 1997.

Meeks, Wayne A. *The First Urban Christians: The Social World of the Apostle Paul.* New Haven: Yale University Press, 1983.

The Origins of Christian Morality: The First Two Centuries. New Haven: Yale University Press, 1993.

Meier, John P. *A Marginal Jew,* volume I: *Rethinking the Historical Jesus.* New York: Doubleday, 1991.

A Marginal Jew, volume II: *Mentor, Message, and Miracles.* New York: Doubleday, 1994.

Merback, Mitchell B. *The Thief, The Cross, and the Wheel: Pain and the Spectacle of Punishment in Medieval and Renaissance Europe.* London: Reaktion Books, 1999.

The Methodist Worship Book. Peterborough, England: Methodist Publishing House, 1999.

Moffett, Samuel Hugh. *A History of Christianity in Asia,* volume I: *Beginnings to 1500.* San Francisco: HarperSanFrancisco, 1992.

Mollenkott, Virginia Ramey. *The Divine Feminine: The Biblical Imagery of God as Female.* New York: Crossroad, 1988.

Neville, Robert Cummings. *God the Creator: On the Presence and Transcendence of God.* Chicago: University of Chicago Press, 1968. Second edition with a new preface, Albany: State University of New York Press, 1992.

The Cosmology of Freedom. New Haven: Yale University Press, 1974. New edition, Albany: State University of New York Press, 1992.

Soldier, Sage, Saint. New York: Fordham University Press, 1978.

Creativity and God. New York: The Seabury Press, 1980. New edition, Albany: State University of New York Press, 1995.

Reconstruction of Thinking. Albany: State University of New York, 1981.

The Tao and the Daimon. Albany: State University of New York Press, 1982.

Recovery of the Measure. Albany: State University of New York Press, 1989.

A Theology Primer. Albany: State University of New York Press, 1991.

Behind the Masks of God. Albany: State University of New York Press, 1991.

The Highroad around Modernism. Albany: State University of New York Press, 1992.

Eternity and Time's Flow. Albany: State University of New York Press, 1993.

Normative Cultures. Albany: State University of New York Press, 1995.

The Truth of Broken Symbols. Albany: State University of New York Press, 1996.

Boston Confucianism. Albany: State University of New York Press, 2000.

Religion in Late Modernity. Albany: State University of New York Press, 2002.

Neville, Robert Cummings. Editor. *The Human Condition*. Albany: State University of New York Press, 2001.

Ultimate Realities. Albany: State University of New York Press, 2001.

Religious Truth. Albany: State University of New York Press, 2001.

The Recovery of Philosophy in America: Essays in Honor of John Edwin Smith. see Kasulis, Thomas P.

Niebuhr, H. Richard. *Christ and Culture*. New York: Harper & Brothers, 1951.

The Meaning of Revelation. New York: Macmillan, 1960.

Oberman, Heiko A. *The Roots of Anti-Semitism: In the Age of Renaissance and Reformation*. Translated by James I. Porter. Philadelphia: Fortress, 1984.

Oden, Thomas C. *The Living God: Systematic Theology*, volume 1. San Francisco: Harper & Row, 1987.

Ogden, Schubert. *Christ without Myth: A Study Based on the Theology of Rudolf Bultmann*. New York: Harper & Row, 1961.

Panikkar, Raimundo. *The Trinity and the Religious Experience of Man: Icon, Person, Mystery*. London: Darton, Longman & Todd, 1973.

The Vedic Experience: Mantramanjan. Berkeley: University of California Press, 1977.

The Unknown Christ of Hinduism. Revised edition; Maryknoll, NY: Orbis Books, 1981.

The Silence of God, The Answer of the Buddha. Translated from the Italian by Robert R. Barr. Maryknoll, NY: Orbis Books, 1989.

Park, Andrew Sung. *The Wounded Heart of God: The Asian Concept of Han and the Christian Doctrine of Sin*. Nashville: Abingdon, 1993.

Peabody, Francis Greenwood. *Jesus Christ and the Social Question: An Examination of the Teaching of Jesus in Its Relation to Some of the Moral Problems of Modern Social Life*. New York: Macmillan, 1900.

Peirce, Charles S. *The Collected Papers of Charles Sanders Peirce*, edited by Charles Hartshorne and Paul Weiss. Volume II; Cambridge, MA: Harvard University Press, 1932.

Pelikan, Jaroslav. *The Emergence of the Catholic Tradition (100–600)*. Volume I of *The Christian Tradition: A History of the Development of Doctrine*. Chicago: University of Chicago Press, 1971.

The Spirit of Eastern Christendom. Volume II of *The Christian Tradition: A History of the Development of Doctrine*. Chicago: University of Chicago Press, 1974.

The Growth of Medieval Theology (600–1300). Volume III of *The Christian Tradition: A History of the Development of Doctrine*. Chicago: University of Chicago Press, 1978.

Reformation of Church and Dogma (1300–1700). Volume IV of *The Christian Tradition: A History of the Development of Doctrine*. Chicago: University of Chicago Press, 1984.

Christian Doctrine and Modern Culture (since 1700). Volume V of *The Christian Tradition: A History of the Development of Doctrine*. Chicago: University of Chicago Press, 1989.

The Illustrated Jesus through the Centuries. New Haven: Yale University Press, 1997.

Pepin, Jean. "Cosmic Piety," in Armstrong, *Classical Mediterranean Spirituality.*

Perrin, Norman. *Jesus and the Language of the Kingdom: Symbol and Metaphor in New Testament Interpretation.* Philadelphia: Fortress Press, 1976.

Placher, William C. *A History of Christian Theology: An Introduction.* Louisville: Westminster, 1983.

Polkinghorne, John, and Michael Welker. Editors. *The End of the World and the Ends of God: Science and Theology on Eschatology.* Harrisburg: Trinity Press International, 2000.

Quinn, Daniel. *Ishmael: An Adventure of the Mind and Spirit.* New York: Bantam, 1992.

Rambuss, Richard. *Closet Devotions.* Durham, NC: Duke University Press, 1998.

Rauschenbusch, Walter. *The Social Principles of Jesus.* New York: Association Press, 1916.

Ricoeur, Paul. *The Symbolism of Evil.* Translated by Emerson Buchanan. New York: Harper & Row, 1967. Paperback edition; Boston: Beacon, 1969.

Robinson, James M. *New Quest for the Historical Jesus.* London: SCM Press, 1959.

Romer, John. *Testament: The Bible and History.* London: Michael O'Mara, 1988.

Rorty, Richard. *Philosophy and the Mirror of Nature.* Princeton: Princeton University Press, 1979.

Royce, Josiah. *The Problem of Christianity.* New York: Macmillan, 1918. New edition, with an introduction by John E. Smith, Chicago: University of Chicago Press, 1968.

Saldarini, Anthony J. "Ultimate Realities: Judaism: God as a Many-sided Ultimate Reality in Traditional Judaism," in Neville, *Ultimate Realities.*

Sampley, J. Paul. *Walking between the Times: Paul's Moral Reasoning.* Minneapolis: Fortress Press, 1991.

Sanders, E. P. *Jesus and Judaism.* Philadelphia: Fortress Press, 1985.

The Historical Figure of Jesus. London: Penguin, 1993.

Schillebeeckx, Edward. *Jesus: An Experiment in Christology.* New York: The Seabury Press, 1979.

Schuessler Fiorenza, Elisabeth. *In Memory of Her: A Feminist Theological Reconstruction of Christian Origins.* New York: Crossroad, 1983.

Jesus, Miriam's Child, Sophia's Prophet: Critical Issues in Feminist Christology. New York: Continuum, 1995.

Schulkin, Jay. *Roots of Social Sensibility and Neural Function.* Cambridge, MA: Massachusetts Institute of Technology Press, 2000.

Schulkin, Jay and Louis A. Schmidt. Editors. *Extreme Fear, Shyness, and Social Phobia.* Cambridge: Cambridge University Press, 1999.

Schwartz, Regina M. *The Curse of Cain: The Violent Legacy of Monotheism.* Chicago: University of Chicago Press, 1997.

Schweitzer, Albert. *The Quest of the Historical Jesus.* New York: Charles Scribner's Sons, 1951. Original edition, 1906.

Segundo, Juan Luis. *The Historical Jesus of the Synoptics*. Maryknoll, NY: Orbis Books, 1985.

Christ in the Spiritual Exercises of St. Ignatius. Maryknoll, NY: Orbis Books, 1987.

Sloyan, Gerard S. *The Crucifixion of Jesus: History, Myth, Faith*. Minneapolis: Fortress Press, 1995.

Smart, Ninian. *Dimensions of the Sacred: An Anatomy of the World's Beliefs*. Berkeley: University of California Press, 1996.

Smith, John E. *Royce's Social Infinite*. New York: Liberal Arts Press, 1950.

Sobrino, Jon. *Jesus the Liberator: A Historical-Theological View*. Maryknoll, N.Y.: Orbis Books, 1993.

Sorabji, Richard. *Time, Creation, and the Continuum: Theories in Antiquity and the Early Middle Ages*. Ithaca: Cornell University Press, 1983.

Stanley, Arthur Penrhyn. *Lectures on the History of the Eastern Church*. New edition, New York: Charles Scribner's Sons, 1884.

Stendahl, Krister. *Paul among Jews and Gentiles*. Philadelphia: Fortress Press, 1976.

Sullivan, Andrew. *Love Undetectable: Notes on Friendship, Sex, and Survival*. New York: Random House, 1998.

Thangaraj, M. Thomas. *The Crucified Guru: An Experiment in Cross-Cultural Christology*. Nashville: Abingdon Press, 1994.

Theissen, Gerd. *The Shadow of the Galilean: The Quest of the Historical Jesus in Narrative Form*. Philadelphia: Fortress Press, 1987.

A Theory of Primitive Christian Religion. Translated by John Bowdon. London: SCM Press, 1999.

Tillich, Paul. *The Religious Situation*. Translated by H. Richard Niebuhr. New York: Henry Holt, 1932. Living Age Books edition, New York: Meridian, 1956.

Systematic Theology. Volume I. Chicago: University of Chicago Press, 1951.

The Courage to Be. New Haven: Yale University Press, 1952.

Systematic Theology. Volume II. Chicago: University of Chicago Press, 1957.

Systematic Theology. Volume III. Chicago: University of Chicago Press, 1963.

Tracy, David. *The Analogical Imagination: Christian Theology and the Culture of Pluralism*. New York: Crossroad, 1981.

Pluralism and Ambiguity: Hermeneutics, Religion, Hope. San Francisco: Harper & Row, 1987.

Underhill, Evelyn. *Mysticism*. New York and Cleveland: Meridian Books, 1965.

The United Methodist Hymnal. Nashville: The United Methodist Publishing House, 1989.

Vaught, Carl G. "Theft and Conversion: Two Augustinian Confessions," in Kasulis and Neville, eds., 1997.

Vermes, Geza. *Jesus the Jew: A Historian's Reading of the Gospels*. Philadelphia: Fortress Press, 1981.

The Changing Faces of Jesus. London: Allen Lane/The Penguin Press, 2000.

Ward, Keith. *Religion and Creation*. Oxford: The Clarendon Press, 1996.

Weiss, Johannes. *Jesus' Proclamation of the Kingdom of God*. Edited by Richard H.

270 *Bibliography*

Hiers and D. Larrimore Holland. Philadelphia: Fortress Press, 1971. German original, 1892.

Wesley, John. *The Works of John Wesley*. Volume II. Edited by Albert Outler. Nashville: Abingdon Press, 1987.

Whitehead, Alfred North. *Science and the Modern World*. New York: Macmillan, 1925.

Religion in the Making. New York: Macmillan, 1926.

Process and Reality: An Essay in Cosmology. New York: Macmillan, 1929. Corrected edition by David Ray Griffin and Donald W. Sherburne, New York: Free Press, 1978.

Adventures of Ideas. New York: Macmillan, 1933.

Wildman, Wesley J. "God Is Holy Mystery." Sermon preached at Marsh Chapel, Boston University, September 30, 1993. Texts: Job 8:20–9:20, Revelation 19:11–21.

"God Is Friend." Sermon preached at Marsh Chapel, Boston University, October 20, 1994. Texts: Isaiah 52:13–53, Psalm 35, Mark 10:35–45.

Fidelity with Plausibility: Modest Christologies in the Twentieth Century. Albany: State University of New York Press, 1998.

"Theological Literacy: Problem and Promise," in *Theological Literacy*, edited by Rodney Petersen. Grand Rapids: Eerdmans, 2002.

Williams, Rowan. *On Christian Theology*. Oxford: Blackwells, 2000.

Lost Icons: Reflections on Cultural Bereavement. Edinburgh: T & T. Clark, 2000.

Witherington, Ben, III. *Jesus the Sage: The Pilgrimage of Wisdom*. Minneapolis: Fortress Press, 1994.

The Jesus Quest: The Third Search for the Jew of Nazareth. Downers Grove, IL: InterVarsity Press, 1995.

Wright, N. T. *Christian Origins and the Question of God*, volume II: *Jesus and the Victory of God*. London: SPCK, 1996.

Index of biblical passages

Genesis
  1   29, 41, 96, 117
  1:1–3 55
  1:26–27 95, 134
  2 117, 136, 187
  2:2–3 146
  2:4–25 136
  2:7 250–51
  3 187
  3:14–19 136
  3:24 189
  5:2–3 95
  6–9 29
  6:1–8 151
  9:1–17 137
  9:4–6 64, 66
  15:1–21 137
  17:1–27 137

Exodus 137
  11–13 67
  12 13
  20:8–10 146
  23:16 238
  24:3–8 65
  32:30–34 230
  34:22 238

Leviticus 137
  1–6 64
  1–7 72
  1:3–9 64
  4:2 230
  16 13, 67
  16:21–22 67
  17:14 66
  23:15–21 25, 238

Numbers 137
  15:27–31 230

Deuteronomy 137
  16:9–12 238

  30:15–16 251
  30:19–20 251
  31:20 251

1 Samuel
  8 26, 86

2 Samuel
  7 137

Job
  1 3
  1:6 129
  2:1 129
  38–41 29

Psalms 25, 122
  29 190
  45 98
  90:4 253
  95 27
  102 98

Proverbs
  1:20–21 96
  8:22–31 96

Ecclesiastes
  1:2–9 221

Song of Solomon
  2:1–2 223

Isaiah
  2 88
  6 3
  23–24 225
  24–27 102, 225
  40–55 131
  45:1 86
  45:22–23 152
  63:16 26
  64:8 26

General index

Aaron, as priest, 66–68
Abraham, 128, 137, 144, 251
absolution, prayer of, 123, 234
abstraction, in metaphysics, 35
absurdity, 104–05, 118
abundance, of life, 250–56
abuse, paternal, 14–15, 248
Abyss, 33, 40, 222, 249
acceptance, unconditional, 114, 123–24
achievement, as past, 44
act, of creation, 33–44, 59, 142, 205–06, 256;
    precedes divine nature, 31–32; singular,
    133–34; of Persons of Trinity in unity, 142,
    158, 258
action, 36; conjoint, 192, 196
actuality, 44–55, 254
Adam, 51, 72, 101, 128, 134–42, 187, 245, 251;
    as living doll, 136–37; as son of God, 95
addiction, 231
adepts, 243
adultery, 145
Advent, 30, 239
advocacy (pro bono publico) organizations,
    182
Advocate (Holy Spirit), 129
Africa, 7, 173
African Independent Churches, 190
African-Americans, 184
afterlife, 78, 81, 194
age, old, 250
agency, defined, 38–40; in substance, 133
AIDS, 204–05
alienation, 93, 107–08, 116–24, 138, 255–56;
    and atonement symbols, 92; from
    community by sin, 65
Alpha and Omega, 21–22, 30, 115, 117–24, 216,
    225 n. 3, 230
altar, of Temple, 61
Altizer, Thomas J. J., 225, 228 n. 4
ambiguities, 254
America, 8

amygdala, 69
Anabaptists, 172
analogy, of eminence, proportion, and proper
    proportionality, 39–40; for God, 37–43; of
    the Sun, in Plato, 106 n. 9; Thomistic, 36
Ananias, 173
Ancient One, 129–30
Andrew, 200–02
angels, xxv, 6, 97, 151, 221–22, 227–28, 235;
    angel of death, 61, 67; failed, 77
anger, 231
Anglicans, 160, 172
animals, 104
anthropocentrism, 221
anthropomorphism, 38–39
apartheid, 185
apocalypse, xxi, 122, 130, 185, 189–91, 224–29;
    and history, 225
apocalypticism, 102, 161
apologists, 159, 185
apophasis, 2, 21, 119, 194–95, 249
apostasy, 151
apostles, xxiii, 25, 101; Apostles' Creed, 26; see
    also disciples
apple, 137
Aquinas, Thomas, 31, 34, 36–40
Arabia, 173
Aramaic, 210
Aratus, 178
arbitrariness, in analogies, 38–40; of life
    chances, 30; see also indifference
archeology, 160
architecture, xiii, 239; as image of creation, 29
Areopagus, 178
Arianism, 128, 132–33, 158
Aristotle, 31, 34, 43
arts, xiii, 142, 239
Ascension, xxi, 98, 149, 172, 190, 239
asceticism, 51
Ashton, Loye, xvi
Asia, 104

275

children, of God, 26, 77, 136, 147, 256 (*see also* image of God); as images of parents, 95–96
China, 7, 143; language of, 87; religions of, 135; sacrifice in, 74; conception of soul in, 104
choice, 37, 43, 232–33, 252; in forming intentionality structure, 218; what versus whether, 113–15
Chosen People, 195
Christ of St. John of the Cross (Dali), xiii
Christ the King, 87–88, 122; *see also* Jesus Christ
Christendom, 171, 173
Christian origins, 162
Christianity, xvii, 10, 99, 166–68, 221; ancient versus late modern, 15–18; as a community of interpretation, 257–58; contemporary, 103; early, xx–xxvi, 25, 60–68, 102–03, 131; as a religion of empire (ancient multiculturalism), 88; Greek and Latin forms, 128; historical, 197; as pluralistic, 173–74; punishment in, 76–77; as a religion, 259; symbols in, 8–9
Christians, Jewish and Gentile, xxii, 60–68, 166–67
Christmas, 239
Christology, xiii–xiv, xvii, 9–10, 16–18, 31–32, 56, 61; atonement, 61–62; of historical Jesus, 159–71; of Jesus as guru, 164; normative, 22–23; starting point for, 24; students of, 245; of symbolic engagement, 160 (*see* engagement, symbolic engagement); theory of, 1–23
Church, xxi–xxii, 31, 93, 130, 148, 168, 234; as body of Christ, 98–99, 141, 166–67; as cosmic, 98–99; definition of, 166–68; early, 238–29 (*see also* Christianity, early); institutional, 239–40, 259; Jesus both in and out of, 149–50, 250; as ritual substance, 86–92; as witness, 7, 203–10
churches, 22
cigars, in Heaven, 233, 244
circumcision, xxiii, 24, 79–80
civilization, 106; price for, 77
clans, 70
class-consciousness, 175
cleanliness, 65; *see also* purity
Cleopas, 202
Close, Frank, 30 n. 8
closure, of nature, 7
coeternality, 130
coherence, of community, 257
collaboration, xv
colonialism, 103, 179

Colossians, xxiv, 79–80, 82; author of, 228
communication, 206–17
communism, 172
community, xix, 8, 195; as conjoint action, 51–52; Christian, xxi, 87–88, 91–92, 143; of friendship, 59; of Jesus, xx–xiv; love in, 204; membership in, 190–91
companionship, 137
compassion, 80
complexity, 120–21
components, 57, 105–15, 133–34, 155, 195, 205, 256, 258 (*see also* harmony, form, existential location, value)
compromise, of justice and deference, 111–12
computers, 12, 206
conceptions, compared with schematized images and symbols, 2–6, 9–10
concerns, proximate versus ultimate, 114–24, 197
condemnation, 197
condition (causal), 133; of temporality, 45–55
confession, 214; of One God and One Lord, 257–58
Confessions (Augustine's), 108
Confucianism, 10 n. 12, 16, 70, 74, 103, 125, 171, 177, 206, 231, 261; self-cultivation in, 76; on ritual, 70
Confucius, 152
congregations, 174–76; contextualized, 250; and the Cultural Way, 240
consciousness, 164–71, 255; divine, 42–43; of pressure and guilt, 68–77; temporal, 248
Constantine I, 171
consumption, 111, 245–46
contexts, 258; ancient versus late modern, 15–17; of interpretation, 15–18, 23; misinterpreted, 259–60; for truth conditions, xiv
contingency, 1, 33–34, 40–43, 59
contrast, the ontological ground of value, 121–22
contrition, 231
control, 69–77; imposed on behavior, 70–79; the source of responsibility, 107–08
controversy, first in the Church, 173
conventions, 137; in symbolic reference, 14–17
conversation, among different perspectives, 182
conversion, 17; Augustine's 117
cooperation, and culture, 69–70
Coptic Church, 173
coram deo (facing God, presenting oneself before God), 74, 76, 78, 148–49, 195, 217, 234
Corban, 146